2019 Georgia Real Estate Exam Prep. Questions and Answers

Study Guide to Passing the Salesperson Real Estate License Exam Effortlessly

Volume One

Written by

Real Estate Exam Professionals, Ltd.

Table of Contents

Introduction

Thank you for purchasing this Real Estate Exam Prep. book. We hope you will learn a great deal from our study guide and that you will study well and pass your exam. It is our purpose to provide you with the most up to date information for your state real estate exam. We have made every effort to present this material as the closest possible example to what you will see on your actual state exam. At times, it will appear to be exactly what you will see on the exam. We have tried very hard to make this book as error and typo free as possible. However, we are not without our faults. Real estate exam material and the real estate exams change rapidly and we are continuously updating this book as these changes occur. You may find a typo here and there, but do not be alarmed. We assure you that if you find one, it will be obvious and it will not prevent you from being able to tell what the correct answer is.

You will find that after you have studied this material as instructed in the *How to Use this Guide Effectively*, you will discover that this is all you need to pass the real estate exam. There are many real estate schools out there such as Allied Real Estate School, Anthony Real Estate School and Kaplan that, although they are good schools, also offer exam cram or exam preparation materials, but are extremely overpriced. Their materials can cost into the $100 and $300 ranges and provide a lot of extra "fluff" material that will not help you pass the exam and will waste your time. This book offers all the same materials in a condensed and precise manner with no fluff. Once you have taken the department of real estate certified classes and passed them, qualified to for a state exam date then you do not need those classroom materials anymore. All you will need are the answers to the state and national real estate exam questions. Study those, nothing else, memorize them, and you will pass your exam on the 1st try. There is no need to buy expensive materials from other schools, no need to sit in live exam cram courses, and there is no need for the Real Estate Exam for Dummies books. We have been offering this material to thousands of licensees for over 10 years with a tremendous amount of positive reviews and feedback.

Please be aware that the materials in this book including any bonus item you have received with this book are copyrighted. No part of this book in part or in whole may be duplicated, distributed or resold without consent of the publishers. Our staff actively searches the internet everyday for sales of real estate media on thousands of websites and online auctions. If our program is found being copied, distributed or resold we will prosecute to the fullest extent of the law.

HOW TO USE THIS GUIDE EFFECTIVELY

Here you will find tried and true steps to help you use this guide effectively and to get the best results while minimizing your study time. Please understand that as you go through the real estate questions we have prepared for you, you may come across a few that you have never seen before. Do not be alarmed. These are questions that are on the state exam, but were never given to you in the real estate class you took or in your class textbooks. This is why there is such a high failure rate for the real estate exam. The actual questions on the state or national real estate exams are NOT created by the same agency that created the college courses or text books. These college courses are designed by regional college accreditation agencies and the state real estate exams are created by the individual state's department of real estate or real estate commissions. It is very frustrating, we know. That is why there publishers like us who create exam cram courses and applications to "bridge the gap" of knowledge for the real estate exams.

STEP 1: Read and understand the VOCABULARY section first. These are very important terms. The key to successful knowledge of real estate is understanding and knowing the vocabulary used. Review them until you are confident to go onto the questions. Do not continue to the questions until you know these terms well.

STEP 2: Now go to the STUDY SECTION and read all the real estate questions with their correct answers and explanations in each exam. There are a lot of questions. Pace yourself and allow time to understand and memorize the correct answers.

STEP 3: Go back to the VOCABULARY section and review. Again, they are VERY important. You must know these forwards and backwards.

STEP 4: Repeat step 2 until you feel you are scoring 90% or better. Then review the VOCABULARY section again.

STEP 5: Now begin the MATH only portion of the STUDY SECTION. Read the questions with the answers and explanations until you have mastered them just as you did with the regular real estate questions. Make sure you set aside a separate time of the day to ONLY study the math. The reason for this is that the analytical/math function of the human brain works on math problems from different areas of the brain than word problems. When studying it takes approx. 10 min. for the brain to fully switch to a pure analytical/math function. If you are studying word problems and math problems in the same study session, you will be wasting a lot of time and overworking your brain. Time is key here, especially when it comes to the day of the exam, more about that later.

STEP 6: Repeat the MATH ONLY portion in the STUDY SECTION until you feel you are scoring at least 90% or better.

STEP 7: Now you are ready to go on to the TEST SECTION of this book. These questions will simulate what you will find on the actual state exam. You will have a limited time to complete the exam. Set a timer to the amount of time that your state allows for you to complete the state exam. Begin taking one of the exams and write your answers on a blank sheet of paper. When you are finished, check your answers with the correct answers shown in the same exams from the STUDY SECTION and score yourself. Now continue to Step 8.

STEP 8: Did you score 90% or better? If so, congratulations! You are ready to take the actual state exam and pass on your first try. If you did not score 90% or better, review the questions you missed using the STUDY SECTION. Study them, and retake the corresponding exam in the TESTING SECTION.

Continue doing this and review the Vocabulary, if needed, until you are scoring 90% or better.

IMPORTANT!!!

REMEMBER THIS ON THE DAY YOU TAKE YOUR STATE EXAM…

DO NOT ANSWER, OR EVEN READ, THE FIRST 5 QUESTIONS OF THE EXAM. DO THOSE SECOND TO LAST AND ANY MATH RELATED QUESTIONS, VERY LAST!!!

Write the numbers to these questions on a piece of paper to remember to do them later. The reason is that they have placed the hardest questions in the first 5 spots to distract you, make you nervous and frustrated while taking the test. So, do those just before doing the math questions. Do the math questions very last because as we explained earlier, psychologically it takes the brain about 5-10 minutes to go from comprehensive thinking to analytical mathematical thinking. You only have a limited amount of time to complete the real estate exam. Therefore, your time will be very valuable. Do not leave any question unanswered. An unanswered question will be scored as a wrong answer.

Be sure to read the section *"Secrets to Passing the Real Estate Exam"* this section was developed by ex-real estate exam proctors. It will give you more detailed steps and inside information on how to use the above method on the day of your exam. It will also show you how to answer a question correctly even if you have completely forgotten the answer.

Good luck and study well!

REAL ESTATE VOCABULARY

Due to the length of this Real Estate Glossary, we have included it as a link below:

http://www.realestateabc.com/glossary/

You may also download a PDF version here:

http://tinyurl.com/realestatevocab

STUDY SECTION

In this section you will have the Real Estate Vocabulary Exam, Georgia Real Estate Exam, Real Estate Math Exam and the AMP Real Estate Exam. Read through all the questions in each exam according to the *How to Use this Guide Effectively* chapter and ONLY look at the correct answers in each exam. Start with the Vocabulary Exam and read question number one and then read ONLY the correct answer immediately. Continue to do this for each question until you have read all the questions in the first exam. If you go through each exam 3-4 times in this manner, you will then be able to recognize the correct answer right away when it comes to taking the actual exam. If your reading device has the ability to highlight the correct answer in each question, please utilize this feature. It will make it a little easier each time when reading through the exams in this section.

Please understand these are general real estate terms used in almost every state. This is here for practice and review purposes only. Some terms may not be on your exam.

1. Which of the following describes the term "appreciation"?

A.   Kind words expressed to someone about something they did

B.   An increase in the value of property

C.   An item of value owned by an individual

D.   None of the above

Answer: B. Appreciation is the increase in the value of a property due to changes in market conditions, inflation, or other causes.

2. When ownership of a mortgage is transferred from one company or individual to another, it is called

A.   an assumption

B.   an assignment

C.   an assessment

D.   all of the above

Answer: B. When ownership of a mortgage is transferred (assigned) from one company or individual to another, it is called an assignment.

3. A mortgage loan which requires the remaining balance be paid at a specific point in time is called a/an

A. balloon mortgage
B. early due mortgage
C. mortgage of convenience
D. promissory note

Answer: A. A mortgage loan that requires the remaining principal balance be paid at a specific point in time is a balloon mortgage.

4. The following reason accounts for why bridge loans are not used much anymore:

A. More second mortgage lenders now will lend at a high loan to value
B. Sellers would rather accept offers from Buyers who have already sold their property
C. Neither A or B
D. Both A and B

Answer: D. Bridge loans are not used much anymore because more second mortgage lenders now will lend at a high loan to value and sellers often prefer to accept offers from buyers who have already sold their property.

5. A title which is free of liens or legal questions as to ownership of the property is called a _____ title.

A.   good
B.   cloudy
C.   clear
D.   free

Answer: C. A title free of liens or legal questions as to ownership of the property is called a clear title. It is clear because there can be no challenges made to its legality.

6. What is the collateral in a home loan?

A.   The property itself
B.   A person's good name
C.   The amount of savings a person has
D.   The current automobile the person owns

Answer: A. The property itself is the collateral, and the borrower risks losing it if he does not repay according to the terms of the mortgage or deed of trust.

7. The adjustment date on an adjustable-rate mortgage is

A.   the date the interest rate changes
B.   the date the stock market goes up
C.   30 days from the date the mortgage was taken out
D.   all of the above

Answer: A. The adjustment date is the date the interest rate changes (adjusts).

8. What is the deposit made by a potential buyer to show he is serious about buying a house called?

A.   Serious money deposit
B.   Earnest money deposit
C.   "Nothing ventured, nothing gained" deposit
D.   Down payment

Answer: B. The deposit made by a potential buyer to show they are in earnest about purchasing a house is called an earnest money deposit.

9. A right-of-way which gives persons other than the owner access to or over a property is known as an

A.   easement

B.   ingress
C.   egress
D.   none of the above

Answer: A. An easement is a right-of-way to persons other than the owner and gives them legal access.

10. Which best describes a "subdivision"?

A.   Houses in the same neighborhood similar in style and size
B.   A housing development created by dividing a tract of land into individual lots
C.   A development which is "substandard"
D.   None of the above

Answer: B. A subdivision consists of individual lots created from a larger tract (subdivided) and are offered for sale or lease.

11. When someone contributes to the construction or rehabilitation of a property with labor or services rather than cash, that contribution is called

A.   a personal contribution
B.   sweat equity
C.   a big help to the contractors
D.   toil and labor

Answer: B. Sweat equity is the contribution to the construction of or rehabilitation of a property in the form of labor or services rather than cash.

12. A two-step mortgage is defined as

A.   an adjustable rate mortgage with one interest rate for the first five or seven years and a different rate for the remainder of the term.
B.   a mortgage which is both adjustable and fixed
C.   a mortgage which is named after a dance step
D.   all of the above

Answer: A. A two-step mortgage starts out with one rate for the first five or seven years and then changes to a different rate for the remainder of the term of the mortgage amortization.

13. A legal document evidencing a person's right to or ownership of a property is called a:

A.   quitclaim deed
B.   title
C.   yearly lease
D.   accurate appraisal

Answer: B. A title is a legal document evidencing a person's right to or ownership of a property.

14. If you were buying a house that included furnishings, you would receive a written document transferring title to the personal property. This document is called a/an

A.   title
B.   deed
C.   bill of sale
D.   evidence of payment

Answer: C. A bill of sale is a written document that transfers personal property from one owner to another.

15. An oral or written agreement that is binding in a court of law is called a:

A.   gentlemen's agreement
B.   contract
C.   business deal
D.   promissory note

Answer: B. A contract can be oral or written and is binding in a court of law.

16. The part of the purchase price of a property that the buyer pays in cash and does not finance with the mortgage is

called the

A.   deposit
B.   second mortgage
C.   down payment
D.   deed of trust

Answer: C. The down payment is the amount paid down in cash as the initial upfront portion of the total amount due. It is usually given in cash at the time of finalizing the transaction.

17. A female named in a will to administer an estate is called an

A.   executor
B.   executrix
C.   individual representative
D.   able inheritor

Answer: B. The female executor named in a will to administer an estate is called an executrix.

18. The greatest possible interest a person can have in real estate is called

A.   fee complex
B.   fee simple
C.   no additional fees

D.   ownership

Answer: B. The greatest possible interest a person can have in real estate is called fee simple.

19. Required for properties located in federally designated flood areas, this type of insurance compensates for physical property damage resulting from flooding. It is called

A.   water damage insurance
B.   hurricane insurance
C.   there's no such thing
D.   flood insurance

Answer: D. Flood insurance is required in federally designated flood areas and does compensate for physical property damage resulting from flooding.

20. The following is true of a government loan:

A.   It is guaranteed by the Department of Veterans Affairs (VA)
B.   It is guaranteed by the Rural Housing Service (RHS)
C.   It is insured by the Federal Housing Administration (FHA)
D.   All of the above

Answer: D. Government loans are either insured by FHA,

guaranteed by VA or RHS. Mortgages that are not government loans are called conventional loans.

21. The person conveying an interest in real property is called

A.   the buyer
B.   the grantee
C.   the grantor
D.   the mortgagor

Answer: C. The grantor is the person conveying an interest in real property to another party.

22. Insurance that covers in the event of physical damage to a property from fire, wind, vandalism, or other hazards is called

A.   act of God insurance
B.   hazardous insurance
C.   hazard insurance
D.   there is no such insurance

Answer: C. Insurance covering physical damage to a property from fire, wind, vandalism, or other hazards is called hazard insurance.

23. A liquid asset is

A.   an asset which is not in solid form
B.   an asset which cannot be frozen
C.   a cash asset or an asset easily turned into cash
D.   an asset that is hard to get to

Answer: C. A liquid asset is either cash or something easily turned into cash.

24. Another term for the lender in a mortgage agreement is the

A.   banker
B.   mortgagee
C.   mortgagor
D.   private mortgage company

Answer: B. The mortgagee is the lender.

25. If you are buying a house and asking the Seller to provide all or part of the financing, you are asking for _____ financing.

A.   special
B.   owner
C.   personal
D.   non-bank

Answer: B. When the Seller provides all or part of the financing it is called owner financing.

26. A point is

A.   the part of the pen you sign a contract with
B.   a score in a basketball game
C.   the reason for telling the story
D.   1% of the amount of the mortgage

Answer: D. A point is 1% of the amount of the mortgage.

27. What does a power of attorney grant someone?

A.   The ability to attend law school
B.   Complete or limited authority on behalf of someone else
C.   Complete control over which medical facility someone uses
D.   The right to inherit an estate

Answer: B. A power of attorney derives power from a legal document and grants someone complete or limited authority on behalf of someone.

28. The principal is

A.   the amount borrowed or remaining unpaid

B.   part of the monthly payment that reduces the remaining balance of a mortgage

C.   an ethic or value

D.   both A and B

Answer: D. The principal is the amount borrowed or remaining unpaid, as well as the part of the monthly payment that reduces the remaining balance of a mortgage.

29. A promissory note is

A.   a written promise to repay a specified amount over a specified period of time

B.   an oral promise to repay a specified amount over a specified period of time

C.   a note passed back and forth in class

D.   a note you deliver to another telling them of your intentions

Answer: A. A promissory note is a written promise to repay a specific amount over a specified period of time.

30. Which of the following best describes a real estate agent?

A.   A licensed person who negotiates and transacts the sale of real estate

B.   The owner of a real estate firm

C.   A person who negotiates and transacts the sale of real estate but is not licensed

D.   A person who sells both property and insurance

Answer: A. A real estate agent is a licensed person who negotiates and transacts the sale of real estate.

31. When does an assumption take place?

A.   When someone believes something and it turns out to be true

B.   When the buyer assumes the seller's mortgage

C.   When the seller assumes the buyer's mortgage

D.   All of the above

Answer: B. When the buyer assumes the seller's mortgage is a transaction called an assumption.

32. A legal document conveying title to a property is called a/an

A.   sales contract

B.   option to purchase

C.   deed

D.   contract for deed

Answer: C. A deed is a legal document conveying title to property.

33. If you have a loan and transfer the title to another individual without informing the lender, it is likely that the lender will demand payment of the outstanding loan balance. He is able to do this because of a clause in your mortgage called the

A.   due on demand clause
B.   acceleration clause
C.   amortization schedule
D.   both A and B

Answer: B. An acceleration clause allows the lender to demand payment, most commonly if the borrower defaults on the loan or transfers title to someone without informing the lender.

34. The most common type of bankruptcy is called

A.   Chapter 11 bankruptcy
B.   Chapter 11 no asset bankruptcy
C.   Chapter 7 no asset bankruptcy
D.   Chapter 7 bankruptcy

Answer: C. The most common type for an individual is a "Chapter 7 No Asset" bankruptcy, which relieves the borrower of most types of debts.

35. Which of the following best describes a "broker"?

A.   Someone who owns a real estate firm
B.   Some real estate agents working for brokers
C.   Someone who acts as an agent and brings two parties
together for a transaction and earns a fee for this
D.   All of the above

Answer: D. A broker can own a real estate firm, work for
another broker who owns the firm, broker loans in the mortgage
industry, but basically is defined as anyone who acts as an
agent, bringing two parties together for any type of transaction
and earns a fee.

36. A normal contingency in a real estate contract would be that the

A.   purchaser is able to obtain a satisfactory home inspection
from a qualified inspector.
B.   seller is allowed to come back and spend 2 weeks in the
house each year
C.   purchaser is able to have occupancy as soon as the sales
contract is signed
D.   seller is allowed to dig up some of the landscaping and
take it with him

Answer: A. A normal contingency in a sales contract would be
that the purchaser is able to obtain a satisfactory home
inspection from a qualified inspector. This condition has to be

met before the contract is legally binding.

37. If you go to a bank or mortgage company to apply for a home, what type of mortgage would you be applying for?

A.   Government
B.   Conventional
C.   American
D.   Adjustable rate

Answer: B. Home loans which are not VA or FHA are called conventional loans.

38. A report of someone's credit history which is prepared by a credit bureau and used by a lender in the loan qualification process is called a

A.   personal affidavit
B.   credit card history
C.   savings account history
D.   credit report

Answer: D. A report of an individual's credit prepared by a credit bureau and used by a lender in determining a loan applicant's creditworthiness is called a credit report.

39. If you have not made your mortgage payment within 30

days of the due date, the mortgage is considered to be in

A.   arrears
B.   default
C.   trouble
D.   bankruptcy

Answer: B. Failure to make the mortgage payment within a specified period of time, usually 30 days for first mortgages or first trust deeds, causes the loan to be in default.

40. A term used by appraisers to estimate the physical condition of a building. It may be different from the building's actual age.

A.   Estimated age
B.   Longevity
C.   Preferred age
D.   Effective age

Answer: D. An appraiser's estimate of the physical condition of a building is called effective age. Its actual age may be shorter or longer than the effective age.

41. The difference between the fair market value of a property and the amount still owed on the mortgage and other liens is the owner's financial interest in the property and is called his

A. equity
B. balance due
C. indebtedness
D. none of the above

Answer: A. A homeowner's financial interest in a property is called his equity. It is the difference between fair market value and what is still owed on the mortgage and any other liens.

42. You put in a new driveway to your property, but in the process the paving goes across your property line onto your neighbor's property a few inches. This is called an

A. illegal driveway
B. extra benefit for your neighbor
C. encroachment
D. easement

Answer: C. An improvement that intrudes illegally on another's property is called an encroachment. An easement would be a LEGAL intrusion.

43. A government loan that is not a VA loan would be a/an

A. FHA mortgage
B. FDA mortgage
C. This type loan does not exist

D.   ARM mortgage

Answer: A. A mortgage which is insured by the Federal Housing Administration (FHA) and is the other type of government loan besides a VA loan is an FHA mortgage.

44. If you convey an interest in real property to a relative, that person is known as the

A.   receiver
B.   mortgagor
C.   grantee
D.   lucky relative

Answer: C. The person to whom an interest in real property is conveyed is the grantee.

45. You decide you want to buy a boat and you want to borrow against the equity in your home. You would get a mortgage loan up to a specified amount which is in second position to your first mortgage. This arrangement is called a

A.   perfectly acceptable way to buy a boat
B.   leverage against your house
C.   home equity line of credit
D.   line of credit for personal purposes

Answer: C. A mortgage loan, usually in second position, which allows the borrower to obtain cash drawn against the equity of his home, up to a predetermined amount, is known as a home equity line of credit.

46. You are your sister are joint tenants in a home your mother left you. Your sister has three children in her will and you have one. If she dies first, who does the property go to?

A.   It is divided equally between her three children
B.   It goes entirely to you
C.   It is divided equally between her three children and your one
D.   It goes into her estate

Answer: B. In the event of death in joint tenancy, the survivor owns the property in its entirety.

47. What is the best description of a lien?

A.   Something that doesn't stand up straight in a house
B.   Something that's illegal
C.   A legal claim against property that must be paid off when it's sold
D.   None of the above

Answer: C. A lien, such as a mortgage or first trust deed, is a legal claim against a property that must be paid off when it is sold.

48. What is a lock-in?

A.   A gated community which locks the gate at midnight
B.   An agreement from a lender guaranteeing a specific interest rate for a specific time at a certain cost
C.   What parents do with wayward children
D.   A type of key available at most hardware stores

Answer: B. A lock-in is a rate guaranteed by the lender for a certain period of time at a certain cost to the buyer.

49. The right of a government to take private property for public use upon payment of its fair market value. It is the basis for condemnation proceedings.

A.   Eminent domain
B.   Governmental domain
C.   Encroachment
D.   Both A and B

Answer: A. Eminent domain is the right of the government to take private property for public use upon payment of its fair market value.

50. A mortgage with a lien position subordinate to the first

mortgage on a piece of property is called a

A. second mortgage
B. first subordinate mortgage
C. mortgage which isn't legal
D. lien position mortgage

Answer: A. A second mortgage is a mortgage with a lien position subordinate to the first mortgage.

51. An adjustable-rate mortgage, also known as an ARM is

A. one in which the interest rate is fixed over time
B. one in which the interest rate changes periodically, depending on index changes
C. one in which the interest rate changes periodically, depending on the stock market
D. a type of mortgage that the mortgagor can adjust himself

Answer: B. An adjustable rate mortgage in one in which the interest rate adjusts periodically, according to corresponding fluctuations in an index.

52. A schedule that shows how much of each payment will be applied to principal and how much toward interest over the life of the loan is called a/n

A.   amortization schedule
B.   annual percentage rate
C.   assumption
D.   both A and C

Answer: A. An amortization schedule is a table showing how much of each payment is applied to interest and how much to principal. It also shows the gradual decrease of the loan balance until it reaches zero.

53. The term applied to a mortgage in which you make the payments every two weeks, thereby making thirteen payments a year rather than twelve. This mortgage is paid off faster than a normal mortgage.

A.   Twice-monthly mortgage
B.   Accelerated mortgage
C.   Bi-weekly mortgage
D.   None of the above

Answer: C. A mortgage in which you make payments every two weeks instead of once a month is called a bi-weekly mortgage.

54. The limitation of how much an adjustable rate mortgage may adjust over a six-month period, annual period, and over the life of the loan is called a

A. buy-down
B. high point
C. top stop
D. cap

Answer: D. The limitation on how much the loan may adjust over a period of time and for the life of the loan is a cap.

55. When is a real estate transaction considered to be "closed"?

A. When the buyer has signed all the sales contracts
B. When the closing documents have been recorded at the local recorder's office
C. When all the documents are signed and money changes hands
D. Both B and C.

Answer: D. In some states "closed" means when the documents are recorded at the courthouse, and in others it is a meeting where the documents are signed and money changes hands.

56. A record of an individual's repayment of debt, reviewed by mortgage lenders in determining credit risk is called a

A. credit affidavit
B. credit history

C.   there is no such record

D.   credit worthiness

Answer: B. A record of an individual's repayment of debt is called a credit history.

57. If you sell your property to a neighbor and the lender demands repayment in full, this means you have a _____ in your mortgage.

A.   seller pays all provision

B.   buyer pays all provision

C.   due-on-sale provision

D.   none of the above

Answer: C. A provision in a mortgage which allows the lender to demand repayment in full if the borrower sells the property that serves as security for the mortgage is called a due-on-sale provision.

58. The sum total of all the real and personal property owned by an individual at time of death is called their

A.   estate

B.   probate

C.   will

D.   all of the above.

Answer: A. The sum total of all the real and personal property owned by an individual at time of death is called an estate.

59. If you list your property with a real estate agent and sign a written agreement that they are the only ones entitled to a listing for a specific time you have given them an

A.   exclusive listing
B.   exclusive right to advertise
C.   exclusive right to show
D.   inclusive listing

Answer: A. A written contract giving a licensed real estate agent the exclusive right to sell a property for a specified time is called an exclusive listing.

60. Fair market value could be defined as

A.   how much a property is worth, determined by a realtor's market analysis
B.   the most a buyer, willing, but not compelled to buy, would pay
C.   the least a seller, willing, but not compelled to sell, would take
D.   both B and C

Answer: D. Fair market value is the highest price that a buyer, willing but not compelled to buy, would pay, and the lowest a seller, willing but not compelled to sell, would accept.

61. If a lender agrees to make a loan to a specific borrower on a specific property, he has made a

A.   decision to make the loan
B.   statement that both the buyer and the property pass inspection
C.   firm commitment
D.   both B and C

Answer: C. A lender's agreement to make a loan to a specific borrower on a specific property is called a firm commitment.

62. If you buy a house and build cabinets into the wall, then sell that house, the cabinets stay because they have become a

A.   type of attachment
B.   fixture
C.   part of the house
D.   none of the above

Answer: B. Personal property becomes real property when attached in a permanent manner to real estate and is called a fixture.

63. A home inspection is

A.   a thorough inspection by a professional which evaluates the structural and mechanical condition of a property
B.   not required by law
C.   often a contingency in a contract that it turns out satisfactorily
D.   both A and C

Answer: D. A home inspection is a thorough inspection by a professional that evaluates the structural and mechanical condition of the property. A satisfactory home inspection is often a contingency.

64. An insurance policy which combines personal liability insurance and hazard insurance coverage for a dwelling and its contents is called

A.   homeowner's insurance
B.   buyer's insurance
C.   errors and omissions insurance
D.   all of the above

Answer: A. Homeowner's insurance combines personal liability insurance and hazard insurance coverage for a dwelling and its contents.

65. Which of the following is true of a lease-option?

A.   It is an alternative financing option
B.   Each month's rent may also consist of an additional
amount applied toward the purchase
C.   The price is already set in the beginning
D.   All of the above

Answer: D. A lease-option is an alternative financing option
that allows home buyers to lease a home with an option to buy.
Each month's rent payment may consist of not only the rent, but
an additional amount which can be applied toward the down
payment on an already specified price.

66. In simple terms, a sum of borrowed money (principal) usually repaid with interest is called a

A.   mortgage
B.   loan
C.   conventional loan
D.   alternative mortgage

Answer: B. A sum of borrowed money generally repaid with
interest is simply a loan.

67. A property description which is recognized by law and is sufficient to locate and identify the property without oral testimony is known as the property's

A.   address
B.   911 address
C.   legal description
D.   identifying information

Answer: C. A legal description describes the property and is recognized by law. It is sufficient to locate and identify the property without oral testimony.

68. The date on which the principal balance of a loan, bond, or other financial instrument becomes due and payable is called

A.   its due date
B.   maturity
C.   end of the paper trail
D.   delivery

Answer: B. The date on which the principal balance of a loan, bond, or other financial instrument becomes due and payable is called maturity.

69. The person borrowing money in a mortgage agreement is called the

A.   mortgagor
B.   mortgagee

C.   borrower
D.   lessee

Answer: A. The borrower in a mortgage agreement is called the mortgagor.

70. Which of the following is true about an origination fee?

A.   It applies to both government and conventional loans

B.   It is usually 1% on a government loan
C.   It is usually 2% on a conventional loan
D.   Both A and B

Answer: D. Origination fees apply to government and conventional loans. A government loan origination fee is one percent of the loan amount, but additional points may be charged which are called "discount points". In a conventional loan, the origination fee refers to the total number of points a borrower has to pay.

71. Which of the following falls under the term "personal property"?

A.   A garage attached to a house
B.   A sofa
C.   The front porch of a home

D.   The windows in a home

Answer: B. Personal property is any property that is not part of the real property. A, C, an D are all parts of the house.

72. In some cases if a borrower pays off a loan before it is due he may encounter a penalty called a

A.   penalty for early withdrawal
B.   loan to value penalty
C.   prepayment penalty
D.   there is never a penalty for paying a loan off early

Answer: C. A fee that may be charged to a borrower who pays off a loan before it is due is known as a prepayment penalty.

73. Which of the following statements is true regarding the term "pre-approval"?

A.   It applies only to the property
B.   It is done before the loan application is complete
C.   It s a loosely used term
D.   None of the above

Answer: C. Pre-approval is a loosely used term generally taken to mean a borrower has completed a loan application and provided debt, income, and savings documentation which an underwriter has reviewed and approved.

74. PITI reserves applies to

A.   a cash amount the borrower must have on hand after down payment and closing Costs.

B.   an amount which is financed with the mortgage

C.   both A and B

D.   none of the above

Answer: A. PITI reserves must equal the cash amount that the borrower would have to pay for principal, interest, taxes, and insurance for a predefined number of months.

75. Why would a public auction take place?

A.   It's a good way to buy property

B.   To inform the public about property for sale

C.   To help auctioneers get employment

D.   To sell property to repay a mortgage in defaults

Answer: D. A public auction is a meeting in an announced public location to sell property to repay a mortgage that is in default.

76. The term "realtor" applies to

A.   any real estate agent who has passed the state exam
B.   any real estate agent whose license is active
C.   any real estate agent who is a member of a local real estate board affiliated with the National Association of Realtors.
D.   any real estate agent who belongs to his local board

Answer: C. A realtor is defined as an agent, broker, or associate who holds active membership in a local real estate board which is affiliated with the National Association of Realtors.

77. "Remaining term" refers to

A.   the remaining school term for a real estate class
B.   the original amortization term minus the number of payments that have been applied
C.   the months left in a pregnancy
D.   all of the above

Answer: B. The remaining term applies to the original amortization term minus the number of payments that have been applied.

78. Which of the following is not true of a "revolving debt"?

A.   It is a type of credit arrangement, like a credit card
B.   It revolves around no interest for the first six months
C.   A customer borrows against a pre-approved line of credit

D.   The customer is billed for the amount borrowed plus any interest due

Answer: B. Revolving debt is a credit arrangement, such as a credit card, which allows a customer to borrow against a pre-approved line of credit when purchasing goods and services. The borrower is billed for the amount that is actually borrowed plus any interest due.

79. Which of the following does a survey not show?

A.   Precise legal boundaries of a property
B.   Location of improvements, easements, rights of way
C.   Encroachments
D.   Location of furnishings within the dwelling

Answer: D. A survey is a drawing or map showing the precise legal boundaries of a property, the location of improvements, easements, rights of way, encroachments, and other physical features.

80. What is meant by "seller carry-back"?

A.   The seller physically carries his furnishings out of the house on the day of closing
B.   The seller agrees to be on the mortgage with the buyer
C.   the seller provides financing, often in combination with

an assumable mortgage

D.   The seller carries the principal, but not the interest on a loan

Answer: C. A seller carry-back is an agreement in which the owner of a property provides financing, often in combination with an assumable mortgage.

81. A title company is one which

A.   is usually not needed in a real estate transaction
B.   is not called upon until one year after the sale is closed
C.   specializes in examining and insuring titles to real estate
D.   specializes in preparing deeds and deeds of trust

Answer: C. A title company specializes in examining and insuring titles to real estate.

82. A state or local tax which is payable when title passes from one owner to another is called a

A.   title tax
B.   transfer tax
C.   revenue stamps
D.   real estate tariff

Answer: B. State or local tax payable when title passes from one owner to another is called a transfer tax.

83. What is Truth-in-Lending?

A.   A state law requiring lenders to fully disclose in writing all terms and conditions of a mortgage
B.   A federal law requiring lenders to fully disclose in writing all terms and conditions of a mortgage
C.   A local law requiring lenders to fully disclose in writing all terms and conditions of a mortgage
D.   None of the above

Answer: B. Truth-in-Lending is a federal law requiring lenders to fully disclose in writing the terms and conditions of a mortgage, including the annual percentage rate and other charges.

84. A VA mortgage

A.   is a conventional mortgage for the state of Virginia
B.   is guaranteed by the Department of Veterans Affairs
C.   originates in Texas but ends up in Virginia
D.   in available to anyone applying for a mortgage

Answer: B. A VA mortgage is guaranteed by the Department of Veterans Affairs.

85. Which of the following is not true of "amortization"?

A.   Over time the interest portion increases as the loan balance decreases
B.   Over time the interest portion decreases as the loan balance decreases
C.   Over time the amount applied to principal increases so the loan is paid off in the specified time
D.   None of the above

Answer: A. The loan payment consists of a portion which will be applied to pay the accruing interest on a loan, with the remainder being applied to the principal. Over time the interest portion decreases as the loan balance decreases and the amount applied to principal increases so that the loan is paid off (amortized) in the specified time.

86. The valuation placed on property by a public tax assessor for taxation purposes is called

A.   real value
B.   fair market value
C.   assessed value
D.   predicted value

Answer: C. The valuation placed on property by a public tax assessor for purposes of taxation is called assessed value.

87. If a veteran is eligible for a VA loan, he or she would receive a document from the VA called

A.   Certificate of Authenticity
B.   Certificate of Approval
C.   Certificate of Met Requirements
D.   Certificate of Eligibility

Answer: D. A certificate of eligibility is a document issued by the Veteran's Administration that certifies a veteran's eligibility for a VA loan.

88. Which of the following usually earns the largest commissions in a real estate transaction?

A.   Attorneys
B.   Realtors
C.   Loan officers
D.   Home warranty companies

Answer: B. Realtors generally earn the largest commissions, followed by lenders.

89. An unwritten body of law based on general custom in England and used to an extent in some states is called

A.   common law
B.   uncommon law

C.   casual law

D.   it isn't law if it's not written down

Answer: A. An unwritten body of law based on general custom in England and used to an extent in some states is called common law.

90. If a real estate agent is trying to determine the market value of a property, one thing they would use is recent sales of similar properties or

A.   neighbors' estimates of the value of the property

B.   records from several years back in the same neighborhood

C.   comparable sales

D.   sales they estimate to happen in the future

Answer: C. Recent sales of similar properties in nearby areas and used to help determine the market value of a property are called comparable sales, or "comps."

91. A person to whom money is owed is known as a

A.   debtor

B.   creditor

C.   mortgagee

D.   lender

Answer: B. A creditor is a person to whom money is owed.

92. Discount points refer to

A.   a system of figuring out how much the property will be discounted
B.   points paid in addition to the one percent loan origination fee
C.   usually only FHA and VA loans
D.   both B and C

Answer: D. This term is usually used in reference to only government loans (FHA and VA). Discount points are any points paid in addition to the one percent loan origination fee.

93. Which of the following can the Equal Credit Opportunity Act (ECOA) not discriminate against?

A.   Race, color or religion
B.   National origin
C.   Age, sex, or marital status
D.   All of the above

Answer: D. ECOA is a federal law requiring lenders and other creditors to make credit equally available without discrimination based on race, color, religion, national origin, age, sex, marital status, or receipt of income from public assistance programs.

94. An exclusive listing is one which gives a licensed real estate agent the exclusive right to sell a property

A.   until it sells
B.   until the owner takes it off the market
C.   for a specified period of time
D.   none of the above

Answer: C. An exclusive listing gives a licensed real estate agent the exclusive right to sell a property for a specified period of time.

95. Which of the following is true about Fannie Mae's Community Home Buyer's Program?

A.   It is an income-based community lending model
B.   It has flexible underwriting guidelines to increase low to moderate income family's buying power
C.   Borrows who participate must attend pre-purchase home-buyer education sessions
D.   All of the above

Answer: D. Fannie Mae's Community Home Buyer's Program is an income-based community lending model, under which mortgage insurers and Fannie Mae offer flexible underwriting guidelines to increase a low or moderate income family's buying power and to decrease the total amount of cash needed to purchase a home. Participating borrows are required to attend pre-purchase home-buyer education sessions.

96. The mortgage that is in first place among any loans recorded against a property and usually refers to the date in which loans are recorded, but not always, is called a

A. primary mortgage
B. first in line mortgage
C. first mortgage
D. both A and B

Answer: C. The mortgage that is in first place is a first mortgage.

97. The legal process by which a borrower in default under a mortgage is deprived of his or her interest in the mortgaged property is called a

A. takeover by the mortgage company
B. public auction
C. foreclosure
D. proceeds sale

Answer: C. The legal process by which a borrower in default under a mortgage is deprived of his or her interest in the mortgaged property is called a foreclosure.

98. Loans against 401K plans are

A.   not allowed for down payments on property
B.   an acceptable source of down payment for most types of loans
C.   too great a risk for most people to take
D.   only allowed if you're accumulated $50,000 in the plan

Answer: B. Some administrators of 401(k)/403B plans allow for loans against the monies you have accumulated in these plans. Loans against 401k plans are an acceptable source of down payment for most types of loans.

99. A late charge is

A.   the penalty a borrower pays when a payment is late a stated number of days
B.   usually put into play when the payment is fifteen days late on a first mortgage
C.   usually not applicable to most people
D.   both A and B

Answer: D. A late charge usually kicks in after fifteen days on a first mortgage and is a penalty a borrower must pay.

100. A person's financial obligations are known as his

A.   payments
B.   assets
C.   liabilities
D.   credit risks

Answer: C. A person's financial obligations are called liabilities and include long-term and short-term debt and any other amounts owed to others.

101. Which of the following is not true of annual percentage rate (APR)?

A.   It is the note rate on your loan
B.   It is not the note rate on your loan
C.   It is a value created according to a government formula intended to reflect the true cost of borrowing and expressed as a percentage
D.   It is always higher than the actual note rate on your loan

Answer: A. Annual percentage rate is not the note rate on your loan. It is a value created according to a government formula intended to reflect the true annual cost of borrowing, expressed as a percentage. The APR is always higher than the actual note rate on your loan.

102. An individual qualified by education, training, and experience to estimate the value of real property and personal property and who usually works independently is called an

A. estimator of value
B. appraiser
C. on-site inspector
D. underwriter

Answer: B. An appraiser is an individual qualified by education, training, and experience to estimate the value of real and personal property. Some work for lenders, but most are independent.

103. Which of the following best describes a "balloon payment"?

A. Payment delivered with a "bang"
B. First of many payments on a mortgage
C. The final lump sum payment due at the termination of a balloon mortgage
D. Payments which go higher and higher each year

Answer: C. A balloon payment is the final lump sum payment due at the termination of a balloon mortgage.

104. When a borrower refinances his mortgage at a higher amount than the current loan balance with the intention of pulling out money for personal use, it is referred to as a

A.   refinance extra
B.   cash-out refinance
C.   home equity refinance
D.   adjustable lump sum refinance

Answer: B. A cash-out refinance is when a borrow refinances his mortgage at a higher amount than the current loan balance because he wants to pull our money for personal use.

105. A certificate of deposit is

A.   the same as a down payment
B.   a liquid asset
C.   a deposit held in a bank paying a certain amount of interest to the depositor over a certain time
D.   a deposit held in a bank which pays double the amount of normal interest over time

Answer: C. A certificate of deposit is a time deposit held in a bank which pays a certain amount of interest to the depositor.

106. Common area assessments are

A.   sometimes called Homeowners Association Fees
B.   paid by individual owners of condominiums or planned unit developments
C.   used to maintain the property and common areas
D.   all of the above

Answer: D. Common area assessments are also sometimes called Homeowners Association Fees and are paid by the individual owners of condos or planned unit developments and are used to maintain the property and common areas.

107. A short-term interim loan for financing the cost of construction is called a

A.   flexible loan
B.   convertible loan
C.   construction loan
D.   not a loan, but a promissory note

Answer: C. A short-term interim loan for financing the cost of construction is called a construction loan. The lender makes payments to the builder at periodic intervals as the work progresses.

108. In simple terms, debt is

A.   credit extended to someone
B.   an amount owed to another
C.   an amount owed to another with interest
D.   repayable

Answer: B. Debt is an amount owed to another

109. Which of the following is not true of the term "depreciation"?

A.   It is a decline in the value of property
B.   It is an accounting term showing the declining monetary value of an asset
C.   It is a true expense where money is actually paid
D.   Lenders add back depreciation expense for self-employed borrowers and count it as income

Answer: C. Depreciation is not a true expense where money is actually paid. It is a decline in the value of property and an accounting term showing the declining monetary value of an asset. Lenders add back depreciation expense for self-employed borrowers and count it as income.

110. Which of the following would not be paid by escrow disbursements?

A. Real estate taxes
B. Hazard insurance
C. Mortgage insurance
D. Personal property taxes

Answer: D. Personal property taxes are not a typical escrow disbursement, but real estate taxes, hazard insurance and mortgage insurance are.

111. The lawful expulsion of an occupant from real property is called

A. conviction
B. divorce from bed and board
C. eviction
D. there is no way to lawfully remove an occupant from real property

Answer: C. The lawful expulsion of an occupant from real property is called eviction.

112. If you have a loan in which the interest rate does not change during the term of the loan you have a _____ mortgage.

A. fixed-rate
B. conventional fixed-rate
C. owner financing
D. all of the above

Answer: A. A loan in which the interest rate does not change during the term is called a fixed-rate mortgage.

113. The following is true of a Home Equity Conversion Mortgage (HECM).

A. It is also known as reverse annuity mortgage
B. You don't make payments to the lender, the lender makes payments to you
C. It enables older homeowners to convert their equity into cash
D. All of the above

Answer: D. Usually called a reverse annuity mortgage, this mortgage is unique in that instead of making payments to a lender, the lender makes payments to you, allowing older homeowners to convert their equity to cash. The loan does not have to be repaid until the borrower no longer occupies the property.

114. A written agreement between property owner and

tenant stipulating the conditions under which the tenant may possess the property for a specified period of time and the payment due is called a/an

A.   contract
B.   option
C.   lease
D.   lease-option

Answer: C. A written agreement between property owner and tenant laying out the terms of the agreement including payment and period of time is called a lease.

115.   A lender is

A.   the firm making the loan
B.   the individual representing the firm making the loan
C.   the individual offering owner financing
D.   both A and B

Answer: D. A lender is the firm making the loan or an individual representing the firm making the loan.

116. A margin is

A.   a measurement of error
B.   an artificial line not to write in on a loan document
C.   both A and B

D.   the difference between the interest rate and the index on an adjustable rate mortgage

Answer: D. A margin is the difference between the interest rate and the index on an adjustable rate mortgage which remains stable over the life of the loan.

117. Which of the following is the best definition of a mortgage broker?

A.   A mortgage company which originates loans, then places with other lending institutions
B.   A mortgage company which originates loans, then keeps them in house
C.   An individual which originates loans, then sells on the secondary market
D.   Much like a real estate broker, receives a commission on loans

Answer: A. A mortgage broker is a mortgage company which originates loans, then places with a variety of other lending institutions with whom they usually have pre-established relationships.

118. The term "note rate" refers to:

A.   the speed at which a musician plays scales

B.   the interest rate stated on a mortgage note
C.   the interest rate stated on a personal loan
D.   the rate at which a note is amortized

Answer: B. Note rate means the interest rate stated on a mortgage note.

119. If you have not made your mortgage payment, you are likely to receive which of the following?

A.   Notice of non-payment
B.   A written eviction notice
C.   Notice of default
D.   A letter from an attorney

Answer: C. You are likely to receive a formal written notice, called a notice of default, that a default has occurred and legal action may be taken.

120. A payment that is not sufficient to cover the scheduled monthly payment on a mortgage loan is called a

A.   late payment
B.   partial payment
C.   "too little, too late" payment
D.   a drop in the bucket

Answer: B. A payment insufficient to cover the scheduled monthly payment on a mortgage loan is a partial payment, normally not accepted by the lender, but in times of hardship a borrower can make a request of the loan servicing collection department.

121. PITI stands for

A.   principal, interest, taxes and insurance

B.   principle, interest, taxes and insurance
C.   prepayment, interest, tariff and insurance
D.   none of the above

Answer: A. PITI is principal, interest, taxes and insurance.

122. Which of the following describes "prepayment"?

A.   An amount paid to reduce the interest on a loan before the due date
B.   An amount paid to reduce the principal on a loan before the due date
C.   Can result from a sale, owner's decision to pay off the loan, or foreclosure
D.   Both B and C

Answer: D. A prepayment reduces the principal on a loan before the due date and can result from a sale, the owner's decision to pay off the loan early, or foreclosure.

123. What is private mortgage insurance?

A.   Mortgage insurance that is arranged for by the buyer privately

B.   Mortgage insurance provided by a private mortgage insurance company

C.   Insurance required for loans with a loan-to-value percentage in excess of 80%

D.   Both B and C

Answer: D. A prepayment reduces the principal on a loan before the due date and can result from a sale, the owner's decision to pay off the loan early, or foreclosure.

124. If you were trying to buy a home you and the seller would need to sign a written contract called a/an

A.   purchase agreement
B.   down payment agreement
C.   option to purchase
D.   all of the above

Answer: A. A written contract signed by buyer and seller stating the terms and conditions under which a property will be sold is called a purchase agreement.

125. What is a recorder?

A.   A public official who keeps records of real property transactions
B.   The county clerk
C.   The registrar of deeds
D.   All of the above.

Answer: D. A recorder is a public official who keeps records of real property transactions in their area and is also known by the names "county clerk" and "registrar of deeds".

126. The principal balance on a mortgage is

A.   the outstanding balance of principal and interest
B.   the outstanding balance of principal only
C.   the amount the mortgage has been paid down
D.   none of the above

Answer: B. The principal balance is the outstanding balance of principal only on a mortgage and does not include interest or any other charges.

127. Which of the following is not true about qualifying ratios?

A. There are two types of ratios—"top" or "front" and "back" or "bottom"

B. The "top" ratio is a calculation of the borrower's monthly housing costs (principal, taxes, insurance, mortgage insurance, homeowners' association fees) as a percentage of monthly income

C. the "back" ratio includes all monthly costs as well as "back" taxes

D. Both calculations are used in determining whether a borrower can qualify for a mortgage

Answer: C. The "back" or "bottom" ratio includes housing costs as well as all other monthly debt.

128. The definition of "real" property is

A. property that has nothing artificial on it, only natural materials

B. land and appurtenances, including anything of a permanent nature such as structures, trees and minerals

C. things located within houses such as furniture, accessories, appliances, and clothing

D. all of the above

Answer: B. Real property is defined as land and appurtenances, including anything of a permanent nature such as structures, trees, minerals, and the interest, benefits, and inherent rights thereof.

129. In joint tenancy, if one person dies and the other inherits the property, this is called

A.   tenants in common
B.   whatever is stated in the will
C.   following the wishes of the deceased
D.   right of survivorship

Answer: D. In joint tenancy the right of survivors to acquire the interest of a deceased joint tenant is called right of survivorship.

130. A secured loan is

A.   backed by collateral
B.   when the borrower promises something of value to the lender
C.   when the bank is not in danger of failing
D.   when the bank has been bailed out

Answer: A. A secured loan is backed by security, also called collateral.

131. A mortgage or other type of lien that has a priority lower than that of the first mortgage is called

A.   a second mortgage
B.   subordinate financing
C.   first subordinate financing
D.   all of the above

Answer: B. Subordinate financing is any mortgage or other lien that has a priority lower than the first mortgage.

132. If you were buying a house and wanted to protect yourself against any loss arising from disputes over ownership of your property, you would purchase

A.   hazard insurance
B.   errors and omissions insurance
C.   title insurance
D.   deed insurance

Answer: C. Insurance that protects the lender (lender's policy) or the buyer (owner's policy) against loss arising from disputes over ownership of a property is title insurance.

133   Which of the following is true of the Veteran's

Administration (VA)?

A.   It encourages lenders to make mortgages to veterans
B.   It is an agency of the federal government which guarantees residential mortgages made to eligible veterans
C.   The guarantee protects the lender against loss
D.   All of the above

Answer: D. An agency of the federal government, the VA guarantees residential mortgages made to eligible veterans of the military services. This guarantee protects the lender against loss and thus encourages lenders to make mortgages to veterans.

134. The form used to apply for a mortgage loan, which contains information about a borrower's income, savings, assets, debts, and more is called a/an

A.   application for funds
B.   income documentary
C.   both A and B
D.   application

Answer: A. The form used to apply for a mortgage loan containing information about a borrower's income, savings, assets, debts, and more is called an application.

135. An assessment does which of the following?

A.   Places a value on property for the purpose of real estate sales

B.   Is the same as a competitive market analysis

C.   Places a value on property for the purpose of taxation

D.   Is usually carried out by the mayor of a town

Answer: C. An assessment places a value on property for the purpose of taxation.

136. Which of the following is not true about the "bond market"?

A.   It refers to the daily buy and selling of thirty-year treasury bonds

B.   Lenders do not usually follow this market closely

C.   The same factors that affect the bond market affect mortgage rates at the same time

D.   Fluctuations in this market cause mortgage rates to change daily

Answer: B. Lenders actually do follow this market closely because the same factors that affect the Treasury Bond market also affect mortgage rates at the same time.

137. What does the term "buydown" mean?

A.   Usually refers to a fixed rate mortgage where the interest rate is "bought down" for a temporary period, usually one to three years.
B.   A lump sum is paid and held in an account used to supplement the borrower's monthly payment
C.   These funds can sometimes come from the seller to induce someone to buy their property
D.   All of the above

Answer: D. A buy-down refers to a fixed rate mortgage where the interest rate is "bought down" for a temporary period. The funds for this can come from the seller, the lender, or some other source. The lump sum is paid and held in an account used to supplement the borrower's monthly payment for a time and after that time the borrower's payment is calculated at the note rate.

138. Certificate of Reasonable Value (CRV) applies to

A.   an FHA loan
B.   a conventional loan
C.   a VA loan
D.   a car loan

Answer: C. Once the appraisal has been done on a property being bought with a VA loan, the VA issues a CRV.

139. If you are buying a piece of property and have someone else who is obligated on the loan and is on the title to the property, that person is called a

A.   spouse
B.   family member or friend who shares the property and payments with you
C.   co-borrower
D.   none of the above

Answer: C. An additional individual who is both obligated on the loan and is on the title to the property is called a co-borrower.

140. How would you define "collection"?

A.   A plate, usually at church, where money is donated
B.   It goes into effect when a borrower falls behind
C.   It applies to several or many things in the same category on a loan application
D.   It only applies to trash

Answer: B. When a borrower falls behind, the lender contacts them in an effort to bring the loan current. The loan then goes to "collection" and the lender must mail and record certain documents in case they have to foreclose on the property.

141. Which of the following is true of "condominium"?

A.   It applies to ownership, not to construction or development

B.   It is a type of ownership where all of the owners own each other's interior units

C.   It is an ownership where owners own the property, common areas, and buildings together

D.   both A and C

Answer: D. A condominium is real property where all the owners own the property, common areas and building together, with the exception of the interior of the unit to which they have title. Mistakenly referred to as a type of construction or development, it actually refers to type of ownership.

142. An organization which gathers, records, updates, and stores financial and public records information about the payment records of individuals being considered for credit is called a

A.   credit repository

B.   credit reporting agency

C.   mortgage company

D.   bank

Answer: A. A credit repository is an organization which gathers, records, updates, and stores financial and public records information about the payment records of individuals being considered for credit.

143. In some states a recorded mortgage is replaced by a

A.   contract for deed
B.   promissory note
C.   deed of trust
D.   deed

Answer: C. Some states do not record mortgages but do record a deed of trust which is essentially the same thing.

144. If you have failed to pay mortgage payments when they are due, it is called

A.   delinquency
B.   foreclosure
C.   collections
D.   no big deal

Answer: A. Failure to make mortgage payments when they are due is called delinquency. Most are due on the first day of the month, and even though they may not charge a "late fee" for a number of days, the payment is considered to be late and the loan delinquent.

145. Which of the following would not be considered an "encumbrance", limiting the fee simple title, on a piece of property?

A.   Leases
B.   Mortgages
C.   Easements or restrictions
D.   Furniture not paid for

Answer: D. Encumbrances include mortgages, easements, leases, or restrictions.

146. An earnest money deposit is put into this until delivered to the seller when the transaction is closed.

A.   the realtor's bank account
B.   the attorney's bank account
C.   the buyer's bank account
D.   an escrow account

Answer: D. An earnest money deposit is put into escrow until delivered to the seller when the transaction is closed.

147. Which of the following is true of the Federal National

Mortgage Association (Fannie Mae)?

A.   It is the nation's largest supplier of mortgages
B.   It is congressionally chartered, shareholder owned
C.   It is the same as Freddie Mac
D.   both A and B

Answer: D. Fannie Mae is a congressionally chartered, shareholder-owned company that is the nation's largest supplier of home mortgage funds.

148. An employer-sponsored investment plan allowing individuals to set aside tax-deferred income for retirement or emergency purposes is called a _____ plan.

A.   436(k)/401B
B.   339(k)/372B
C.   401(k)/403B
D.   both A and B

Answer: C. 401(k)/403B plans are employer-sponsored investment plans allowing individuals to set aside tax-deferred income for retirement or emergency purposes. Private corporations provide 401(k) plans; 403B plans are provided by not for profit organizations.

149. Which of the following is true of the Government National Mortgage Association, also known as Ginnie Mae?

A.   It is government owned
B.   It was created by Congress on September 1, 2002
C.   Provides funds to lenders for making home loans
D.   Both A and C

Answer: D. Ginnie Mae is government owned, created by Congress on September 1, 1968. Ginnie Mae performs the same roles as Fannie Mae and Freddie Mac in providing funds to lenders for home loans, but it provides funds for government loans (FHA and VA).

150. At what amount is a loan considered to be a "jumbo" loan, which exceeds Fannie Mae's and Freddie Mac's loan limits? It is also known as a non-conforming loan.

A. $417,000
B. $227,150
C. $300,000
D.   Jumbo refers to the percentage borrowed, not the amount

Answer: A. A jumbo loan is anything over $417,000.

151. Usually part of a homeowner's insurance policy, this type insurance offers protection against claims alleging that

a property owner's negligence or inappropriate action resulted in bodily injury or property damage to another party.

A.   Malpractice insurance
B.   Liability insurance
C.   Hazard insurance
D.   Collision insurance

Answer: B. Liability insurance protects against claims against a property owner for negligence or bodily injury or property damage to another party.

152. A lender refers to the process of getting new loans as

A.   selling his product
B.   loan origination
C.   his bread and butter
D.   more than just a job

Answer: B. A lender refers to the process of getting new loans as loan origination.

153. The percentage relationship between the amount of the loan and the appraised value or sales price (whichever is lower) is called

A.   value to loan
B.   first-time homebuyer's loan
C.   loan to value
D.   both B and C

Answer: C. The percentage relationship between the amount of the loan and the appraised value or sales price is called loan to value.

154. If you are applying for a loan, the lender gives and guarantees you a specific interest rate for a specific time. This period of time is called the

A.   period of no return
B.   rate-freeze period
C.   lock-in period
D.   period at which you cannot seek other financing

Answer: C. The time during which the lender has guaranteed a certain rate is called the lock-in period.

155. A credit report which reports the raw data pulled from two or more of the major credit repositories is called a

A.   multi-credit report
B.   merged credit report
C.   this is not legal

D.   none of the above

Answer: B. A merged credit report reports the raw data pulled from two or more of the major credit repositories.

156. Sometimes, called a first trust deed, this is a legal document pledging a property to the lender as security for payment of a debt.

A.   promissory note
B.   deed of trust
C.   owner financing document
D.   mortgage

Answer: D. A mortgage is a legal document pledging a property to the lender as security for payment of a debt.

157. Which of the following is not true of mortgage insurance?

A.   It covers the lender against some of the losses incurred resulting from default on a home loan
B.   It is sometimes is mistakenly referred to a PMI (private mortgage insurance)
C.   It is required on all loans having a loan to value of more than 90%
D.   No "MI" loans are usually made at higher rates

Answer: C. Mortgage insurance is required on all loans having a loan to value of more than 80%.

158   A no-point loan has an interest rate

A.   lower than if you pay one point
B.   the same as if you pay one point
C.   higher than if you pay one point
D.   a no-point loan does not exist

Answer: C. The interest rate on a "no points" loan is approximately a quarter percent higher than on a loan where you pay one point.

159. The total amount of principal owed on a mortgage before any payments are made is called the

A.   total amount due
B.   original principal balance
C.   a lot less than you'll actually pay
D.   your down payment times ten

Answer: B. The total amount of principal owed on a mortgage before any payments are made is called the original principal balance.

160. A planned unit development (PUD) is different from a condominium because

A.   a condominium usually has more amenities

B.   there are fewer units in a condominium development

C.   in a condominium the individual owns the airspace of the unit

D.   all of the above

Answer: C. A planned unit development is a type of ownership where individuals actually own the building or unit they live, but common areas are owned jointly with the other members of the development or association. In a condominium, an individual owns the airspace of his unit, but the buildings and common areas are owned jointly with the others in the development.

161. The term that means a limit on the amount that the interest rate can increase or decrease over the life of an adjustable rate mortgage is

A.   term cap

B.   life cap

C.   ARM cap

D.   none of the above

Answer: B. A life cap limits the amount the interest rate can increase or decrease over the life of the mortgage.

162. If a commercial bank or other financial institution extends you credit up to a certain amount for a certain time, you are receiving a

A.   line of credit
B.   personal loan
C.   unsecured loan
D.   both B and C

Answer: A. A line of credit is given by a commercial bank or other financial institution for a certain time and certain amount.

163. The term "modification" means

A.   a change in your mortgage without having to refinance
B.   a change in house plans before building begins
C.   the right of the bank to modify the interest rate without telling you
D.   both B and C

Answer: A. Occasionally a lender will agree to modify the terms of your mortgage without requiring you to refinance.

164. Which of the following is true of the term "mortgage banker"?

A.   They are generally assumed to originate and fund their own loans

B.   It is a loosely applied term to those who are mortgage brokers or correspondents

C.   They usually sell loans on the secondary market to Fannie Mae, Freddie Mac, or Ginnie Mae.

D.   All of the above.

Answer: D. A mortgage banker is generally assumed to originate and fund their own loans, which are then sold on the secondary market. Firms loosely apply this term to themselves, whether they are true mortgage bankers or simply mortgage brokers or correspondents.

165. Which of the following describes "prime rate"?

A.   It is the interest rate banks charge to their preferred customers

B.   The same factors that influence the prime rate also affect interest rates of mortgage loans

C.   Changes in the prime rate are usually not widely publicized in the news media

D.   Both A and B

Answer: D. Prime rate is the interest rate banks charge to their preferred customers. Changes in the prime rate are widely publicized in the news media and the same factors that influence prime rate also affect interest rates of mortgage loans.

166. A no cash-out refinance is

A.   intended to put cash in the hands of the borrower
B.   calculated to cover the balance due on the current loan and any costs associated with obtaining the new mortgage
C.   often referred to as a "rate and term refinance"
D.   both B and C

Answer: D. A no cash-out refinance is not intended to put cash in the hands of the buyer, but the new balance is calculated to cover the balance due on the current loan and any costs associated with obtaining the new mortgage. It is often referred to as a "rate and term refinance".

167. A legal document requiring a borrower to repay a mortgage loan at a stated interest rate during a specified period of time is called a

A.   note
B.   deed of trust
C.   mortgage
D.   both B and C

Answer: A. A note is a legal document requiring a borrower to repay a mortgage loan at a stated interest rate during a specified period of time.

168. The date when a new monthly payment amount takes effect on an adjustable-rate mortgage or graduated-payment mortgage is called the

A.   new payment date
B.   payment change date
C.   new payment due date
D.   change payment date

Answer: B. The date when a new monthly payment amount takes effect on an adjustable-rate mortgage or graduated-payment mortgage is called the payment change date.

169. A quitclaim deed does which of the following?

A.   Transfers with warranty whatever interest or title a grantor may have at the time the conveyance is made
B.   Transfers without warranty whatever interest or title a grantor may have at the time the conveyance is made
C.   Does not transfer interest at all
D.   Quitclaim deeds are no longer used

Answer: B. A quitclaim deed transfers without warranty whatever interest or title a grantor may have at the time the conveyance is made

170. In a refinance transaction, what happens?

A.   One loan is paid off with the proceeds from a new loan using the same property as security
B.   An additional loan is added to the present loan
C.   The loan's interest rate changes
D.   The term of the loan is increased

Answer: A. A refinance transaction is the process of paying off one loan with the proceeds from a new loan using the same property as security.

171. The amount of principal that has not yet been repaid is called the

A.   amount owed
B.   balance of the loan
C.   remaining balance
D.   all of the above

Answer: C. The amount of principal that has not yet been repaid is called the remaining balance.

172. If you made an arrangement to repay delinquent installments or advances, you would be setting up a

A.   good faith payment plan
B.   repayment plan
C.   another loan to pay off
D.   oral contract

Answer: B. A repayment plan is an arrangement made to repay delinquent installments or advances.

173. Your neighbor has given you a right of first refusal on a piece of land he plans to sell. What does this mean?

A.   He has given you the first opportunity to purchase it before he offers it for sale to others
B.   He expects you to refuse to buy it
C.   He expects you to pay more for it than anyone else
D.   None of the above

Answer: A. A right of first refusal is a provision in an agreement that requires the owner of a property to give another party the first opportunity to purchase or lease the property before he offers it for sale or lease to others.

174. You are selling the house you live in, but the house you're moving to is not completed. You need to stay on in

the house a while after closing. You work out a deal with the new purchaser called a

A.   no-rent lease agreement
B.   delayed possession for the new purchaser
C.   sale-leaseback
D.   lease for one year past closing

Answer: C. A sale-leaseback is a technique in which a seller deeds property to a buyer for a consideration, and the buyer simultaneously leases the property back to the seller.

175. In a tenancy in common

A.   ownership passes to the survivors in the event of death
B.   ownership does not pass to the survivors in the event of death
C.   there are no provisions made for the death of the owners
D.   when one person dies, the others have to move

Answer: B. In a tenancy in common ownership does not pass to the survivors in the event of death.

176. The duties of a "servicer" include

A.   collecting principal and interest payments from borrowers
B.   managing borrowers' escrow accounts

C. usually a servicer services mortgages purchased by an investor in the secondary mortgage market

D. all of the above

Answer: D. A servicer is an organization that collects principal and interest payments from borrowers and manages borrowers' escrow accounts. The servicer often services mortgages that have been purchased by an investor in the secondary mortgage market.

177. In "third-party origination"

A. an independent political party originates a loan

B. a lender uses another party to completely or partially originate, process, underwrite, close, fund, or package the mortgages it plans to deliver to the secondary mortgage market.

C. three parties are involved in the loan process

D. all of the above

Answer: B. A lender uses another party to completely or partially originate, process, underwrite, close, fund, or package the mortgages it plans to deliver to the secondary mortgage market.

178. A title search of a property would show the following to be true:

A. the seller is the legal owner of the property
B. there are no liens or other claims against the property
C. the previous owners came over on the Mayflower
D. both A and B

Answer: D. A title search would show that the seller is the legal owner and there are no outstanding liens or other claims against the property.

179. A trustee

A. is known to be trustworthy
B. is someone who has a great deal of trust in others
C. is a fiduciary who holds or controls property for the benefit of another
D. is usually a job for relatives

Answer: C. A trustee is a fiduciary who holds or controls property for the benefit of another.

180. When a person is "vested" he can

A. use a portion of a fund such as an individual retirement fund
B. use a portion of a fund without paying taxes on it
C. have access to a bulletproof vest when in dangerous situations

D.   both A and C

Answer: A. A person who is "vested" can use a portion of a fund such as an individual retirement fund, but must pay taxes on funds that are withdrawn. If someone is 100% vested, they can withdraw all the funds set aside for them in a retirement fund.

181. Which of the following is not true of the term "appraised value"?

A.   It usually comes out lower than the purchase price when using comparable sales
B.   It is an opinion of a property's fair market value
C.   It is based on comparable sales
D.   None of the above

Answer: A. The appraised value usually comes out at the purchase price because the most recent sale is the one on the property in question.

182. If a buyer qualifies and is able to take over the seller's mortgage when buying his home, this type of mortgage is called

A.   "pass on down" mortgage
B.   assumable mortgage

C.   owner financing
D.   both B and C

Answer: B. A mortgage that can be assumed by the buyer when a home is sold is called an assumable mortgage. Usually the borrower must qualify in order to assume.

183. A call option is most similar to

A.   a lifetime cap
B.   a buy-down
C.   an acceleration clause
D.   all of the above

Answer: C. A call option is most similar to an acceleration clause.

184. A "chain of title" would show

A.   the transfers of title to a piece of property over the years
B.   members of the "chain gang" who had previously owned the property
C.   neither A nor B
D.   both A and B

Answer: A. A chain of title is an analysis of the transfers of title to a piece of property over the years.

185. Which of the following is true of a cloud on title?

A.   It usually cannot be removed except by deed, release, or court action

B.   It is the result of conditions revealed by a title search that adversely affect the title to real estate

C.   both A and B

D.   neither A nor B

Answer: C. A cloud on title is any condition revealed by a title search that adversely affects the title to real estate. Usually clouds cannot be removed except by deed, release, or court action.

186. Which of the following applies to "closing costs"?

A.   They are divided into two categories—"non-recurring closing costs" and "pre-paid items"

B.   Lenders try to estimate the amounts of non-recurring and pre-paids on a Good Faith Estimate shortly after receiving the loan application

C.   Pre-paids are items which recur over time, such as property taxes and homeowners insurance

D.   All of the above

Answer: D. Closing costs are either "non-recurring" or "pre-paids." "Pre-paids" occur over time, like property taxes and homeowners insurance. Lenders try to estimate both categories and give a Good Faith Estimate within three days of receiving a home loan application.

187. What is "community property"?

A.   Property that is owned by an entire condominium development
B.   Property that is owned by an entire subdivision of single-family homes
C.   Property acquired by a married couple during the marriage and considered to be jointly owned
D.   Both A and B

Answer: C. Community property, an outgrowth of the Spanish and Mexican heritage of the area, determines that property acquired by a married couple during their marriage is considered to be jointly owned.

188. If an apartment complex is converted to a condominium, this is called

A.   a condominium conversion
B.   an apartment conversion
C.   either an apartment or condominium conversion
D.   fewer options for people to rent

Answer: A. Changing the ownership of an existing building (usually a rental project) to the condominium form of ownership is called a condominium conversion.

189. This is an adjustable rate mortgage that allows the borrower to change the ARM to a fixed rate mortgage within a specific time.

A.   due-to-change ARM
B.   convertible ARM
C.   fixed rate ARM
D.   two-fold mortgage

Answer: B. A convertible ARM is an adjustable rate mortgage that allows the borrower to change the ARM to a fixed rate mortgage within a specific time.

190. If someone gives you "credit," you are

A.   agreeing to receive something of value in exchange for a promise to repay the lender at a later date
B.   getting something you deserve for something you did
C.   very lucky, because this doesn't happen often
D.   both B and C

Answer: A. Credit is an agreement in which a borrower receives something of value in exchange for a promise to repay the lender at a later date.

191. In an effort to avoid foreclosure (which may or may not happen), you might give the lender

A.   the payments he is due, all at one time
B.   your car and any other valuable personal property you have
C.   a "deed in lieu" (of foreclosure)
D.   a "deed in lieu" (of foreclosure), which then will not affect your credit badly

Answer: C. A "deed in lieu of foreclosure" conveys title to the lender when the borrower is in default and wants to avoid foreclosure. The lender may or may no stop foreclosure proceedings. Regardless, the avoidance and non-repayment of debt will most likely show on a credit history. The "deed in lieu" may prevent having the documents preparatory to a foreclosure becoming a matter of public record by being recorded.

192. When a lender performs this calculation annually to make sure the correct amount of money for anticipated expenditures is being collected, the lender is performing

A.   checks and balances
B.   an escrow analysis

C. a detailed loan analysis

D. lenders don't do this

Answer: B. Once a year your lender will perform an "escrow analysis" to make sure they are collecting the correct amount of money for the anticipated expenditures.

193. The report on the title of a property from the public records or an abstract of the title is called

A. a title report

B. an examination of title

C. an examination of deed, survey and title

D. title insurance

Answer: B. The report on the title of a property from the public records or an abstract of the title is called an examination of title.

194. A consumer protection law that regulates the disclosure of consumer credit reports by consumer/credit reporting agencies and establishes procedures for correcting mistakes on one's credit record is called the

A. Credit Reporting Act

B. Fair Credit Reporting Act

C. Consumer Protection Act

D.   Truth-in-Lending Act

Answer: B. The Fair Credit Reporting Act is a consumer protection law that regulates the disclosure of consumer credit reports by consumer/credit reporting agencies and establishes procedures for correcting mistakes on one's credit record.

195. If you inherit from someone, the best type of estate to inherit is called

A.   a fee simple estate
B.   general, all-encompassing estate
C.   life estate
D.   none of the above

Answer: A. A fee simple estate is an unconditional unlimited estate of inheritance that represents the greatest estate and most extensive interest in land that can be enjoyed and is of perpetual duration.

196. A homeowner's association does which the following?

A.   It manages the common areas of a condominium project or planned unit development
B.   It owns title to the common elements in a condominium development
C.   It doesn't own title to the common elements in a planned

unit development

D.   All of the above

Answer: A. A homeowner's association manages the common areas of a condominium project or planned unit development, owns title to the common elements in a planned unit development but doesn't in a condo development.

197. In simple terms a judgment is

A.   a personal opinion about real estate
B.   an individual's way of making decisions about legal matters
C.   a decision made by a court of law
D.   an opinion of an attorney

Answer: C. A judgment is a decision made by a court of law. In repayment of a debt, the court may place a lien against the debtor's real property as collateral for the judgment's creditor.

198. This is a way of holding title to a property wherein the mortgagor does not actually own the property but rather has a recorded long-term lease on it.

A.   contract for deed
B.   rent-to-own contract
C.   long-term lease

D.   leasehold estate

Answer: D. A leasehold estate is a way of holding title to a property when the mortgagor does not actually own the property but rather has a recorded long-term lease on it.

199. Which of the following are duties of a loan officer?

A.   The solicitation of loans
B.   Representation of the lending institution
C.   Representation of the borrower to the lending institution
D.   All of the above

Answer: D. A loan officer, sometimes called a lender, loan representative, loan "rep," or account executive solicits loans, represents the lending institution, and represents the borrower to the lending institution.

200. The amount paid by a mortgagor for mortgage insurance, either government or private is called

A.   mortgage insurance premium
B.   private mortgage insurance premium
C.   FHA insurance premium
D.   VA insurance premium

Answer: A. The mortgage insurance premium is paid by a

mortgagor for mortgage insurance, either to a government agency such as the Federal Housing Administration (FHA) or to a private mortgage insurance (MI) company.

201. Which of the following statements is not true of mortgage life and disability insurance?

A.   It begins immediately after someone becomes disabled

B.   It pays off the entire debt if someone dies during the life of the mortgage

C.   It is a type of term life insurance often bought by borrowers

D.   In this type insurance, the amount of coverage decreases as the principal declines

Answer: A. Be careful to read the terms of coverage because often it does not start immediately upon the disability, but after a specified period, sometimes forty-five days.

202. Which is the best definition of "multi-dwelling units"?

A.   They are properties that provide separate housing units for more than one family with several different mortgages

B.   They are properties that provide separate housing units for more than one family, but with a single mortgage

C.   They are properties that provide separate housing units for more than one family, but are leased rather than owned

D.   They are properties that provide separate housing units for more than one family on a lease-option basis

Answer: B. Multi-dwelling units provide separate housing units for more than one family, although they secure only a single mortgage.

203. Which of the following is true of "negative amortization"?

A.   It is also called "deferred interest"
B.   Because some ARM's allow the interest rate to fluctuate, the borrower's minimum payment may not cover all the interest
C.   The unpaid interest is added to the balance of the loan and the loan balance grows larger instead of smaller
D.   All of the above

Answer: D. Because some adjustable rate mortgages allow the interest rate to fluctuate independently of a required minimum payment, if a borrower makes the minimum payment it may not cover all the interest. The borrower is deferring the interest payment, called "deferred interest." It is then added to the balance, making it grow larger, and thus the term "negative amortization.

204. For someone to be determined to be "pre-qualified" for a loan, what has taken place?

A.   The person has given a written statement saying he can afford the loan

B.   A loan officer has given a written opinion of the borrower's ability to qualify based on debt, income, or savings

C.   The loan officer has reviewed a credit report on the borrower

D.   The information given to the loan officer is in the form of written documentation

Answer: B. Pre-qualification usually refers to the loan officer's written opinion of the ability of a borrower to qualify for a home loan, after the loan officer has made inquiries about debt, income, and savings. This information provided to the loan officer may have been presented verbally or in the form of documentation, and the loan officer may or may not have reviewed a credit report on the borrower.

205. The four components of a monthly mortgage payment on impounded loans are

A.   principal, interest, taxes, maintenance
B.   principal, interest, insurance, bank fees
C.   principal, interest, taxes, miscellaneous charge
D.   principal, interest, taxes, insurance

Answer: D. The four components of a monthly mortgage payment on impounded loans are principal, interest, taxes and insurance (PITI). While taxes and insurance are usually paid into an escrow account until they're due, principal refers to the part of the monthly payment that reduces the remaining balance and interest is the fee charged for borrowing money.

206. The term "periodic rate cap" refers to

A.   an adjustable rate mortgage
B.   a limit on the amount the interest rate can increase or decrease during any one adjustment period
C.   conventional fixed-rate loans
D.   both A and B

Answer: D. For an adjustable rate mortgage, a limit on the amount that the interest rate can increase or decrease during any one adjustment period, regardless of how high or low the index might be is called a periodic rate cap.

207. The acquisition of property through the payment of money or its equivalent is called

A.   a purchase money transaction
B.   having a down payment and mortgage
C.   simply, buying property
D.   a sales transaction

Answer: A. The acquisition of property through the payment of money or its equivalent is called a purchase money transaction.

208. What is a recording?

A.   A sound file of music to study real estate by
B.   Details of a properly executed legal document noted in the registrar's office
C.   A document, such as a deed or mortgage note which becomes public record
D.   Both B and C

Answer: D. The noting in the registrar's office of the details of a properly executed legal document, such as deed, mortgage note, satisfaction of mortgage, or extension of mortgage, thereby making it a part of the public record is called a recording.

209. If a landlord wants to protect himself against loss or rent or rental value due to fire or other casualty that would render the premises unusable for a time he would purchase

A.   hazard insurance
B.   fire insurance
C.   rent-loss insurance
D.   there is no such insurance

Answer: C. Rent loss insurance protects a landlord against loss or rent or rental value due to fire or other casualty that renders the leased premises unavailable for use and as a result of which the tenant is excused from paying rent.

210. The right to enter or leave designated premises is called

A.   the right of ingress or egress
B.   the right to enter or leave
C.   the right of non-trespass
D.   an easement

Answer: A. The right to enter or leave designated premises is called the right of ingress or egress.

211. "Secondary market" means

A.   a market which is not as important as the primary market
B.   the buying and selling of existing mortgages, usually as part of a "pool" of mortgages
C.   a market of lower real estate values
D.   none of the above

Answer: B. The buying and selling of existing mortgages, usually as a "pool," is called the secondary market.

212. The property that will be pledged as collateral for a loan is called

A.   the back-up plan
B.   the credit
C.   security
D.   the borrower's former home

Answer: C. Security is the property that will be pledged as collateral for a loan.

213. If you were purchasing a piece of property, either you or your bank would want to know if you were paying a fair price and would order

A.   a market analysis by a realtor
B.   an appraisal
C.   survey
D.   termite inspection

Answer: B. An appraisal is a written justification of the price paid for a property, primarily based on an analysis of comparable sales of similar homes nearby.

214. Which of the following is an example of "transfer of ownership"?

A.   The purchase of property "subject to" the mortgage
B.   Joint tenancy

C.	The assumption of the mortgage debt by the property purchaser
D.	Both A and C

Answer: D. Lenders consider the following to be a transfer of ownership: the purchase of a property "subject to" the mortgage, the assumption of the mortgage debt by the property purchaser, and any exchange of possession of the property under a land sales contract or any other land trust device.

215. Which of the following does not apply the Treasury index?

A.	An index used to determine interest rate changes for certain fixed-rate loans
B.	It is based on the results of auctions that the U. S. Treasury holds for its Treasury bills and securities
C.	derived from the U. S. Treasury's daily yield curve
D.	None of the above

Answer: A. The Treasury index is an index used to determine interest rate changes for certain adjustable rate loans.

216. What are assets?

A.	Items of value owned by an individual
B.	Items that can be quickly converted into cash are called

"liquid assets"

C.   Real estate, personal property, and debts owed to someone by others

D.   All of the above.

Answer: D. Assets are items of value owned by an individual. Assets quickly converted to cash are considered "liquid assets" and include bank accounts, stocks, bonds, mutual funds, etc. Other assets include real estate, personal property, and debts owed to an individual by others.

217. One who establishes the value of a property for taxation purposes is called

A.   a government tax appraiser
B.   an assessor
C.   an appraiser
D.   all of the above

Answer: B. A public official who establishes the value of a property for taxation purposes is called an assessor.

218. A certificate of deposit index is

A.   one of the indexes used for determining interest rate changes on some adjustable rate mortgages
B.   is an average of what banks are paying on certificates of

deposit
C.   both A and B
D.   neither A nor B

Answer: C. A certificate of deposit index is used for determining interest rate changes on some adjustable rate mortgages. It is an average of what banks are paying on certificates of deposit.

219. Which of the following is true of "common areas"?

A.   They include swimming pools, tennis courts, and other recreational facilities
B.   They are portions of a building, land, and amenities owned or managed by a planned unit development or condominium project's homeowners' association
C.   They have shared expenses by the project owners for the operation and maintenance
D.   all of the above

Answer: D. Common areas include portions of a building, land, and amenities owned by or managed by a planned unit development or condo project's homeowners' association (or a cooperative project's cooperative corporation) that are used by all of the unit owners, who share in the common expenses of their operation and maintenance. They include swimming pools,, tennis courts, and other recreational facilities, as well as common corridors of buildings, parking areas, means of ingress and egress, etc.

220. In a condominium hotel you would find the following:

A.   Rental or registrations desks
B.   Daily cleaning services
C.   No individual ownership
D.   Both A and B

Answer: D. Often found in resort areas, this is a condominium project with rental or registration desks, short-term occupancy, food and telephone services, and daily cleaning services. It is operated like a commercial hotel even though the units are individually owned.

221. A type of multiple ownership where the residents of a multi-unit housing complex own shares in the cooperative corporation that owns the property and gives each resident the right to occupy a specific apartment or unit is called

A.   an investment condominium
B.   an investment planned unit development
C.   a cooperative
D.   a government-run housing project

Answer: C. A cooperative (co-op) is a type of multiple ownership where the residents of a multi-unit housing complex own shares in the cooperative corporation that owns the property and gives each resident the right to occupy a specific unit.

222. Which is true of the cost of funds index (COFI)?

A.   It represents the weighted-average cost of savings, borrowings, and advances of the financial institutions such as banks and savings & loans in the 11th District of the Federal Home Loan Bank

B.   It is one of the indexes used to determine interest rate changes for certain government fixed rate mortgages

C.   It is an index used to determine interest rate changes for certain adjustable-rate mortgages

D.   Both A and C

Answer: D. The cost of funds index is one of the indexes used to determine interest rate changes for certain adjustable-rate mortgages. It represents the weight-average cost of savings, borrowings, and advances of the financial institutions such as banks and savings and loans, in the 11th District of the Federal Home Loan Bank.

223. Once you buy a house, the amount you pay each month includes an extra amount above principal and interest. This extra money is held in a special account to pay your taxes and homeowners insurance when it comes due. This account

is called

A.   an escrow account
B.   a savings account
C.   a regular checking account
D.   both B and C

Answer: A. Once you close your transaction, you probably have an escrow account with your lender which is composed of extra money taken from your monthly payments to be put in escrow and pay your taxes and insurance when they come due. The lender pays them with your money instead of you paying them yourself.

224. Which of the following does the Federal Housing Administration do?

A.   Lends money and plans and constructs housing
B.   Insures residential mortgage loans made by government lenders
C.   Sets standards for construction and underwriting
D.   None of the above

Answer: C. The main activity of the FHA is the insuring of residential mortgage loans made by private lenders. It sets standards for construction and underwriting but does not lend money or plan or construct housing.

225. If you purchase a type of insurance called homeowner's warranty, you would do so because

A.   It will cover repairs to certain items, such as heating or air conditioning if they break down within the coverage period
B.   The seller will sometimes pay for it
C.   Both A and B
D.   Neither A nor B

Answer: C. Homeowner's warranty will cover repairs to certain items like air conditioning or heating during the coverage period. The buyer often requests the seller to pay for this, but either party can pay.

226. A type of foreclosure proceeding used in some states that is handled as a civil lawsuit and conducted entirely under the auspices of a court is called

A.   a legal foreclosure
B.   a court-appointed foreclosure
C.   a judicial foreclosure
D.   a civil foreclosure

Answer: C. A type of foreclosure proceeding used in some states that is handled as a civil lawsuit and conducted entirely under the auspices of a court is called a judicial foreclosure.

227. Which of the following is not part of loan servicing?

A.   Processing payments, sending statements
B.   Managing the escrow account
C.   Handling pay-offs and assumptions
D.   Sending a monthly statement to the owner

Answer: D. The company you make your loan payments to is "servicing" your loan by processing payments, sending statements, managing the escrow account, providing collection efforts on delinquent loans, making sure insurance and property taxes are made, handling pay-offs and assumptions and other services.

228. A period payment cap applies to

A.   any mortgage taken out in the U.S.
B.   adjustable rate mortgages
C.   fixed-rate loans
D.   government loans

Answer: B. The period payment cap applies to an adjustable-rate mortgage where the interest rate and the minimum payment amount fluctuate independently of one another. It is a limit on the amount that payments can increase or decrease during any one adjustment period.

229. The commitment issued by a lender to borrower or other mortgage originator guaranteeing a specified interest rate for a specified period of time at a specific cost is called

A.   a rate lock
B.   under lock and key
C.   a promissory note
D.   a deed of trust

Answer: A. A rate lock is a commitment from a lender to the borrower or other mortgage originator guaranteeing a specific rate for a specific time at a specific cost.

230. A fund set aside for replacement of common property in a condominium, PUD, or cooperative project, particularly that which has a short life expectancy, such as carpet or furniture is called

A.   a capital improvements fund
B.   a replacement reserve fund
C.   a savings fund
D.   a contingency fund

Answer: B. The fund set aside for replacement of common property in a condominium, PUD or cooperative project is called a replacement reserve fund.

231. The term "servicing" describes

A.   the collection of mortgage payments from borrowers
B.   what the mechanic does to your car
C.   duties of a loan servicer
D.   both A and C

Answer: D. Servicing is the collection of mortgage payments from borrowers and related responsibilities of a loan servicer.

232. A two- to-four family property

A.   consists of a structure that provides living space for two to four families and ownership is evidenced by two to four deeds
B.   consists of a structure that provides living space for two to four families and ownership is evidenced by a single deed
C.   is not a deeded property
D.   is an illegal form of ownership

Answer: B. A two-to-four family property consists of a structure that provides living space for two to four families and ownership is evidenced by a single deed.

1. In a dual agency situation, a broker may collect a commission from both the seller and the buyer if:

A. both parties are represented by attorneys.

B. the broker has written authority from the Real Estate Commission.

C. the buyer and the seller are represented by different agents.

D. both parties give their informed consent in writing to the dual compensation.

Answer: D. The answer is both parties give their informed consent in writing to the dual compensation. A broker may receive compensation from both a buyer and a seller only if both parties give their informed consent in writing to the dual compensation. Brokers create a designated agency situation when they appoint different agents to represent the seller and the buyer. The Real Estate Commission is not involved in compensation arrangements. A broker represents both parties in a dual agency situation; the parties are not represented by an attorney.

Reference: Real Estate Practice in Georgia > Listings and Agency

2. In Georgia, errors and omissions insurance is:

A. required for all companies with more than ten licensees.

B. required for all licensees.

C. required for all companies with more than one office.

D. not required.

Answer: C. The answer is not required. In Georgia, errors and omissions insurance is not required. However, may brokers carry the insurance as a cost of doing business, as the insurance company will defend the broker and pay legal costs and judgments in a lawsuit against the broker.

Reference: Real Estate Practice in Georgia > Real Estate Practice

3. When a seller asks a listing broker to keep certain information confidential,:

A. the broker can ignore the request if doing so will quicken a sale.

B. the broker should inform the seller that the broker is bound to keep all information from any client confidential.

C. the broker must honor the seller's request unless it relates to adverse material facts that the buyer is entitled to know.

D. the broker should inform the seller that the broker has no responsibility of confidentiality.

Answer: C. The answer is the broker must honor the seller's request unless it relates to adverse material facts that the buyer is entitled to know. BRRETA states that brokers owe their client the duty of confidentiality. However, BRRETA requires brokers to disclose any adverse material fact that they know to the parties in a transaction. Brokers must make full disclosure of adverse material defects.

Reference: Real Estate Practice in Georgia > Listings and Agency

4. A buyer purchased a house and moved in the day after the closing but did not record his deed. Two weeks later, he was shocked to learn that the seller had now sold the house to a second buyer who has recorded his deed. Who now owns the house?:

A. The first buyer does, because his deed has an earlier date.

B. The second buyer is the owner, because he was the first to record.

C. The first buyer owns the house, because his occupancy affords constructive notice even though he did not record his deed.

D. The original seller is still the owner, because his dual sales were fraudulent and, therefore, are canceled.

Answer: C. The answer is the first buyer owns the house, because his occupancy affords constructive notice even though he did not record his deed. The first buyer owns the house, because his occupancy affords constructive notice even though he did not record his deed. Recording the deed would avoid any controversy over ownership.

5. A seller listed his house for sale with a broker on February 1. The listing agreement was to last five months. In April, the seller decided that the house was no longer for sale. Which statement is TRUE?:

A. The Georgia Real Estate Commission will decide if the seller's action is justifiable.

B. The seller has withdrawn the broker's authority to sell the property and may be responsible for the broker's expenses.

C. The seller has canceled the agreement and there are no penalties.

D. The seller is required by law to leave his house on the market until June.

Answer: C. The answer is the seller has withdrawn the broker's authority to sell the property and may be responsible for the broker's expenses. The listing agreement may be canceled and the house taken off the market, but the seller may be responsible for the broker's expenses in marketing the property. The seller may agree to pay such expenses, or the broker may have to take the seller to court to force the seller to pay the expenses. The Georgia Real Estate Commission will not be involved.

Reference: Real Estate Practice in Georgia > Listings and Agency

6. In Georgia, which statement is TRUE in regard to local jurisdictions that impose a business license fee?:

A. Real estate companies must pay for the business license in jurisdictions where they have offices.

B. Real estate companies are exempt from business license fees.

C. A business license might be required in any jurisdiction where the real estate company has listings.

D. A real estate company cannot be required to have more than one license.

Answer: A. The answer is real estate companies must pay for the business license in jurisdictions where they have offices.

Real estate companies must pay for the business license in jurisdictions where they have offices. A business license may be imposed by a local city, county, or other jurisdiction in addition to the required real estate license for a real estate firm.

Reference: Real Estate Practice in Georgia > Real Estate Practice

7. How is a broker's commission determined in a real estate sales transaction?:

A. It will be determined through arbitration by the Georgia Real Estate Commission.

B. It is determined according to the standard rates set by local real estate brokers.

C. It must be stated in the brokerage agreement and is negotiated between the broker and the broker's client.

D. It is established by the state real estate association.

Answer: C. The answer is it must be stated in the brokerage agreement and is negotiated between the broker and the broker's client. The broker's commission must be stated in the listing agreement and is negotiated between the broker and the seller. Broker's establishing a standard commission rate is a violation of antitrust laws. Neither the Commission nor a state association sets a standard commission rate.

Reference: Real Estate Practice in Georgia > Real Estate Practice

8. With regard to the use of a property condition disclosure form in Georgia:

A. the buyer must be given the form before signing an offer.

B. the use of a specific form is recommended but is not a legal requirement.

C. the seller must fill out and sign the form when the property is listed.

D. if the seller refuses to sign the form, the broker should sign on the seller's behalf.

Answer: B. The answer is the use of a specific form is recommended but is not a legal requirement. Georgia law does not require a particular seller disclosure form, but using a specific form for all sellers is recommended. It is not advisable that the broker sign the form if the seller will not. Georgia does not require when a seller must complete the form or that a form be given to a buyer, but listing brokers protect themselves and the seller by requiring the seller to complete a disclosure form. Most listing brokers will require a seller to complete the form when listing a house or before the house is shown to buyers.

Reference: Real Estate Practice in Georgia > Real Estate Practice

9. A salesperson with LMN Realty has a buyer prospect who wishes to be shown a property listed by XYZ Realty. All of the following statements are true EXCEPT:

A. the salesperson can act as a subagent of the seller with the seller's permission.

B. the salesperson may work with the buyer as a customer.

C. the listing broker must give permission for the showings.

D. the salesperson can acquire an agency relationship with the buyer by way of an express, verbal contract.

Answer: D. The answer is the salesperson can acquire an agency relationship with the buyer by way of an express, verbal contract. BRRETA requires a written, not a verbal, contract to establish an agency relationship. The salesperson can act as a subagent of the seller with the seller's permission, usually granted in the listing agreement with the broker. The salesperson can work with the buyer as a customer. The listing broker must give permission for the showings.

Reference: Real Estate Practice in Georgia > Listings and AgencyThe answer is the salesperson can acquire an agency relationship with the buyer by way of an express, verbal contract. BRRETA requires a written, not a verbal, contract to establish an agency relationship. The salesperson can act as a subagent of the seller with the seller's permission, usually granted in the listing agreement with the broker. The salesperson can work with the buyer as a customer. The listing broker must give permission for the showings.

Reference: Real Estate Practice in Georgia > Listings and Agency

10. The principal method of delineating property boundaries or legal descriptions in Georgia is known as the:

A. rectangular survey system.

B. system of metes and bounds.

C. colonial block grant system.

D. system of principal meridians and base lines.

Answer: B. The answer is system of metes and bounds. The principal method of delineating property boundaries or legal descriptions in Georgia is known as the system of metes and bounds. Two forms of legal description are used in Georgia: (1) metes and bounds, and (2) the recorded plat.

Reference: Real Estate Practice in Georgia > Real Estate Practice

11. Under BRRETA, if an agency agreement does not contain a termination date, which of the following is TRUE?:

A. It will automatically end after one year.

B. It is not a valid agreement.

C. It cannot continue beyond 120 days.

D. It might last indefinitely.

Answer: A. The answer is it will automatically end after one year. According to BRRETA, an agency agreement will automatically end after one year if the agreement does not contain a termination date or if the task required in the agreement has not been performed. An agency agreement usually ends when the time limit in the agreement has expired, when the task has been performed, or by mutual agreement of the parties.

Reference: Real Estate Practice in Georgia > Listings and AgencyThe answer is it will automatically end after one year. According to BRRETA, an agency agreement will automatically end after one year if the agreement does not contain a termination date or if the task required in the agreement has not been performed. An agency agreement usually ends when the time limit in the agreement has expired, when the task has been performed, or by mutual agreement of the parties.

12. Contract forms in general use in Georgia make use of the concept of "due diligence." How does "due diligence" affect the purchase and sales agreement?:

A. It assures the buyer that the title search will be reliable.

B. It makes both listing and selling agents accountable for any mistakes.

C. It obligates the seller to make all necessary repairs.

D. It obligates the buyer to remove contingencies within a stated time frame or cancel the contract.

Answer: D. The answer is it obligates the buyer to remove contingencies within a stated time frame or cancel the contract. Due diligence requires that a person use good-faith efforts to perform any obligations stated in a purchase and sale agreement. Sales contracts usually include specific time periods in which due diligence must be exercised by the parties to the contract.

13. A sales contract is signed on May 1. Closing takes place on June 10, and the security deed is recorded on June 15. The borrower's first payment is due on August 30. When is the soonest that the broker might receive a commission check?:

A. 1-May

B. 15-Jun

C. 10-Jun

D. 30-Aug

Answer: C. The answer is June 10. In Georgia, it is customary that funds are disbursed and commission checks received at the closing. June 10 is the soonest that brokers would receive their commission check.

Reference: Real Estate Practice in Georgia > Real Estate Practice

14. When should a landlord first present the rules and regulations for tenants of leased property?:

A. When the tenant first violates them

B. At any time during the rental agreement

C. When the tenant requests them

D. At the time the tenant enters into the rental agreement or at the time the rules or regulations are adopted

Answer: D. The answer is at the time the tenant enters into the rental agreement or at the time the rules or regulations are adopted. The landlord should present the rules when the tenant is entering into the rental agreement or whenever the rules are adopted.

Reference: Real Estate Practice in Georgia > Real Estate Practice

15. After a tenant's lease terminates, the tenant is entitled to the return of the security deposit:

A. with no deduction withheld.

B. within six weeks, including interest.

C. within three weeks, including interest.

D. within 30 days, minus deductions for any damages as provided for in the lease agreement.

Answer: D. The answer is within 30 days, minus deductions for any damages as provided for in the lease agreement. Georgia law requires that a tenant's security deposit be returned within one month after the tenant has vacated the property and returned the keys to the landlord. The landlord may deduct amounts for damages to the property as provided for in the lease agreement. The landlord must provide a written explanation to the tenant prior to making deductions from the security deposit.

Reference: Real Estate Practice in Georgia > Real Estate Practice

16. In any real estate sales transaction that a broker negotiates on behalf of a seller, the broker is required to do all of the following EXCEPT:

A. make sure that the written purchase and sale agreement includes all the terms of the parties' agreement.

B. keep copies of all documents involved in the transaction in her files for three years after the year in which the transaction was closed.

C. make sure that the closing statement is accurate and that a copy of it is delivered to both buyer and seller.

D. inform the buyer of her personal opinion of the condition of the seller's title to the property.

Answer: D. The answer is inform the buyer of her personal opinion of the condition of the seller's title to the property. The broker may not offer a title opinion, which could be an authorized practice of law. The broker should make sure that all terms agreed to by the parties have been included in the sales contract. The broker is responsible for the accuracy of the closing statement. The broker should keep documents related to the transaction in her files for three years.

17. What type of insurance must a Georgia licensee carry if managing community associations and if at any time handling more than $60,000?:

A. Trust fund insurance

B. Fire and extended coverage insurance

C. Fidelity insurance

D. Personal liability insurance

Answer: C. The answer is fidelity insurance. Under Georgia license law, fidelity insurance is required of any Georgia licensee if managing community associations and if at any time handling more than $60,000. A broker managing community associations who at any time handles more than $60,000 must have a separate fidelity bond or policy for each association managed.

Reference: Real Estate Practice in Georgia > Community Association Management

18. Which type of agency is recognized in Georgia?:

A. Undisclosed dual agency

B. Fiduciary agency

C. Transaction brokerage

D. Designated agency

Answer: D. The answer is designated agency. In Georgia, designated agency is specifically recognized and defined. Dual agency is permitted only if both parties agree to the dual representation. BRRETA defines the duties of agents and does not use the term "fiduciary" as found in the common law agency. Transaction brokerage occurs when a licensee acts only as a facilitator in a transaction, and the agent does not represent either party to the transaction.

Reference: Real Estate Practice in Georgia > Listings and Agency

19. All of the following agreements must be in writing EXCEPT:

A. an exclusive-agency listing.

B. a 10-year commercial lease.

C. an exclusive-right-to-sell listing.

D. an open listing.

Answer: D. The answer is an open listing. An open listing does not have to be in writing. BRRETA requires that exclusive agency listings be in writing. All leases with a term over one year must be in writing to be enforceable.

Reference: Real Estate Practice in Georgia > Listings and Agency

20. Two agents who work for the Realty Company find themselves working on the same transaction, one with the

seller as a client and one with the buyer as a client. In this situation, under Georgia's Brokerage Relationships in Real Estate Transactions Act (BRRETA),:

A. the broker can authorize both agents to continue to give full service to their respective clients.

B. the brokerage firm is practicing dual agency.

C. one of the two clients must be referred to another brokerage firm.

D. no material facts may be exchanged by the agents.

Answer: A. The answer is the broker can authorize both agents to continue to give full service to their respective clients. BRRETA defines this situation as "designated agency," not dual agency. The two agents are still bound to disclose any adverse material facts that may influence either party in the transaction.

Reference: Real Estate Practice in Georgia > Listings and Agency

21. Under Georgia law, written disclosure of an agency relationship must be made:

A. at an open house.

B. at the closing table.

C. as soon as reasonably possible.

D. at the time an offer is made.

Answer: D. The answer is at the time an offer is made. Under Georgia law, written agency disclosure must be made no later than at the time an offer is made. Georgia law does require that an agency disclosure be made as soon as reasonably possible in a transaction, but the law does not require that disclosure to be in writing.

Reference: Real Estate Practice in Georgia > Listings and Agency

22. Under Georgia agency law, a material fact is defined as:

A. a fact a party does not know but would reasonably want to know.

B. a fact that a party could readily discover but might have failed to observe.

C. any fact that could be verified in public records.

D. a fact that a party would find of minor importance in a transaction.

Answer: A. The answer is a fact a party does not know but would reasonably want to know. Under BRRETA, Georgia's agency law, a material fact is defined as a fact a party to a transaction does not know, could not reasonably discover, and would reasonably want to know.

Reference: Real Estate Practice in Georgia > Listings and Agency

23. In Georgia, the age of legal competence is:

A. 21 years old.

B. 19 years old.

C. 18 years old.

D. 20 years old.

Answer: C. The answer is 18 years old. The age of legal competence in Georgia is 18 years old. A person must be at least 18 years old to enter into a legal contract in Georgia.

Reference: Real Estate Practice in Georgia > Sales Contracts

24. In making a listing presentation, a licensee is told by a seller that the commission rate he is quoting seems somewhat high. How should he reply?:

A. "The board of REALTORS® recommends this rate."

B. "This is the rate my company charges for its services."

C. "It is the going rate in our market."

D. "This rate is endorsed by the real estate commission."

Answer: C. The answer is "This is the rate my company charges for its services." A brokerage may establish its own compensation policy, but any other answer violates antitrust law. The licensee must avoid any remarks that might indicate price-fixing or group boycotting.

Reference: Real Estate Practice in Georgia > Real Estate Practice

25. Georgia real estate salespersons may lawfully collect compensation from:

A. their employing broker only.

B. a licensed real estate broker only.

C. either a buyer or a seller.

D. any party to the transaction or the party's representative.

Answer: A. The answer is their employing broker only. Salespeople may only collect compensation from their employing brokers. They may not receive compensation from parties to a transaction or another broker.

**26. In the purchase and sales agreement, the responsibility
for a satisfactory inspection for termites and other wood-
destroying insects rests with:**

A. the buyer.

B. the seller.

C. the listing company.

D. no one, as the inspection is no longer deemed necessary.

Answer: A. The answer is the buyer. Georgia law does not
require a standard contract form be used in all real estate
transactions. The purchase and sales agreement provided by the
Georgia Association of REALTOR®, commonly used in
transactions in Georgia, includes due diligence clauses that
require the buyer to inspect the property and the neighborhood.
The contract forms require the seller to keep all utilities,
systems, and equipment operable so that the buyer or the

buyer's representative may conduct inspections of the property.

Reference: Real Estate Practice in Georgia > Real Estate Practice

27. In Georgia, which statement is TRUE regarding instructors who teach prelicense classes?:

A. A school may teach prelicense courses without Commission approval if the courses are taught by approved prelicense instructors.

B. Prelicense instructors do not have a continuing education requirement.

C. Instructors wishing to teach prelicense classes must be licensed by the Commission.

D. Prelicense instructor licenses must be renewed every two years.

Answer: C. The answer is instructors wishing to teach prelicense classes must be licensed by the Commission. A person teaching Georgia prelicense courses must be approved by the Commission as a prelicense instructor. Prelicense instructors renew their approval every four years, and are required to complete instructor continuing education courses. Prelicense instructors may only teach courses at a school approved by the Commission.

Reference: Real Estate Practice in Georgia > Real Estate Practice

28. In Georgia, a broker is representing a couple who has purchased a lot and is contemplating the construction of a new home. The broker should advise them on all of the following EXCEPT:

A. having a plan that provides for required setbacks.

B. having the contract for the construction reviewed by an attorney before signing.

C. how the couple should take title.

D. providing protection against future mechanics' liens.

Answer: C. The answer is how the couple should take title. The couple should be advised to see an attorney for title advice. However, the broker should advise the couple to see that the plan has appropriate setbacks, to have the contract reviewed by an attorney, and to ask for a lien waiver, which would provide protection against future mechanics' liens.

Reference: Real Estate Practice in Georgia > Listings and Agency

29. The types of agency relationships that a company offers are stated in:

A. the company's policy manual.

B. the Georgia license law.

C. the rules and regulations of the Georgia Real Estate Commission.

D. Georgia's Brokerage Relationships in Real Estate Transactions Act (BRRETA).

Answer: A. The answer is the company's policy manual. Georgia law requires that real estate brokerage firms must have a written policy stating the types of agency relationships to be practiced by the broker and their agents. BRRETA defines the statutory duties of agents to their clients but does not mandate what types of agency companies may practice. Neither the license law nor the Commission's rules require real estate companies to enter into specific types of agency relationships.

Reference: Real Estate Practice in Georgia > Listings and Agency

30. A buyer contacts a real estate office and indicates an interest in purchasing a nearby home. Without entering into an agency relationship with the buyer, a salesperson from the real estate office can do all of the following EXCEPT:

A. give the buyer maps showing local schools, hospitals, and shopping centers.

B. inform the buyer of the brokerage firm's agency policies.

C. prequalify the buyer for a mortgage.

D. provide the buyer with information on properties for sale in the area.

Answer: C. The answer is prequalify the buyer for a mortgage. The salesperson may not prequalify the buyer for a mortgage, as doing so would require gaining confidential information from the buyer without first entering into a buyer agency relationship. The salesperson may provide the buyer with maps, information on available properties, and the firm's agency policies.

Reference: Real Estate Practice in Georgia > Listings and Agency

31. A buyer's broker is showing a house that is for sale by owner. The owner has agreed to the showing and is willing to pay a commission if a sale results from the showing. This means that the broker:

A. has no agency relationship with the seller even though the seller will pay a commission.

B. is acting as a dual agent.

C. is acting as a subagent of the seller.

D. is acting as the listing agent.

Answer: A. The answer is has no agency relationship with the seller even though the seller will pay a commission. While the broker represents the buyer, the owner is not represented. The buyer broker is not an agent of the buyer. Agency representation is determined by who hires the broker, and not by who pays the broker's commission.

Reference: Real Estate Practice in Georgia > Listings and Agency

32. A seller has been presented with an offer to purchase that includes a provision that the seller will be willing to make a 20% purchase money mortgage loan. The seller asks the listing broker for advice about any risk involved with taking back purchase money loan. The broker should tell the seller that:

A. the risk is minimal if a credit report is presented.

B. it would be best to consult an attorney.

C. there is no risk involved since the property will be security for the loan.

D. it would be illegal for the seller to lend as much as 20% of the purchase price.

Answer: B. The answer is it would be best to consult an attorney. Because the seller is asking a legal question, the broker should advise the seller to consult with an attorney. Providing advice on this matter to the seller would be an unauthorized practice of law and a violation of the license law.

Reference: Real Estate Practice in Georgia > Real Estate Practice

33. A broker has agency agreements with both a seller and a buyer. The buyer wants to make an offer on the seller's property. Can the broker represent the buyer in this transaction?:

A. No, because the real estate company would then be a dual agent

B. No, the buyer should be advised to offer on a different property

C. Yes, if company policy permits "designated agency"

D. Yes, if the seller has agreed to pay the commission

Answer: C. The answer is yes, if company policy permits "designated agency." The Georgia's Brokerage Relationships in Real Estate Transactions Act (BRRETA) allows the broker to appoint two separate agents within the company to individually represent the seller and the buyer in the same transaction. The law classifies this arrangement as "designated agency." Commissions may be paid by either the seller or the buyer, or by both. BRETTA does not define this relationship as dual agency.

Reference: Real Estate Practice in Georgia > Listings and Agency

34. A salesperson may accept compensation from someone other than the broker with whom the salesperson is affiliated only if:

A. the compensation comes from a former employing broker as a commission earned on a contract negotiated before the change of employment.

B. the compensation comes from a cooperating broker with whom the salesperson shared a transaction.

C. the salesperson is paid directly by a buyer who was a client.

D. the compensation is a bonus voluntarily paid by a grateful client.

Answer: A. The answer is the compensation comes from a former employing broker as a commission earned on a contract negotiated before the change of employment. A salesperson may accept compensation from someone other than the broker with whom the salesperson is affiliated only if the compensation comes from a former employing broker as a commission earned on a contract negotiated before the change of employment.

Reference: Real Estate Practice in Georgia > Real Estate Practice

35. In Georgia, any interest earned on a tenant's security deposit:

A. should be distributed as stated in the lease agreement.

B. is shared evenly between landlord and tenant.

C. is illegal, since security deposits must be kept in non-interest-bearing accounts.

D. must be repaid to the tenant.

Answer: A. The answer is should be distributed as stated in the lease agreement. Unless a lease contract states otherwise, interest earned on a tenant's security deposit will belong to the landlord. A lease agreement specifies how any interest on a tenant's security deposit will be distributed.

Reference: Real Estate Practice in Georgia > Real Estate Practice

36. In Georgia, a buyer brokerage agreement may be canceled by:

A. the broker if having given 30 days' notice in writing.

B. the broker if having given 30 days' notice in writing.

C. either party with written notice at any time.

D. either party with at least 30 days' written notice.

Answer: C. The answer is either party with written notice at any time. In Georgia, buyer brokerage agreement forms provide that the agreement can be canceled by either party, with written notice, at any time. A broker, however, can claim the right to compensation for properties shown to the buyer before the buyer brokerage agreement was cancelled.

Reference: Real Estate Practice in Georgia > Listings and Agency

37. In Georgia, residential sales contracts generally afford to buyers some confidence about the structural condition of the property, because the offer may be made subject to a(n):

A. broker's price opinion.

B. inspection by a home inspector.

C. survey prepared by a licensed surveyor.

D. appraisal.

Answer: B. The answer is inspection by a home inspector. Residential sales contracts in Georgia usually contain a clause stating that the buyer's offer is contingent upon a property inspection by a qualified home inspector. An appraisal is an estimate of value by a state classified appraiser, and a broker's price opinion is a broker's competitive market analysis of the property. Neither an appraisal, a broker's price opinion, nor a survey provide any protection for the buyer concerning the actual structural condition of the property.

Reference: Real Estate Practice in Georgia > Sales Contracts

38. A listing broker delivers a buyer's contract to her seller, and the seller accepts the offer. The next day, the seller

notifies the broker that he withdraws the acceptance of the buyer's offer. In this situation, the broker:

A. is without recourse, because the transaction was never completed.

B. is entitled to collect a commission.

C. may retain the deposit as commission.

D. may sue the buyer.

Answer: B. The answer is is entitled to collect a commission. The broker earned the commission since she has procured a ready, willing, and able buyer for the seller. The deposit must be returned to the buyer. The broker may not take her commission from the earnest money that was deposited into the broker's trust account.

Reference: Real Estate Practice in Georgia > Listings and Agency

39. A real estate salesperson is representing a buyer in the buyer's search for a new home. After helping the buyer

negotiate for his dream home, the salesperson might perform other services, including:

A. accepting a gratuity from the lender chosen by the buyer.

B. recommending several sources for mortgage loans.

C. advising the buyer not to order a home inspection.

D. accepting a bonus from the listing salesperson.

Answer: B. The answer is recommending several sources for mortgage loans. The buyer's agent may recommend several sources for mortgage loans. Accepting a gratuity from the lender who is chosen by the buyer would be an illegal kickback. Salespersons may only receive compensation from their employing broker. In most cases, a buyer's agent should advise a buyer to order a home inspection.

Reference: Real Estate Practice in Georgia > Listings and Agency

40. In the purchase and sale agreement forms used in Georgia, the question of how a commission will be divided between listing and selling brokers:

A. is not included; rather, it is noted in a separate agreement.

B. provides for a 50-50 split.

C. is included as an obligation, but the percentages are left up to the closing attorney.

D. is included and has blanks for filling in the percentage each is to receive.

Answer: A. The answer is is not included; rather, it is noted in a separate agreement. The commission split between brokers is not included in the purchase and sale agreement form; rather, it is noted on a separate agreement. The commission split is negotiated between the brokers involved in the transaction.

Reference: Georgia Real Estate Practice in Georgia > Sales Contracts

41. Routine real estate services that do NOT require a licensee's professional judgment or skill are referred to as:

A. material acts.

B. transactional brokerage acts.

C. ministerial acts.

D. routine brokerage acts.

Answer: C. The answer is ministerial acts. BRRETA defines ministerial acts as acts that do not require a licensee's professional judgment or skills. A real estate license is required to perform brokerage acts for a client or to act as a transaction broker or agent for parties to a real estate transaction.

Reference: Real Estate Practice in Georgia > Listings and Agency

42. In Georgia, an exclusive-right-to-sell listing contract:

A. must extend for at least 30 days.

B. must provide for the seller's written consent for "For Sale" signs are to be posted.

C. becomes the property of the broker's affiliated licensee.

D. can be written to last "until sold."

Answer: B. The answer is must provide for the seller's written consent for "For Sale" signs are to be posted. The salesperson must have written permission to post a For Sale sign. A listing contract in Georgia must have a definite termination date and can be for any period of time agreed to by the seller and the broker. The listing belongs to the broker and is a contract between the seller and the broker.

Reference: Real Estate Practice in Georgia > Listings and Agency

43. Official maps indicating that a property might be all or partially in a floodplain are available from:

A. FEMA.

B. the state planning department.

C. county health departments.

D. local planning departments.

Answer: A. The answer is FEMA. Official maps indicating that a property might be all or partially in a floodplain are available online from the Federal Emergency Management Agency (FEMA).

Reference: Real Estate Practice in Georgia > Real Estate Practice

44. A leasing agent's primary responsible is to:

A. hire the owner's employees.

B. make property repairs.

C. spend the profits.

D. find a qualified tenant.

Answer: D. The answer is find a qualified tenant. A property manager's first duty is to find qualified tenants, collect rents, and be sure the principal makes money. Property repairs may or may not be done by the property manager. A property manager would not be responsible for hiring the owner's employees or spending the owner's profits.

Reference: Real Estate Practice In Georgia > Property Management

45. With regard to the use of preprinted real estate contract forms in Georgia, which of the following is TRUE?:

A. The printed language on a form takes precedence over anything written in.

B. Real estate licensees may fill in the blanks or cross out inappropriate language without being accused of practicing law.

C. The Georgia Real Estate Commission requires that approved forms be used.

D. A licensee may prepare a contract form if a preprinted form does not suit the transaction.

Answer: B. The answer is real estate licensees may fill in the blanks or cross out inappropriate language without being accused of practicing law. Real estate licensees may fill in the blanks of a preprinted real estate contract form without being guilty of practicing law. Licensees who draft a contract on their own are guilty of practicing law and in violation of the license law. The Commission does not require standard forms. Brokers use preprinted forms drafted or approved by attorneys so that agents do not practice law. Anything in a person's handwriting takes precedence over printed language in a contract.

Reference: Real Estate Practice in Georgia > Sales Contracts

46. In Georgia, properties are assessed for tax purposes at:

A. 40% of market value.

B. 75% of market value.

C. market value, as established by the assessor.

D. 25% of market value.

Answer: A. The answer is 40% of market value. In Georgia, properties are assessed for tax purposes at 40% of market value. In some states, the assessed value is equal to the market value. States may select a percentage of market value as the assessed value provided each property in a taxing district is treated equally.

Reference: Real Estate Practice in Georgia > Real Estate Practice

47. A seller's listing agreement has expired, and the seller lists with a different brokerage firm. The original listing agent now has a buyer interested in the seller's property. The original listing agent:

A. is a dual agent.

B. cannot represent the buyer.

C. cannot disclose to the buyer information about the physical condition of the property.

D. cannot disclose to the buyer offers received on the seller's property while it was listed with him.

Answer: D. The answer is cannot disclose to the buyer offers received on the seller's property while it was listed with him. The original agent no longer has an agency relationship with the seller, and the agent is now free to represent the buyer. Agents must always disclose information about the physical condition of the property, but confidential information, such as the amount of a previous offer, must remain confidential.

Reference: Real Estate Practice in Georgia > Listings and Agency

48. A broker has obtained an offer to purchase a residence that is listed with his firm. Two days after the offer has been accepted and become a binding agreement, another offer is received that is higher in price than the one the seller accepted. Which statement is TRUE?:

A. The offer must be presented and can be accepted only as a backup in case the first offer does not close.

B. The broker should write "rejected" on the offer and return it to the offeror.

C. The broker need not present the second offer since there is now a firm contract.

D. The broker can present the offer and suggest ways in which the seller might get out of the first contract.

Answer: A. The answer is the offer must be presented and can be accepted only as a backup in case the first offer does not close. The second offer must be presented and can be accepted only as a backup in case the first offer does not close. A broker must present all offers to the seller, even if there is a binding agreement in place. In this situation, the higher offer can only be accepted by the seller if the binding agreement does not close.

Reference: Real Estate Practice in Georgia > Real Estate Practice

49. Georgia's Brokerage Relationships in Real Estate Transactions Act (BRRETA) requires that a licensee, when taking a listing, must disclose to the seller all of the following EXCEPT:

A. the names of the company's officers and directors.

B. the company's policy regarding agency relationships.

C. whether the broker will share compensation paid by the client to another broker representing another party.

D. any brokerage relationship that would conflict with the interests of the prospective client.

Answer: A. The answer is the names of the company's officers and directors. The licensee does not have to disclose the names of the company's officers and directors. However, the licensee is required to disclose the company's agency policies, the company's policy with regard to sharing compensation with other brokers, and whether the company has any brokerage relationship with another party that would create conflict of interest for the prospective client. Reference: Real Estate Practice in Georgia > Listings and Agency

50. Commissions earned by brokers in a real estate sales transaction:

A. are based on a schedule of commission rates set by the Georgia Real Estate Commission.

B. may be deducted from the earnest money deposit and claimed by the broker as soon as the buyer and seller execute the purchase and sale agreement.

C. may be shared with an unlicensed person, provided that such person aided the broker in bringing the buyer and seller together.

D. are determined by agreement of the brokers and their principal.

Answer: D. The answer is are determined by agreement of the brokers and their principal. Commissions are always negotiable between the principal and the broker and are not determined by custom or law. The commission may not be deducted from the earnest money deposit and may not be shared with an unlicensed party.

Reference: Real Estate Practice in Georgia > Real Estate Practice

51. A salesperson represents a seller in a transaction. When prospective buyers ask the salesperson to show them the property, the salesperson must:

A. tell them that they must be represented by a designated agent from her firm.

B. make a written disclosure of the agency relationship with the seller in a timely manner.

C. show the property without any agency disclosure to protect the interests of the seller.

D. tell them that they must first enter into a buyer representation agreement with another firm.

Answer: B. The answer is make a written disclosure of the agency relationship with the seller in a timely manner. Georgia regulations require that brokers or salespersons disclose in writing their agency relationship with a seller to a buyer in a timely manner, but no later than the time of an offer being made by the buyer. This disclosure must be made so that the buyer understands that the salesperson does not represent the buyer. A buyer is not required to be represented by any broker, and the seller's agent can work with an unrepresented buyer as a customer.

Real Estate Practice in Georgia > Listings and Agency

52. Which of the following is an example of a ministerial act under Georgia's agency law?:

A. Arguing the merits of an offer on behalf of a prospective buyer.

B. Assisting a buyer through the closing process.

C. Responding to general questions about the price and location of a specific property.

D. Advising a prospective buyer on how much to offer for a property.

Answer: C. The answer is responding to general questions about the price and location of a specific property. Generally speaking, providing published information, like the price and location of a property, is considered ministerial in nature. However, negotiating on behalf of a buyer, helping buyers determine a price range, or assisting a buyer through closing requires a real estate license in Georgia. A ministerial act is any act that does not require the exercise of a licensee's professional judgment or skill.

Reference: Real Estate Practice in Georgia > Listings and Agency

53. A real estate licensee has signed a brokerage agreement with a tenant who is looking for an apartment to rent. The licensee does not charge a fee to the prospective tenant; rather, the licensee receives a commission from the landlord. The licensee tells the landlord that the prospective tenant could probably pay a somewhat higher rent than what the landlord is asking. In this situation,:

A. the licensee's disclosure was appropriate.

B. the licensee must receive a commission from his client.

C. the licensee owes a duty to disclose the buyer's financial condition to the landlord.

D. the licensee has violated his statutory duties owed to the tenant.

Answer: D. The answer is the licensee has violated his statutory duties owed to the tenant. BRRETA, Georgia's agency law, requires a licensee to keep confidential the tenant's financial condition, as the tenant is the client in this situation. The licensee may receive a commission from either party in the transaction. The licensee's agency relationship is determined by being hired by the tenant, not by the fact that the landlord pays the licensee's commission.

Reference: Real Estate Practice in Georgia > Listings and Agency

54. Upon obtaining a listing, a broker or licensed salesperson is obligated to:

A. cooperate with every real estate office wishing to participate in the marketing of the listed property.

B. create a listing file and number it in compliance with Georgia real estate license law and rules.

C. place advertisements in the local newspapers.

D. give the person or persons signing the listing a legible, signed, true, and correct copy.

Answer: D. The answer is give the person or persons signing the listing a legible, signed, true, and correct copy. Giving the seller a legible, signed, true, and correct copy is required, but numbering files or advertising is not. Other brokers are not required to participate in the marketing of the property.

Reference: Real Estate Practice in Georgia > Listings and Agency

55. A "short form" legal description, often used in Georgia documents and contracts, is a(n):

A. government survey land description.

B. abbreviated metes-and-bounds description.

C. reference to recorded subdivision maps, noting book and page number of the recorded information.

D. surveyor's description.

Answer: C. The answer is reference to recorded subdivision maps, noting book and page number of the recorded information. A "short form" legal description, often used in

Georgia documents and contracts, is a reference to recorded subdivision maps, noting book and page number of the recorded information. This short form of legal description is commonly referred to as the recorded plat.

Reference: Real Estate Practice in Georgia > Real Estate Practice

56. Every Georgia real estate office is required to:

A. maintain trust account records for five years.

B. keep transaction records for three years.

C. employ at least one salesperson.

D. display signage at the office location.

Answer: B. The answer is keep transaction records for three years. Georgia license law requires brokers to keep trust and transaction records for three years. Brokers are not, however, required to display a sign at the office location or employ any salespeople.

Reference: Real Estate Practice in Georgia > Real Estate Practice

57. Developers of new homes and subdivisions in metropolitan areas of Georgia may be required to pay "impact fees." Impact fees are:

A. fees charged by local jurisdictions to pay for new schools and utilities arising from projected increases in the local population.

B. fees charged by the police to provide extra security to job sites.

C. charges to support the work of the local planning departments.

D. charges by the Department of Transportation to offset the damage construction equipment will do to roads.

Answer: A. The answer is fees charged by local jurisdictions to pay for new schools and utilities arising from projected increases in the local population. "Impact fees" are fees charged by local jurisdictions to pay for new schools and utilities expected due to the increase in local populations. Such increases often occur as a result of the availability of new homes and subdivisions.

Reference: Real Estate Practice in Georgia > Real Estate Practice

58. In Georgia, a qualifying broker is responsible for all of the following duties EXCEPT:

A. making sure that all salespeople are actively licensed.

B. reviewing all contracts of affiliates within 30 days.

C. providing health insurance to all agents and staff.

D. retaining all contracts and documents for at least three years.

Answer: C. The answer is providing health insurance to all agents and staff. Georgia license law requires that qualifying brokers review all contracts within 30 days, retain records for three years, and make sure agents are properly licensed. Health insurance is not a requirement, as most licensees are employed as independent contractors.

59. Buyer-brokerage contracts in Georgia:

A. are illegal.

B. must be in writing to be enforceable.

C. must be on specific forms.

D. are not regulated under the license laws.

Answer: C. The answer is must be in writing to be enforceable. The buyer-brokerage contract is an employment contract between the buyer and the broker and must be in writing to be enforceable. Buyer-brokerage contracts are legal under BRRETA and are regulated, just as are listing agreements between a seller and the broker. BRRETA does not dictate specific forms for agency agreements, but brokers and agents should only use forms that have been drafted and approved by an attorney.

60. Anxious to acquire a particularly desirable listing, a broker tells a seller that he will buy the property himself if it does not sell within 60 days. Which statement is TRUE?:

A. The broker must arrange for another licensee to manage the sales transaction between the parties.

B. Licensees should never buy properties they have listed.

C. The plan is legal if the promise to purchase is put into writing in a sales agreement that will accompany the listing.

D. This type of inducement is illegal in Georgia.

Answer: D. The answer is the plan is legal if the promise to purchase is put into writing in a sales agreement that will accompany the listing. The broker must include this promise in writing in a sales agreement that accompanies the listing. The broker and his firm may negotiate and manage the sale if the broker purchases the property.

61. In Georgia, which statement is TRUE regarding the gross receipts tax imposed by some local jurisdictions?:

A. The tax can be imposed on any transaction in which a party of the transaction resided in the jurisdiction.

B. The tax is due only on transactions that occur within the jurisdiction.

C. The tax can be imposed on every transaction closed by a company that has an office in the jurisdiction.

D. Real estate companies are exempt from gross receipts taxes.

Answer: B. The answer is the tax is due only on transactions that occur within the jurisdiction. The gross receipts tax can only be imposed on transactions that occur within the specific jurisdiction. The tax does not apply to transactions outside of the jurisdiction.

62. A salesperson is working with a buyer prospect who does not wish to enter into a buyer agency agreement. The buyer wants to make an offer on a property that is "for sale by owner." The salesperson approaches the seller about listing the property with her real estate company, but the seller does not want to list his property with any broker. The salesperson agrees to help the buyer and seller complete the transaction. The salesperson in this situation is acting as a:

A. transaction broker.

B. dual agent.

C. buyer's broker.

D. designated agent.

Answer: A. The answer is transaction broker. According to Georgia's Brokerage Relationships in Real Estate Transactions Act (BRRETA), the salesperson is acting as a transaction broker, which can be defined as a licensee who is treating both parties to the transaction as customers, not clients (i.e., acting as a facilitator). As a transaction broker, the salesperson owes to the parties only ministerial acts and must disclose to the parties any adverse material facts.

Reference: Real Estate Practice in Georgia > Listings and Agency

63. A buyer who is a broker's client wants to purchase a house that the broker has listed with a seller. In this situation,:

A. the broker may proceed with the transaction if both parties give informed, written consent.

B. the broker should refer the buyer to another broker to negotiate the sale.

C. an illegal dual agency is created.

D. the buyer should not have been shown a house listed by the broker.

Answer: A. The answer is the broker may proceed with the transaction if both parties give informed, written consent. BRRETA, Georgia's agency law, does not explicitly forbid dual agency. However, a broker may represent both parties to a transaction only with the informed, written consent of both parties to the transaction. BRRETA does permit the broker to appoint different salespersons or associate brokers to represent the seller and the buyer as designated agents.

Reference: Real Estate Practice in Georgia > Listings and Agency

64. If a minor enters into a contract in Georgia, what is the statutory period within which they may legally void the contract after reaching the age of majority?:

A. They have six months after reaching the age of majority.

B. There is no statutory period, but courts have held that the action must be taken within a reasonable time after coming of age.

C. They have one year to void a contract.

D. The contract may be voided only up to the date when the minor reaches the age of majority; after that date, the contract is binding.

Answer: B. The answer is there is no statutory period, but courts have held that the action must be taken within a reasonable time after coming of age. There is no statutory period in Georgia, but courts have held that the action must be taken within a reasonable time after coming of age. A minor wishing to disaffirm a contract must do so while still a minor or within a reasonable time after reaching maturity.

Reference: Real Estate Practice in Georgia > Sales Contracts

65. A licensed salesperson is holding an open house in a property he has listed. A couple, who are prospective buyers and not represented by a licensee, visits the property and shows some interest. In this situation, the salesperson:

A. becomes a dual agent.

B. should explain that he represents the seller and will be treating the couple as customers.

C. must have written permission from the buyers to proceed.

D. can share with the couple the lowest price the sellers will accept for the house.

Answer: B. The answer is should explain that he represents the seller and will be treating the couple as customers. The salesperson represents the seller and will be treating the buyers as customers. He should disclose his agency relationship with the seller to the couple before proceeding to show them the house. In this situation, the salesperson does not represent the buyers, so no dual agency is created. The salesperson may work with the couple as customers without any written permission. However, to disclose the lowest price the sellers will accept would violate the salesperson's statutory duties to the seller, his client.

Reference: Real Estate Practice in Georgia > Listings and Agency

66. Which method of describing real estate is NOT used in Georgia?:

A. The recorded plat

B. The "short form" description

C. Rectangular survey system

D. Metes and bounds

Answer: C. The answer is rectangular survey system. The rectangular survey system is not used in Georgia. The "short form" description also is referred to as the recorded plat.

Reference: Real Estate Practice in Georgia > Real Estate Practice

67. Georgia's Brokerage Relationships in Real Estate Transactions Act (BRRETA) requires that certain disclosures must be made to any client with whom a licensee is entering into a brokerage engagement. These disclosures include:

A. whether the brokerage firm has a conflict of interest in the transaction.

B. the name of the financial institution where trust funds are held.

C. the names of the real estate company's officers and directors.

D. the number of licensees in the company.

Answer: A. The answer is whether the brokerage firm has a conflict of interest in the transaction. BRRETA requires that the licensee disclose whether the brokerage firm has a conflict of interest. The licensee does not have to identify the names of the real estate company's officers and directors, the name of the financial institution where trust funds are held, or the number of licensees in the company.

Reference: Real Estate Practice in Georgia > Listings and Agency

1. A wife dies intestate, leaving her husband and three grown children, what percentage of her estate might the husband expect to receive?:

A. One-half of the estate

B. One-fourth of the estate

C. All of the estate, because only minor children inherit

D. One-third under the Georgia law of descent

Answer: D. The answer is one-third under the Georgia law of descent. When the wife dies intestate (without a will or testament), leaving a husband and three grown children, the husband can expect to receive one-third under the Georgia law of descent. The remaining two-thirds is distributed among the three children.

Reference: State Laws and Rules > Substantive Regulations

2. In Georgia, support personnel may perform all of the following activities EXCEPT:

A. compute commission checks.

B. assemble legal documents required for a closing.

C. schedule appointments with an owner for a licensee to show listed real estate.

D. explain contract terms to prospective buyers.

Answer: D. The answer is explain contract terms to prospective buyers. Explaining contract terms to prospective buyers is a service that may only be performed by a licensee. Assembling legal documents (a secretarial act) and computing commission checks (a bookkeeping act) may be performed under the direction of a licensee. Unlicensed support personnel also may schedule appointments for showing real estate.

Reference: State Laws and Rules > Required Licensure

3. To renew a license in Georgia after July 1, 2015, a real estate licensee must:

A. have had a real estate license on active status for at least two years.

B. have completed 36 hours of approved continuing education.

C. pay the required renewal fee for each year of active status.

D. have completed at least 24 hours of approved continuing education.

Answer: B. The answer is have completed 36 hours of approved continuing education. On or after July 1, 2015, a real estate licensee must have completed 36 hours of approved continuing education courses in order to renew a license. Prior to that date, a licensee must have completed 24 hours of continuing education courses. The continuing education requirement applies to anyone having an active license at the time of renewal. The renewal fee applies whether a licensee is on active or inactive status.

Reference: State Laws and Rules > Required Licensure

4. A landlord in Georgia finds that he faces a substantial increase in property taxes. His tenants have leases on their apartments. Which statement is TRUE?:

A. He can raise the rents after paying tax for four months, whether or not the leases have expired.

B. He cannot raise rents because of a property tax increase.

C. He cannot raise the rents until the leases expire.

D. He can raise the rents immediately but only enough to offset the tax increase.

Answer: C. The answer is he cannot raise the rents until the leases expire. Although the landlord has experienced an increase in property taxes, the landlord cannot raise the rents until the leases expire. The landlord is bound by the terms of the lease until expiration of the lease.

Reference: State Laws and Rules > Substantive Regulations

5. If a broker with a Tennessee broker license has a client who wishes to purchase a home in Georgia, the broker may legally do any of the following EXCEPT:

A. by agreement work under the direction of a Georgia broker.

B. refer the client to a Georgia broker and receive a referral fee.

C. hold a nonresident Georgia license and give the client full service.

D. petition the Georgia Real Estate Commission for a temporary license.

Answer: D. The answer is petition the Georgia Real Estate Commission for a temporary license. There is no temporary license. By agreement, the Tennessee broker may work under the direction of a Georgia broker if the Georgia broker agrees to be responsible for the Tennessee broker's action. Alternatively, the Tennessee broker can hold a nonresident Georgia license and give the client full service or refer the client to a Georgia broker and receive a referral fee.

Reference: State Laws and Rules > Required Licensure

6. The sale of unimproved lots is regulated by:

A. state law only.

B. both federal law for interstate sales and Georgia law.

C. the federal Interstate Land Sales Full Disclosure Act only.

D. only by local city or county jurisdictions.

Answer: B. The answer is both federal law for interstate sales and Georgia law. The sale of unimproved lots is regulated by both federal law for interstate sales and Georgia laws for intrastate sales of unimproved property. The laws dictate in part what disclosures must be made to purchasers of those lots.

Reference: State Laws and Rules > Substantive Regulations

7. Which action is legal and does NOT violate license law?:

A. Encouraging a seller to reject an offer because the prospective buyer is Oriental

B. Entering into a dual agency situation with written consent from both parties

C. Having an unlicensed assistant host an open house

D. Advertising that a property is four acres in size when in fact it is only three acres

Answer: B. The answer is entering into a dual agency situation with written consent from both parties. Entering into a dual agency situation with written consent from both parties is legal. However, a broker may not encourage a decision based on race or national origin. Falsely advertising the size of the property or having an unlicensed host an open house is illegal.

Reference: State Laws and Rules > Unfair Practices

8. A real estate broker representing a seller knows that the property has a cracked foundation and that its former owner committed suicide in the kitchen. The broker must disclose:

A. the cracked foundation, but disclosing the suicide is not required.

B. both facts.

C. the suicide but not the cracked foundation.

D. neither fact.

Answer: A. The answer is the cracked foundation, but disclosing the suicide is not required. The broker must disclose any known latent defect in a property, which in this case is the cracked foundation. According to Georgia's Stigmatized Property Act, the broker is not required to disclose the suicide. However, if a buyer directly asks the broker if a suicide has been committed on the property, the broker must answer the question truthfully to the best of her knowledge.

Reference: State Laws and Rules > Substantive Regulations

9. In Georgia, the real estate license law is administered by the:

A. Georgia Association of REALTORS.

B. Georgia Governor's Office of Consumer Affairs.

C. Georgia Real Estate Commission.

D. Department of Housing and Urban Development.

Answer: C. The answer is Georgia Real Estate Commission. In Georgia, the license law is administered by the Georgia Real Estate Commission. The Georgia Association of REALTORS is a trade association, not a government agency.

Reference: State Laws and Rules > Commission Organization and Procedures

10. Many local jurisdictions in Georgia give extra property tax exemptions to property owner-occupants who:

A. have minimum incomes.

B. are elderly or handicapped.

C. are supporting large families.

D. have served in the armed forces.

Answer: B. The answer is are elderly or handicapped. Many local jurisdictions in Georgia give extra property tax exemptions to property owner-occupants who are elderly or handicapped. The exemptions may apply to all or some of the property taxes levied by the jurisdiction. Some jurisdictions have specific exemptions for disabled veterans.

Reference: State Laws and Rules > Substantive Regulations

11. Which statement regarding the Georgia Real Estate Commission is FALSE?:

A. All of the members of the real estate commission must hold active real estate broker's licenses.

B. The examinations that must be taken by all applicants for real estate licensing are administered by an independent testing company.

C. The operation of the commission's activities is administered by an executive director specifically hired for that purpose.

D. The commission makes and enforces the rules by which all real estate licensees must abide.

Answer: A. The answer is all of the members of the real estate commission must hold active real estate broker's licenses. One member of the commission is always an unlicensed person who represents consumers. The commission makes and enforces the rules by which all real estate licensees must abide. A testing service administers the exam, and an executive director administers the operation of the commission.

Reference: State Laws and Rules > Commission Organization and Procedures

12. A broker is convicted on May 1 of possession and distribution of a controlled substance. Both the crime and the conviction took place out of state. On June 15, the broker calls the Georgia Real Estate Commission and leaves a message informing the commission of the conviction. Based on these facts, which statement is TRUE?:

A. The broker was required to notify the commission within 10 days after the conviction.

B. Because the conviction did not occur in Georgia, it is not evidence of unworthy conduct.

C. The broker has properly informed the commission within 60 days after the conviction, and the broker's license may be renewed.

D. The conviction will result in an automatic license revocation.

Answer: A. The answer is the broker was required to notify the commission within 10 days after the conviction. Georgia license law requires that the Commission be notified within 10 days. The licensee's license is automatically revoked within 60 days of the conviction unless the licensee makes a written request for a hearing within the 60-day period.

Reference: State Laws and Rules > Substantive Regulations

13. The area designated to be billed for a special assessment under property tax law to pay for construction of a new sidewalk, sewer, or street lighting is called a(n):

A. construction zone.

B. urban renewal project.

C. improvement district.

D. special tax zone.

Answer: C. The answer is improvement district. The area designated to be billed for a special assessment is called an improvement district or assessment district. The property within that district bears the cost of specific improvements benefitting the people of that district.

Reference: State Laws and Rules > Substantive Regulations

14. A salesperson is showing houses to a buyer who is her client. The houses are listed with other firms. The salesperson is primarily responsible for her actions to the:

A. broker with whom she is affiliated.

B. listing brokers.

C. buyer who is her client.

D. sellers.

Answer: A. The answer is broker with whom she is affiliated. Salespersons are primarily responsible to the broker with whom they are affiliated. The salesperson in this case owes statutory duties to the buyer, who is a client of her broker.

Reference: State Laws and Rules > Substantive Regulations

15. An individual has sued a licensee for fraud and has been awarded a judgment in the amount of $65,000. An attempt to collect on the judgment lien was unsuccessful, so now the Commission's recovery fund might pay:

A. a maximum of $50,000.

B. half of the $65,000 owed.

C. a maximum of $25,000.

D. all of the $65,000 owed.

Answer: C. The answer is a maximum of $25,000. The maximum that an aggrieved individual can obtain from the recovery fund is $25,000. The maximum amount that may be paid from the fund for the actions of any one licensee is $75,000.

Reference: State Laws and Rules > Real Estate Education, Research and Recovery Fund

16. The redemption period for a tax sale in Georgia is:

A. nine months.

B. two years.

C. six months.

D. one year.

Answer: D. The answer is one year. In Georgia, when a tax delinquency occurs, a tax sale is held and the redemption period follows the sale. The redemption period for a tax sale in Georgia is one year. At the tax sale, a tax certificate or certificate of sale in the amount of the unpaid taxes is sold. The purchaser is entitled to a deed to the property provided the delinquent taxpayer does not step forward and redeem it during the redemption period. A person or institution holding a lien on the property also may redeem it.

Reference: State Laws and Rules > Substantive Regulations

17. Georgia law requires that all approved continuing education courses include an element of instruction in the subject of:

A. license law.

B. ethics.

C. contracts.

D. agency.

Answer: B. The answer is ethics. In order for continuing education courses to be approved in Georgia, they must include an element of instruction in the subject of ethics related to the course's content.

Reference: State Laws and Rules > Qualifications and Fees

18. The Georgia Real Estate Commission can refuse to grant a license to an applicant who:

A. is not a resident of Georgia.

B. makes a false statement on the application.

C. has a record of traffic violations.

D. does not plan to work full-time.

Answer: B. The answer is makes a false statement on the application. The Commission may deny a license to a person making a false statement on a license application. The Commission does issue out-of-state licenses. Georgia law does not regulate the work hours for licensees. While the Commission does not consider routine traffic violations in the application process, the Commission may refuse to grant a license to an applicant who has been convicted of numerous DUIs.

Reference: State Laws and Rules > Qualifications and Fees

19. Georgia real estate licenses are automatically revoked for:

A. commingling others' money or property with their own money.

B. failing to respond to a request for information from a real estate commission investigator when a complaint has been filed.

C. failing to perform as promised in a guaranteed sales plan.

D. having been found responsible for acts that resulted in a payout from the Georgia Real Estate Recovery Fund.

Answer: D. The answer is having been found responsible for acts that resulted in a payout from the Georgia Real Estate Recovery Fund. When licensees are found responsible for acts that resulted in a payout from the Georgia Real Estate Recovery Fund, their license is automatically revoked. Failing to respond to a request from the real estate commission investigator, failing to perform as promised in a guaranteed sales plan, or commingling others' money or property with their own may be grounds for disciplinary action by the Commission , but they are not grounds for automatic revocation of a license.

20. A broker's unlicensed assistant worked late nights and weekends to help ensure the successful closing of a difficult transaction. The assistant's extra work included making several phone calls to the prospective buyers and encouraging them to accept the seller's counteroffer. Largely because of the assistant's efforts, the sale went through with no problem. Now, the broker wants to pay the assistant a percentage of the broker's commission, "because the assistant has really earned it." Under Georgia law, the broker may:

A. pay a commission to the assistant only if the assistant is an independent contractor.

B. only collect a fee for the assistant separate from the broker's commission.

C. pay the assistant a percentage of the commission for contributing to the sale.

D. not pay a commission to an unlicensed person, and the broker may be subject to disciplinary action because of the actions of the unlicensed assistant.

Answer: D. The answer is not pay a commission to an unlicensed person, and the broker may be subject to disciplinary action because of the actions of the unlicensed assistant. Unlicensed support personnel are not permitted to advise or negotiate with buyers. Both the unlicensed assistant and the broker are in violation of the license law. A broker may not pay a commission to an unlicensed person.

Reference: State Laws and Rules > Required Licensure

21. When a salesperson decides to terminate affiliation with the employing broker,:

A. the Georgia Real Estate Commission will arbitrate any dispute that arises between the broker and the departing salesperson.

B. the salesperson is entitled to take her own active listings to a new firm.

C. the transferring broker may forward the license to the new broker and notify the Commission in writing of that action.

D. the broker may pay the salesperson any pending commissions from the broker's trust account.

Answer: C. The answer is the transferring broker may forward the license to the new broker and notify the Commission in writing of that action. When a salesperson terminates affiliation with the employing broker, the transferring broker may forward the license of that person to the Commission, or the transferring broker may forward the license to the new broker and notify the Commission in writing of that action. A broker may not pay the salesperson commissions directly from the trust account. The listings belong to the firm, not to the salesperson. The Commission does not arbitrate disputes between brokers and their affiliated licensees.

Reference: State Laws and Rules > Substantive Regulations

22. A real estate license is NOT required for an individual who is:

A. listing luxury properties.

B. selling mobile homes that are not attached to the land.

C. selling real properties at auction sales.

D. marketing new homes for various builders.

Answer: B. The answer is selling mobile homes that are not attached to the land. Selling mobile homes that are not attached to the land does not require a real estate license. However, a real estate license is required to market new homes for various builders, list luxury properties, and sell real property at auction sales.

Reference: State Laws and Rules > Required Licensure

23. A Georgia real estate licensee who is guilty of illegal discrimination may have violated:

A. federal, state, local, and license law.

B. state law only.

C. federal law only.

D. local law only.

Answer: A. The answer is federal, state, local, and license law. A violation of fair housing law can bring about action under federal, state, and local laws and can also result in disciplinary action by the Commission against the real estate licensee. Commission regulations prohibit discrimination because of race, color, religion, sex, disability, national origin, or familial status and define such discrimination as an unfair practice, subject to disciplinary action by the Commission.

Reference: State Laws and Rules > Fair Housing Laws

24. A husband is survived by his wife and their two daughters. The couple's community property is worth $50,000, but the husband also has left a separate estate worth $150,000. Because the husband died suddenly without leaving a will, how will his estate be distributed?:

A. The estate will be distributed according to the state law of descent.

B. The wife will inherit the entire estate.

C. The wife will have to abide by any decision the probate court might make.

D. The wife will inherit the separate property, and the children will share the community property.

Answer: A. The answer is the estate will be distributed according to the state law of descent. Because the husband died suddenly without leaving a will, the estate will be distributed according to the state law of descent. The surviving spouse and the children will be the dominant recipients of all the husband's assets. Georgia does not practice community property law.

Reference: State Laws and Rules > Substantive Regulations

25. A broker intends to open a branch office in a neighboring town. The broker applies for a branch office license, giving a name that clearly identifies its relationship with her main office. The broker names a licensed real estate salesperson as the branch office manager. Will the Commission likely grant approval for the branch office?:

A. No, because a branch office manager must hold a broker's license.

B. Yes, because the manager of a branch office does not need to be a licensed real estate broker.

C. No, because under Georgia license law, brokers cannot have branch offices in more than one municipality.

D. Yes, if the firm's qualifying broker spends at least 40% of her time in the branch office.

Answer: B. The answer is yes, because the manager of a branch office does not need to be a licensed real estate broker. Commission regulations do not require that the manager of a branch office be a licensed real estate broker. Brokers can have branch offices in any location. Qualifying brokers remain responsible for the actions of their branch managers.

Reference: State Laws and Rules > Substantive Regulations

26. In Georgia, when a judgment is filed that involves real property, notice to any future prospective buyer for the property is provided by recording a(n):

A. attachment.

B. lis pendens.

C. notice of pending litigation.

D. habeas corpus.

Answer: B. The answer is lis pendens. In Georgia, when a judgment is filed that involves real property, notice to any future prospective buyer for the property is provided by recording a lis pendens. The buyer can still purchase the property but is now informed of the pending judgment against the property.

Reference: State Laws and Rules > Substantive Regulations

27. A real estate salesperson decides to sell his own property without using a broker. When advertising the property, the salesperson:

A. is required to obtain permission from the Commission.

B. must place his license on inactive status.

C. can place an earnest money deposit in a personal bank account.

D. must disclose his licensed status if acting as a private citizen.

Answer: D. The answer is must disclose his licensed status if acting as a private citizen. When a licensee is selling his own property without a broker, the licensee must disclose his licensed status in all advertising in language identical to that stated in the Commission's regulations. The licensee may never place an earnest money deposit in a personal bank account, and is not required to place a license on inactive status. An active salesperson must obtain the written permission of his broker to advertise the property privately and receive approval of any advertisement.

Reference: State Laws and Rules > Substantive Regulations

28. An individual engaged in real estate activities is exempt from real estate licensing requirements if she is a(n):

A. association, partnership, or corporation.

B. real property securities dealer.

C. executor or administrator selling property to liquidate an estate.

D. appraiser.

Answer: C. The answer is executor or administrator selling property to liquidate an estate. Executors or administrators selling property to liquidate an estate are exempt from licensing requirements. If engaging in real estate activities, an appraiser, association, partnership, corporation, and real estate securities dealer must have a real estate license.

Reference: State Laws and Rules > Required Licensure

29. The rules passed by the Georgia Real Estate Commission:

A. are based on the provisions of the license law.

B. are adopted without notice or public comment.

C. are not in effect until approved in the next session of the state legislature.

D. serve to regulate only the activities of the commission's staff.

Answer: A. The answer is are based on the provisions of the license law. The rules passed by the Georgia Real Estate Commission are based on the provisions of the license law. The rules of the Commission have the force of law and are binding on all real estate licensees. The Commission publishes a notice of intent to change Commission regulations with a stated time period for public comment on any changes.

Reference: State Laws and Rules > Substantive Regulations

30. All of the following are exempt from the provisions of the Georgia license law EXCEPT:

A. resident lessees who receive the equivalent of one month in free rent as a "finder's fee" for referring new tenants to the owner.

B. individuals who receive compensation for procuring prospective buyers or renters of real estate.

C. property owners who sell or lease their own property.

D. utility employees responsible for negotiating easements.

Answer: B. The answer is individuals who receive compensation for procuring prospective buyers or renters of real estate. Anyone receiving compensation for procuring prospective buyers or renters of real estate must first obtain a real estate license. Owners, utility employees, and tenants who receive "free" rent for referring new tenants are exempt from this requirement.

Reference: State Laws and Rules > Required Licensure

31. In Georgia, a real estate license might lapse for any of the following reasons EXCEPT:

A. failure to complete the required hours of approved continuing education.

B. failure to score a passing grade on continuing education courses.

C. failure to pay the required renewal fee when it was due.

D. failure to complete the required salesperson post-licensing course in the first year of licensure.

Answer: B. The answer is failure to score a passing grade on continuing education courses. There is no exam requirement for continuing education courses. A license may lapse for failure to pay the required renewal fee when it was due, failure to complete the required approved continuing education, or failure to complete the salesperson post-licensing course in the first year of licensure.

Reference: State Laws and Rules > Required Licensure

32. The qualifying broker of a real estate corporation in Georgia must:

A. hold at least one share of stock in the corporation.

B. be named an officer of the corporation.

C. hold a majority interest in the corporation's stock.

D. be named to the board of directors.

Answer: C. The answer is be named an officer of the corporation. The qualifying broker of a real estate corporation in Georgia must be named an officer of the corporation. Georgia law does not specify the interest in stock or the shares of stock that the qualifying broker must hold in the corporation.

Reference: State Laws and Rules > Substantive Regulations

33. Neighbor A has a 10-foot easement through neighbor B's forested lot for the purpose of walking to the bank of the river. Neighbor A widens the path to 14 feet to accommodate his truck so he can launch his boat. Neighbor B is furious. Which statement is TRUE in this situation?:

A. The additional four feet is a reasonable extension of the original easement and must be granted.

B. The new use is hostile, and if not stopped within seven years, it could become an easement by prescription.

C. If neighbor A uses the extension for 15 years, the original easement is his by adverse possession.

D. Neighbor A's original use is a right; neighbor B can do nothing.

Answer: B. The answer is the new use is hostile, and if not stopped within seven years, it could become an easement by prescription. The new use is hostile and, if not stopped within seven years, could become an easement by prescription. Neighbor A is only entitled to a 10-foot easement. Neighbor B can avoid the easement by prescription by demanding that neighbor A bring the path back to its original 10-foot dimension.

Reference: State Laws and Rules > Substantive Regulations

34. The total amount that can be paid out of the Georgia Education, Research, and Recovery Fund on behalf of one licensee who may have defrauded many people is:

A. $45,000.00

B. $15,000.00

C. $25,000.00

D. $75,000.00

Answer: D. The answer is $75,000. The total amount that can be paid out of the Georgia Education, Research, and Recovery Fund on behalf of one licensee who may have defrauded many people is $75,000. No individual person may receive more than $25,000 from the fund.

Reference: State Laws and Rules > Real Estate Education, Research, and Recovery Fund

35. A broker took a listing for a small office building from the building's owner. Because the property is in excellent condition and produces a good, steady income, one of the broker's salespersons has decided to purchase it as an investment. When making an offer on the property, the salesperson must:

A. resign as the listing broker's agent and make an offer after becoming affiliated with another broker.

B. purchase the property through a third party on the salesperson's behalf.

C. obtain permission from the Georgia Real Estate Commission.

D. inform the owner in writing that the salesperson is a real estate licensee.

Answer: D. The answer is inform the owner in writing that the salesperson is a real estate licensee. The salesperson must inform the owner in writing that the salesperson is a licensee when making an offer, but the salesperson is not required to change brokerage firms. The salesperson should not use a third party and does not have to report the transaction to the Georgia Real Estate Commission.

Reference: State Laws and Rules > Substantive Regulations

36. The required salesperson postlicense course in Georgia:

A. may be completed through any public educational institution.

B. is only offered in accredited colleges and universities.

C. is available online or in a classroom.

D. may be completed only through public agencies or nonprofit entities.

Answer: C. The answer is available online or in a classroom. While schools offering this course do not have to be an accredited college, university, public agency, or nonprofit organization, they must have a license from the Georgia Real Estate Commission.

Reference: State Laws and Rules > Required Licensure

37. Georgia's Fair Business Practices Act is designed to protect consumers against:

A. pyramid schemes.

B. deceptive advertising.

C. price-fixing.

D. misrepresentation.

Answer: B. The answer is deceptive advertising. Georgia's Fair Business Practices Act is designed to protect consumers against deceptive advertising. To prosecute under the Act, a transaction must have taken place that impacted more than an individual consumer.

Reference: State Laws and Rules > Substantive Regulations

38. In Georgia, the prescriptive period to acquire title to real property by adverse possession is:

A. 20 years.

B. 10 years.

C. 15 years.

D. 7 years.

Answer: A. The answer is 20 years. In Georgia, the prescriptive period to acquire title to real property by adverse possession is 20 years. The period is reduced to seven years if the possession has been under "color of title" in which the occupant of the property appears to have some ownership interest.

39. In Georgia, applicants for a broker's license must prove that they have been actively licensed for:

A. at least two years.

B. at least three years.

C. three of the past five years.

D. three of the past ten years.

Answer: C. The answer is three of the past five years. The Georgia license law requires that applicants for a broker's license must have had three years of active licensure in the past five years.

Reference: State Laws and Rules > Substantive Regulations

40. In Georgia, dower and curtesy rights:

A. give a widower a one-third right to property owned at the time of death.

B. have no effect on the estate of either a widow or a widower.

C. permit a surviving spouse to retain the home.

D. give a widow a one-third right to any property owned during the marriage.

Answer: C. The answer is have no effect on the estate of either a widow or a widower. Georgia does not recognize the rights of dower for a widow or curtesy for a widower.

Reference: State Laws and Rules > Substantive Regulations

41. A broker who wishes to place a For Sale sign on a listed property must first:

A. obtain the written consent of the owner of the property.

B. ensure that there are no more than three For Sale signs on the block at any given time.

C. sell the property.

D. obtain the permission of any adjacent neighbors.

Answer: A. The answer is obtain the written consent of the owner of the property. After obtaining written permission, the broker may erect a For Sale sign on the property. The broker does not have to obtain permission from the neighbors, sell the property, or count the number of other For Sale signs before placing a sign on a listed property.

Reference: State Laws and Rules > Unfair Practices

42. A seller advises a listing broker to avoid discussing the air-conditioning system with prospective buyers, because it is old, noisy, and unreliable. The broker should:

A. tell the seller that the system must be repaired or replaced.

B. trust that a home inspection will note the condition of the system.

C. obey the instructions, because the seller is a client.

D. explain to the seller that the defect must be disclosed.

Answer: D. The answer is explain to the seller that the defect must be disclosed. While the seller is not required to repair the system, the broker should explain to the seller that the defect must be disclosed. The seller may choose to sell "as is," without repairing the system. Brokers are required to disclose to all parties in a transaction any material defect of which they have actual knowledge. The broker is required to disclose the defect even if a home inspection will be conducted on behalf of the buyer.

Reference: State Laws and Rules > Substantive Regulations

43. A licensed real estate salesperson has recently married and, as a result, has changed both her name and home address. Notification of these changes must be made to the Georgia Real Estate Commission within:

A. 3 days.

B. 10 days.

C. 30 days.

D. 15 days.

Answer: C. The answer is 30 days. A licensee must report any name or address change to the Georgia Real Estate Commission within 30 days. The Commission provides a change application for such reporting on the Commission's website.

Reference: State Laws and Rules > Substantive Regulations

44. A person applying for a broker's license in Georgia must meet all of the following requirements EXCEPT:

A. being at least 21 years of age.

B. having been actively engaged as a licensed salesperson for at least two years.

C. being of good moral character.

D. having successfully completed 60 hours of an approved broker prelicense course.

Answer: B. The answer is having been actively engaged as a licensed salesperson for at least two years. In order to obtain a broker's license in Georgia, an individual must have had an active license for at least three years, have successfully completed 60 hours of an approved real estate broker prelicense course, be at least 21 years of age, and be of good moral character.

Reference: State Laws and Rules > Required Licensure

45. In Georgia, the time period necessary for establishing a prescriptive easement is:

A. 7 years.

B. 5 years.

C. 10 years.

D. 25 years.

Answer: C. The answer is 7 years. In Georgia, the time period necessary for establishing a prescriptive easement is seven years. The adverse possession must have occurred over a period of seven years for personal real estate and twenty years for public real property.

Reference: State Laws and Rules > Substantive Regulations

46. How old must a citizen of Georgia be before he may prepare a legally binding will?:

A. 14 years old, provided real property is not involved

B. 18 years old

C. Any age, as long as the will is legally witnessed and recorded

D. 21 years old

Answer: A. The answer is 14 years old, provided real property is not involved. A Georgia citizen must be at least 14 years old in order to prepare a legally binding will. In many states, the legal age to prepare a will is 18.

Reference: State Laws and Rules > Substantive Regulations

47. Which statement about Georgia's Uniform Deceptive Trade Practices Act is TRUE?:

A. It cannot be invoked unless an actual transaction takes place.

B. It is more difficult to invoke than the Fair Business Practices Act.

C. Prosecution can result in prison sentences.

D. It is primarily aimed at price-fixing and antitrust activities.

Answer: D. The answer is it is primarily aimed at price-fixing and antitrust. Georgia's Uniform Deceptive Trade Practices Act is primarily aimed at price-fixing and antitrust activities. Making deceptive statements or engaging in unfair practices may be enough for a violation of this Act.

Reference: State Laws and Rules > Substantive Regulations

48. A homeowner has a real estate license that has been on inactive status for almost 10 years. Now, she wants to sell her home. Which statement is TRUE?:

A. The licensee must state in any advertisements and in any contract that she holds a real estate license.

B. Her license will soon expire, because she cannot be inactive for more than 10 years.

C. She will be required to list the home with an active broker.

D. She must activate her license before selling the house.

Answer: A. The answer is the licensee must state in any advertisements and in any contract that she holds a real estate license. The homeowner must indicate in her ads and contracts that she holds a real estate license. This requirement applies to licensees holding active or inactive real estate licenses.

Reference: State Laws and Rules > Substantive Regulations

49. How many witnesses must sign in the presence of a person making a will to fulfill the legal minimum in Georgia?:

A. Four

B. Two

C. Three

D. One

Answer: B. The answer is two. Two competent witnesses must sign in the presence of the person making the will. No one who is a beneficiary named in a will should be a witness to the signing of the will.

Reference: State Laws and Rules > Substantive Regulations

50. Applicants for a real estate salesperson license in Georgia must:

A. show proof of passing the license examination any time up to six months prior to the application.

B. have the signature of the broker with whom they will affiliate on the application.

C. be at least 21 years old.

D. have completed at least two years of college.

Answer: B. The answer is have the signature of the broker with whom they will affiliate on the application. Applicants for a real estate salesperson license in Georgia must be at least 18 years old and have the signature of the broker with whom they will affiliate on the application. College education is not a real estate licensing requirement. License exam scores are valid for one year.

Reference: State Laws and Rules > Required Licensure

51. In Georgia, which of the following requires a real estate license?:

A. A licensed attorney acting under a power of attorney to convey real estate

B. A person offering management services to subdivision communities

C. A government agency employee managing a subsidized housing development

D. A partnership selling a building owned by the partners

Answer: B. The answer is a person offering management services to subdivision communities. A person offering management services to subdivision communities must have a real estate license. Anyone holding a power of attorney has the authority to sign a principal's name and is not required to have a real estate license. Also exempt from real estate license requirements are partners selling their own property, and government agency employees managing a subsidized housing development.

Reference: State Laws and Rules > Required Licensure

52. The Georgia Real Estate Commission may:

A. publish statements or articles to clarify a position.

B. tell a licensee whether a contemplated action would violate the law.

C. adjudicate a dispute between brokerage firms.

D. render legal advice when asked.

Answer: A. The answer is publish statements or articles to clarify a position. The Georgia Real Estate Commission may publish statements or articles online or in printed form to clarify its positions. The Commission and its staff do not give advice. The Commission does not adjudicate disputes between brokerage firms.

Reference: State Laws and Rules > Substantive Regulations

53. In order to collect from the Georgia Education, Research, and Recovery Fund, an aggrieved individual must first do all of the following EXCEPT:

A. obtain a judgment.

B. sue the licensee whose actions have caused harm.

C. have unsuccessfully attempted to collect on the judgment lien.

D. file an appeal with the state supreme court.

Answer: D. The answer is file an appeal with the state supreme court. In order to collect from the Georgia Education, Research, and Recovery Fund, an aggrieved individual does not have to pursue the matter to the state supreme court. The individual must sue the licensee, obtain a judgment, and then attempt to collect on the judgment lien.

Reference: State Laws and Rules > Real Estate Education, Research and Recovery Fund

54. The Georgia Real Estate Commission's Education, Research, and Recovery Fund is used to compensate:

A. citizens who have become homeless because of foreclosure or dispossession actions.

B. individuals who feel that they have been damaged by the illegal actions of a real estate licensee.

C. brokers who find their business enterprises bordering on bankruptcy.

D. licensees who are unable to work because of a job-related illness or injury.

Answer: B. The answer is individuals who feel that they have been damaged by the illegal actions of a real estate licensee. The Georgia Real Estate Commission's Education, Research, and Recovery Fund is used to compensate individuals who feel that they have been damaged by the illegal actions of a real estate licensee. Payments from the fund may not be made to real estate licensees.

Reference: State Laws and Rules > Real Estate Education, Research and Recovery Fund

55. A homeowner wants to sell her own house. Which statement is TRUE?:

A. She does not need a real estate license to sell her house on her own.

B. In Georgia, anyone who sells real property must first have a real estate license issued by the real estate commission.

C. The individual may obtain a temporary real estate license to legally sell her house

D. She may sell her house without obtaining a real estate license only if she is a licensed attorney.

Answer: A. The answer is she does not need a real estate license to sell her house on her own. In Georgia, property owners selling their own property are exempt from real estate licensing requirements.

Reference: State Laws and Rules > Required Licensure

56. When advertising real property, real estate licensees:

A. may simply give a telephone number to call for more information.

B. may state only the licensee's box number or street address.

C. must identify the owner of the property.

D. must include in any advertisement the name of a licensed real estate firm.

Answer: D. The answer is must include in any advertisement the name of a licensed real estate firm. All advertising must include the name of the listing firm. It is not necessary to state the licensee's box number or street address or the name of the property owner. A phone number alone is insufficient.

Reference: State Laws and Rules > Substantive Regulations

57. A broker has converted an older house into small apartments for students at a nearby college. When a blind student asks to rent a unit on the third floor, the broker rejects his application because he feels it would be too risky for the blind student to negotiate a narrow wooden stairway. Is the broker's action lawful?:

A. Yes, because the visually challenged are not a protected class.

B. Yes, because he is responsible for the safety of his tenants.

C. No, because he is discriminating on the basis of handicap.

D. Yes, because he might be sued if there was an accident.

Answer: C. The answer is no, because he is discriminating on the basis of handicap. Although the broker may feel that he is acting in the best interests of the blind student, this refusal would be a violation of the Fair Housing Act. Disabled people are a protected class under fair housing laws and the Georgia license law.

Reference: State Laws and Rules > Fair Housing Laws

58. A broker has received an earnest money check in the amount of $5,000 and has placed the money in an interest-bearing account. Which of the following is TRUE?:

A. Interest on trust funds will always accrue to the broker who holds the account.

B. Earnest money should never be placed in an interest-bearing account.

C. Interest earned will always accrue to the buyer.

D. The contract must provide for an interest-bearing deposit and state to whom the interest will accrue.

Answer: D. The answer is the contract must provide for an interest-bearing deposit and state to whom the interest will accrue. The broker may deposit the money in an interest-bearing account as long as the contract provides for it and states to whom the interest will accrue. Georgia law does not specify to whom the interest belongs, but the contract must clearly state who will receive interest from the account.

Reference: State Laws and Rules > Substantive Regulations

59. An individual who wants to manage a community association on behalf of a broker, but who does not want to represent sellers, buyers, landlords, or tenants in real estate transactions, may apply for a:

A. CAM license.

B. subdivision license.

C. management license.

D. condominium license.

Answer: A. The answer is CAM license. Anyone managing a community association on behalf of a broker may apply for a CAM (Community Association Management) license. The CAM license does not permit the individual to represent clients in sales or leasing transactions.

Reference: State Laws and Rules > Required Licensure

60. A Georgia real estate license that has been placed on inactive status may stay inactive:

A. indefinitely.

B. for ten years.

C. for two years.

D. for the balance of the renewal period.

Answer: A. The answer is indefinitely. An inactive license may remain on inactive status indefinitely, as long as the licensee renews the license and pays renewal fees every four years.

Reference: State Laws and Rules > Qualifications and Fees

61. Acquiring land by adverse possession requires that the land be used:

A. without the owner's permission.

B. privately so as to avoid being seen.

C. for a period of 30 years.

D. with the owner's permission.

Answer: A. The answer is without the owner's permission. Acquiring land by adverse possession requires use of land without the owner's permission for at least 20 years. The claimant must have maintained visible, actual, hostile, continuous, and notorious possession of the property and be publicly claiming ownership to the property.

Reference: State Laws and Rules > Substantive Regulations

62. An airline pilot told a broker about some friends who were looking for a new home. The broker contacted the friends and eventually sold them a home. When may the broker pay the airline pilot for this valuable lead?:

A. The broker may not pay the pilot for the lead

B. Only after the sale closes

C. As soon as a valid sales contract is signed by the parties

D. After the funds are released from escrow

Answer: A. The answer is the broker may not pay the pilot for the lead. The broker can thank the airline pilot but may not pay a referral fee since a broker may only pay a referral fee to someone who holds a real estate license.

Reference: State Laws and Rules > Substantive Regulations

63. A resident of North Carolina who holds a nonresident Georgia real estate broker's license must meet which qualification?:

A. Employ at least one salesperson in Georgia

B. Maintain offices in both North Carolina and in Georgia

C. Provide records of any disciplinary actions in any state

D. Hold an active license in North Carolina

Answer: C. The answer is provide records of any disciplinary actions in any state. Nonresident brokers must provide the Commission with records of any disciplinary action against the broker in their home state, or any other state. The broker is not required to maintain offices in each state, employ one Georgia salesperson, or hold an active license in North Carolina.

Reference: State Laws and Rules > Required Licensure

64. All of the following must appear in a written listing agreement EXCEPT:

A. a disclosure of the listing company's policy regarding agency.

B. the complete legal description of the property being sold.

C. a disclosure of a "conflict of interest" the listing broker has, if any.

D. the time duration of the listing.

Answer: B. The answer is the complete legal description of the property being sold. An adequate description, such as the property address, is required, but not the legal description. A licensee should acquire the proper legal description of the property as soon as possible after listing the property. Listings must have a definite termination date. The broker must disclose any potential "conflict of interest" and discuss the listing company's policy regarding agency.

Reference: State Laws and Rules > Substantive Regulations

65. All advertising a brokerage corporation uses in any media must include the:

A. names and license numbers of the principal officers of the firm.

B. name of the firm's license as registered with the Commission.

C. all trade names used by the firm.

D. the firm's office address.

Answer: B. The answer is name of the firm's license as registered with the Commission. In all advertising, the brokerage must include the firm's name as registered with the Commission. However, it is not necessary to include the other trade names or the names of the firm's officers or principal address.

Reference: State Laws and Rules > Substantive Regulations

66. In Georgia, the term homestead exemption relates to:

A. the fact that homeowners no longer have to pay school taxes if they have no children in school.

B. the fact that the property tax on the home is an exemption to federal income tax.

C. an exemption for the family home from a foreclosure action when the family breadwinner dies.

D. a deduction that an owner-occupant can take from assessed value before calculating a property tax.

Answer: D. The answer is a deduction that an owner-occupant can take from assessed value before calculating a property tax. In Georgia, the term homestead exemption relates to a deduction that an owner-occupant can take from assessed value before calculating a property tax. The homestead exemption reduces the amount of taxes owed on property used as a primary residence.

Reference: State Laws and Rules > Substantive Regulations

67. Salesperson Janet asked the telephone company to list her name in the directory under the Real Estate heading as: "Janet, Real Estate Salesperson, Residential Property My

Specialty!" Based on this information, Janet also is required to include:

A. the expiration date of her license.

B. her street address.

C. the name of her employing broker.

D. her license number.

Answer: C. The answer is the name of her employing broker. Because all advertising is in the employing broker's name, Janet must indicate the name of her employing broker. She does not, however, have to include her license number, expiration date, or street address.

Reference: State Laws and Rules > Substantive Regulations

68. An office manager for a local real estate firm is responsible for the following activities: coordinating the flow of paperwork through the office, preparing forms and advertising copy, and hiring and supervising clerical personnel. The office manager is:

A. exempt from real estate licensing requirements.

B. required to have a CAM license.

C. required to have a salesperson's license.

D. required to have a broker's license.

Answer: A. The answer is exempt from real estate licensing requirements. Georgia law permits an individual who is performing "ministerial acts" to operate without a real estate license. Ministerial acts are acts that do not require a licensee's discretion or advice. The office manager is performing ministerial activities and is, therefore, exempt from licensing requirements.

Reference: State Laws and Rules > Required Licensure

69. Georgia law requires that a buyer be informed of any adverse conditions of which the agent is aware, and that cannot be discovered by the buyer in a diligent inspection, concerning the:

A. land only.

B. land and improvements.

C. land, improvements, and area up to one mile away.

D. land, improvements, and immediate neighborhood.

Answer: C. The answer is land, improvements, and area up to one mile away. Georgia law specifically requires that buyers be informed of any adverse conditions of which their agent is aware that cannot be discovered by the buyers with a diligent inspection of the land, improvements, and neighborhood up to a distance of one mile away. Brokers are required to disclose to all parties in a transaction any adverse conditions of which they are aware. However, brokers are only liable to disclose such conditions if they possess actual knowledge of the conditions and if such conditions could not be discovered by diligent inspection.

Reference: State Laws and Rules > Substantive Regulations

70. Under Georgia license law, a partnership, association, or corporation will be granted a license only if:

A. there are at least three brokers in the company.

B. all papers are filed with the secretary of state.

C. there is one individual who holds a broker's license and who will be named the qualifying broker.

D. every member and officer actively participating in the brokerage business has a broker's license.

Answer: C. "The answer is there is one individual who holds a broker's license and who will be named the qualifying broker. Under Georgia license law, a partnership, association, or corporation will be granted a license only if there is one individual who holds a broker's license and who will be named the qualifying broker. Members actively participating must either have a salesperson's license or an associate broker's license. Filing papers with the secretary of state is a requirement for incorporation, not for real estate licensing.

Reference: State Laws and Rule > Required Licensure

71. Acme Apartments, Inc., a licensed broker providing property management services to owners, is employing Belinda and giving her authority to show apartments to prospects, receive lease applications, and collect rentals at one of the buildings the firm manages. In this position, Belinda needs:

A. no license.

B. a salesperson's license.

C. a broker's license.

D. a CAM license.

Answer: A. The answer is no license. The license law permits a person employed by a broker to show apartments and other leasing activities when the broker has a written management agreement with a property owner. In this case, the on-site manager may be unlicensed if acting under specific instructions from the broker.

Reference: State Laws and Rules > Required Licensure

72. The Georgia Real Estate Commission's rules regarding advertising require that:

A. when advertising in any media, the name and telephone number of the firm be at least as large as the name of any agent.

B. direct mail advertising to people on the government's do-not-call registry is prohibited.

C. property listings on websites be removed within 30 days of the expiration date of the listing.

D. For Sale signs always contain the name and phone number of the listing salesperson.

Answer: A. The answer is when advertising in any media, the name and telephone number of the firm be at least as large as the name of any agent. Commission rules do not require that salespersons' names be on signs. The rules require that listings on the internet must be removed within 10 days of expiration of the permission given that allowed the advertisement. The do-not-call registry applies only to phone calls. The brokerage name and phone number must appear in at least equal size, prominence, and frequency as the name and phone number of any licensee or group of licensees.

Reference: State Laws and Rules > Substantive Regulations

73. In Georgia, the renewal period for real estate licenses is:

A. four years for brokers and every two years for salespersons and community association managers.

B. two years for brokers and every four years for salespersons and community association managers.

C. two years for all licensees.

D. four years for all licensees.

Answer: D. The answer is four years for all licensees. In Georgia, brokers, salespersons, or community association managers renew their license by the last day of their month every four years. Licenses of real estate firms must be renewed by the last day of their anniversary month every four years.

Reference: State Laws and Rules > Required Licensure

74. In Georgia, brokers may have their license suspended or revoked for all of the following actions EXCEPT:

A. depositing earnest money into the firm's trust account.

B. displaying a For Sale sign on a property without the owner's consent.

C. helping another person cheat on the licensing examination.

D. being declared mentally incompetent.

Answer: A. The answer is depositing earnest money into the firm's trust account. It is entirely appropriate to deposit earnest money into the firm's trust account. However, brokers may lose their licenses if they are declared mentally incompetent, if they help someone cheat on the licensing exam, or if they place a For Sale sign on a property without the owner's permission.

Reference: State Laws and Rules > Investigation and Hearing Process

75. Georgia permits mechanic's lien rights to:

A. commercial real estate brokers suing for unpaid commissions.

B. residential real estate brokers suing for unpaid commissions.

C. building trade union officers suing for unpaid compensation from their union.

D. local building inspectors and home inspectors.

Answer: A. The answer is commercial real estate brokers suing for unpaid commissions. The state legislature of Georgia has extended mechanic's lien rights to commercial real estate brokers who sue for unpaid commissions. Contractors, building material providers, architects, surveyors, and engineers are among others who may be entitled to the protection of mechanic's lien laws.

Reference: State Laws and Rules > Substantive Regulations

76. If a nonresident Georgia real estate licensee moves to Georgia and wants to acquire a resident license in Georgia, the licensee must:

A. file a change of status with the Commission.

B. be a resident of Georgia for six months before applying for a resident license.

C. take the state licensing examination.

D. be a resident of Georgia for one year before applying for a resident license.

Answer: A. The answer is file a change of status with the Commission. If the holder of a nonresident Georgia real estate license wants to change the status to resident license, the holder must simply apply for a change of status. The licensee is not required to retake any examination or course of study, or to wait for a period of time to apply for a resident license.

Reference: State Laws and Rules > Required Licensure

77. Under Georgia license law, all of these statements regarding trust or escrow accounts are true EXCEPT:

A. a broker may have as many trust accounts as needed, provided that each is registered with the Georgia Real Estate Commission.

B. interest-bearing trust accounts are prohibited.

C. all trust or escrow deposits must be held in federally insured depositories.

D. keeping a small amount of personal money in the trust account to cover banking charges or required minimum balances is permissible.

Answer: B. The answer is interest-bearing trust accounts are prohibited. Interest-bearing trust accounts are permitted as long as the contract states that the deposit will be held in an interest-bearing account and states to whom the interest will go. A broker can have as many trust accounts as needed, provided that each is registered with the Georgia Real Estate Commission and held in federally insured depositories. The broker may keep a small amount of personal money in the trust account to cover banking charges or required minimum balances.

Reference: State Laws and Rules > Substantive Regulations

78. The Georgia statute of frauds requires that all real estate contracts must be in writing to be enforceable EXCEPT:

A. an exclusive-right-to-sell listing.

B. a lease for one year or less.

C. a purchase and sale agreement.

D. a buyer brokerage agreement.

Answer: B. The answer is a lease for one year or less. A lease for less than one year may be oral and enforceable. Brokerage engagement agreements and sales contracts must be in writing to be enforceable.

Reference: State Laws and Rules > Substantive Regulations

79. Which statement is TRUE regarding the Georgia Education, Research, and Recovery Fund?:

A. New licensees must contribute $100 to the fund at the time of acquiring their first license.

B. All licensees contribute to the fund every time they renew their licenses.

C. If the total amount in the fund falls below $1,000,000, all licensees will contribute to the fund at their next renewal.

D. The fund must always contain a minimum of $500,000.

Answer: C. The answer is if the total amount in the fund falls below $1,000,000, all licensees will contribute to the fund at their next renewal. If the total amount in the Georgia Education, Research, and Recovery Fund falls below $1,000,000, all licensees will contribute to the fund at their next renewal. New licensees pay into the fund at the time of initial application for licensure, but not at the time of renewal unless the fund falls beyond $1,000,000.

Reference: State Laws and Rules > Real Estate Education, Research, and Recovery Fund

80. When an individual is found to be practicing real estate without a license, the Georgia Real Estate Commission may impose any of the following penalties EXCEPT:

A. a fine of $1,000.

B. additional fines for each day a cease and desist order is ignored.

C. a cease and desist order.

D. a one-year jail term.

Answer: D. The answer is a one-year jail term. The Georgia Real Estate Commission cannot impose a jail term. It can, however, issue a cease and desist order, assess a fine of up to $1,000, and impose additional fines for each day a cease and desist order is ignored.

Reference: State Laws and Rules > Investigation and Hearing Process

81. Members of the Georgia Real Estate Commission are appointed by:

A. public election.

B. real estate licensees.

C. the Georgia Association of REALTORS.

D. the governor.

Answer: D. The answer is the governor. The governor makes the appointments, and the Georgia Senate must ratify the appointments. Members of the Georgia Real Estate Commission are not elected by the public or by real estate licensees.

Reference: State Laws and Rules > Commission Organization and Procedures

82. In Georgia, a license is required for all of the following EXCEPT:

A. instructors for approved prelicense classes.

B. real estate appraisers.

C. home inspectors.

D. community association managers.

Answer: C. The answer is home inspectors. There are no real estate license requirements for home inspectors. Licenses are required for association managers, prelicense instructors, and real estate appraisers.

Reference: State Laws and Rules > Required Licensure

83. A buyer has entered into a contract to buy a condominium unit from a person who originally bought the unit from the developer and has lived there for the past 10 years. This new buyer has a right to cancel the contract within how many days?:

A. 5 days of receipt of resale documents

B. 5 days from the date of the new executed contract

C. The new buyer does not have the right to cancel a signed contract in this situation.

D. 15 days of receipt of resale documents

Answer: C. The answer is the new buyer does not have the right to cancel a signed contract in this situation. A condominium buyer has the right to rescind the contract only when purchasing from the original developer. The buyer may rescind the contract up to seven days after receiving all the documents required by law to be provided to the buyer. A person buying a condominium from a condominium owner who is not the developer is bound by the sales contract and may not rescind that contract.

Reference: State Laws and Rules > Substantive Regulations

84. Under Georgia law, an applicant who passes the state licensing exam may begin practicing real estate:

A. after 45 days.

B. after 60 days.

C. after 30 days.

D. as soon as the broker with whom the new licensee will affiliate receives the wall license.

Answer: D. The answer is as soon as the broker with whom the new licensee will affiliate receives the wall license. Under

Georgia law, an applicant can begin practicing real estate as soon as the broker receives the applicant's wall license.

Reference: State Laws and Rules > Required Licensure

85. In Georgia, support personnel:

A. may independently host open houses and home show booths.

B. may show real estate.

C. may type contract forms as directed by the firm.

D. may collect or hold earnest money deposits.

Answer: C. The answer is may type contract forms as directed by the firm. Typing form contracts under the employing broker's supervision and approval is secretarial in nature and does not require licensing; it is a ministerial act. Commission rules prohibit unlicensed support personnel from hosting open houses, showing real estate, or collecting earnest money deposits.

Reference: State Laws and Rules > Required Licensure

86. Georgia, licensees applying for license renewal may pay a reduced fee if the licensees:

A. have held a license for at least 25 years.

B. have a license history free of any disciplinary action during the renewal period.

C. changed their license status with the Commission within the last year.

D. submit the renewal application on the Commission's website.

Answer: D. The answer is submit the renewal application on the Commission's website. The Commission permits online applicants to pay a reduced fee when applying for license renewal. There is no reduced fee based on the length of licensure, nor for a good license history or a change of status.

Reference: State Laws and Rules > Required Licensure

87. All funds received by brokers on behalf of their principal must be deposited in an escrow or trust account:

A. within five working days of receiving the funds.

B. within three business days of receiving the offer.

C. within three days of reaching a binding agreement.

D. as soon as possible unless the contract provides otherwise.

Answer: D. The answer is as soon as possible unless the contract provides otherwise. All funds received by brokers on behalf of their principal must be deposited in an escrow or trust account as soon as possible unless the contract provides otherwise.

Reference: State Laws and Rules > Substantive Regulations

88. In regard to a tenant's security deposit, all of these statements are true EXCEPT:

A. the tenant may use the deposit for paying the rent for the last month of the lease.

B. the landlord may deduct for the cost of repairing damage.

C. the amount of a security deposit is determined by negotiation.

D. a deduction can take place for the tenant's failure to return the landlord's property, such as keys.

Answer: A. The answer is the tenant may use the deposit for paying the rent for the last month of the lease. The tenant may not use the deposit for paying the rent for the last month of the lease. The landlord may deduct from the security deposit for the cost of repairing damage or for the tenant's failure to return the landlord's property, such as keys. The amount of a security deposit is determined by negotiation.

Reference: State Laws and Rules > Substantive Regulations

89. In Georgia, the time period required for terminating a tenancy at will is:

A. 30 days notice if the tenant wishes to terminate, or 60 days notice if the landlord wishes to terminate.

B. 60 days notice if the tenant wishes to terminate, or 30 days notice if the landlord wishes to terminate.

C. 30 days notice from either the landlord or the tenant.

D. 60 days notice from either a landlord or a tenant.

Answer: A. The answer is 30 days notice if the tenant wishes to terminate, or 60 days notice if the landlord wishes to terminate. In Georgia, the time period required for terminating a tenancy at will is 30 days notice if the tenant wishes to terminate, or 60 days notice if the landlord wishes to terminate. A tenancy at will is for an indefinite period of time and can be terminated by either the landlord or the tenant.

Reference: State Laws and Rules > Substantive Regulations

90. Members of the Georgia Real Estate Commission are:

A. appointed by the commissioner of real estate.

B. elected by licensees.

C. appointed by the governor.

D. elected in statewide elections every six years.

Answer: C. The answer is appointed by the governor. The governor appoints the members of the Georgia Real Estate Commission. The members of the commission are not elected by licensees or by the public.

Reference: State Laws and Rules > Commission Organization and Procedures

91. How must a landlord handle a security deposit in Georgia?:

A. A security deposit can only be used for residential units.

B. Unless there have been damages or other charges, the landlord must return the security deposit to the tenant within 30 days of the end of the lease.

C. At the end of the lease, the landlord cannot apply the security deposit to rent owed by the tenant.

D. Landlords must pay tenants interest on their security deposits.

Answer: B. The answer is unless there have been damages or other charges, the landlord must return the security deposit to the tenant within 30 days of the end of the lease. Security deposits may be required for the rental of any kind of property. The landlord does not have to pay interest on the security deposit, and the landlord can apply the security deposit to rent owed by the tenant.

Reference: State Laws and Rules > Substantive Regulations

92. Under Georgia license law, salespersons are entitled to place a large cash deposit received from a buyer in their personal bank account under which of the following circumstances?:

A. If an attempt to reach their broker for instructions was unsuccessful

B. If the buyer insisted that the money be deposited immediately

C. Under no circumstances

D. If the money is received on a Friday night, and the brokerage office will not open until Monday morning

Answer: C. The answer is under no circumstances. Under no circumstances can salespersons place a cash deposit into their personal bank account. A cash deposit received from a buyer may only be placed in a broker's registered trust account. Brokerage offices should have policies in place stating how salespersons should deal with cash deposits during non-office hours.

Reference: State Laws and Rules > Substantive Regulations

93. The Georgia Real Estate Commission has the power to discipline licensees if the licensees:

A. agree to market ranch land with an open listing.

B. deposit a buyer's down payment in their own bank account.

C. enter into an exclusive-listing contract.

D. attempt to represent a buyer.

Answer: B. The answer is deposit a buyer's down payment in their own bank account. Depositing a buyer's down payment in a licensee's own bank account would be commingling of personal and client's funds and is a prohibited practice that could result in fines, or the suspension or revocation of a real estate license. The other actions mentioned are legal in Georgia.

Reference: State Laws and Rules > Investigation and Hearing Process

94. Under Georgia law, a businessman who plans to specialize in selling real property securities must hold:

A. either a real estate license or a securities license.

B. both a real estate license and a securities license.

C. only a securities license.

D. only a real estate license.

Answer: B. The answer is both a real estate license and a securities license. Under Georgia law, a businessman who plans to specialize in selling real property securities must hold both a real estate license and a securities license.

Reference: State Laws and Rule > Required Licensure

95. A licensed salesperson may hold a concurrent license with more than one Georgia broker under which circumstances?:

A. With the permission of the sales manager

B. With the written consent of the brokers being represented

C. Under no circumstances

D. With the permission of the Georgia Real Estate Commission

Answer: C. The answer is under no circumstances. A salesperson may be licensed with only one broker. Neither another broker nor the Commission has the authority to permit an exception.

Reference: State Laws and Rules > Required Licensure

96. In Georgia, when a sales contract fails to close and the parties to the contract cannot agree on how the earnest money should be disbursed, the broker holding the money can do any of the following EXCEPT:

A. keep the money as commission earned.

B. disburse the money on the basis of a "reasonable interpretation" of the contract.

C. comply with a court order determining how the money should be disbursed.

D. enter an interpleader action in court.

Answer: A. The answer is keep the money as commission earned. The broker cannot keep the disputed earnest money as commission earned. The broker can disburse the money on the basis of a "reasonable interpretation" of the contract, enter an interpleader action in court, or comply with a court order determining how the money should be disbursed.

Reference: State Laws and Rules > Substantive Regulations

97. In Georgia, the advertising of a real estate company that has joined a national franchise must include the:

A. number of franchised companies in the area.

B. phone number of the national franchise firm's office.

C. name in which the license was issued.

D. location of the franchise firm's main offices.

Answer: C. The answer is name in which the license was issued. Commission regulations require that the name of the company as registered with the Commission must be included in all advertising. The company's name as registered with the Commission also must appear in all real estate contracts and on any office signs.

Reference: State Laws and Rules > Substantive Regulations

98. In Georgia, all of the following could be grounds for revoking a broker's license EXCEPT:

A. agreeing with a seller to accept a listing for more than the customary commission rate.

B. advertising in a newspaper that they are a member of the trade association when in fact they are not.

C. depositing escrow money in their personal checking account.

D. being convicted of a felony involving moral turpitude.

Answer: A. The answer is agreeing with a seller to accept a listing for more than the customary commission rate. Commission rates are always negotiable between a broker and client. The Georgia Real Estate Commission may, however, revoke a license if the licensee has been convicted of a felony, is engaged in false advertising, or has commingled funds.

Reference: State Laws and Rules > Investigation and Hearing Process

99. The Georgia Real Estate Commission may undertake an investigation of a licensee based on all the following grounds EXCEPT:

A. a motion from Commission members.

B. a random selection of licensees.

C. a written complaint submitted by a member of the public.

D. its own initiative.

Answer: B. The answer is a random selection of licensees. The Georgia Real Estate Commission may not initiate a random search for investigations of licensees. The Commission may initiate an investigation on its own initiative if the Commission suspects unlawful activity, on a motion by Commission members, or on the basis of a written complaint submitted by a member of the public.

Reference: State Laws and Rules > Investigation and Hearing Process

100. When going to court to sue for a commission a seller has refused to pay, a broker must first prove that:

A. the transaction resulted in the sale of the property.

B. he held an active broker license at the time of the transaction.

C. the broker had a valid agency agreement with the seller.

D. a buyer's broker is not responsible for the commission.

Answer: B. The answer is he held an active broker license at the time of the transaction. The broker also may have to show that he had a valid agency agreement with the seller. The broker may have to prove that he brought a willing and able buyer to the transaction, even if the transaction did not result in a sale. The broker may be due a commission even if there was a buyer's broker involved in the transaction.

Reference: State Laws and Rules > Required Licensure

101. When a broker sole proprietor has his license suspended for two years, what effect does this have on the

associate brokers and salespeople affiliated with the proprietor?:

A. Suspension has no effect on the affiliates.

B. The affiliates' licenses also will be suspended for a two-year period.

C. The affiliates' licenses must be returned to the Georgia Real Estate Commission.

D. The affiliates' licenses will be revoked, subject to reinstatement after one year.

Answer: C. The answer is the affiliates' licenses must be returned to the Georgia Real Estate Commission. When a broker's license is suspended for two years and they are a sole proprietor, any affiliate's license is on inactive status until the associate broker or salesperson becomes affiliated by a new broker. The licenses of affiliates are not suspended or revoked because of the broker's suspension.

Reference: State Laws and Rules > Substantive Regulations

102. Which of the following is a requirement to obtain a real estate salesperson's license in Georgia?:

A. Successful completion of a 60-hour approved prelicense course

B. U.S. and Georgia citizenship

C. Successful completion of a 75-hour approved prelicense course

D. An associate's degree or certificate in real estate from an accredited college, university, or proprietary school

Answer: C. The answer is successful completion of a 75-hour approved prelicense course. An applicant must successfully complete a 75-hour approved prelicense course in order to obtain a real estate salesperson's license. The applicant is not required to be a citizen of either the United States or Georgia and is not required to have a college or university degree. The license law does require that an applicant either be a resident of Georgia or apply for a non-resident Georgia license.

Reference: State Laws and Rules > Qualifications and Fees

103. If a broker submits a contract to a lender indicating that the sales price on a property is something above its actual sales price, the:

A. broker can lose his license.

B. buyer is likely to receive an interest rate break.

C. buyer can receive a higher mortgage amount.

D. broker has done nothing wrong as long as the appraisal substantiates this price.

Answer: A. The answer is broker can lose his license. It is an unfair practice to falsify a contract in a real estate transaction. A broker may not falsify a contract for the purpose of obtaining a larger loan. This action could be grounds for fines, or license suspension or revocation.

Reference: State Laws and Rules > Unfair Practices

104. A homeowner paid her general contractor in full for an addition to her house, but the general contractor failed to pay a mason contractor who has now filed a mechanic's lien. Which statement is TRUE?:

A. The homeowner has no responsibility for the lien since he paid for the job in full.

B. The lien was illegally filed since the owner paid for the job in full.

C. The mason contractor can foreclose on the lien as soon as it is filed.

D. The mason contractor must now file suit against the general contractor within the statutory period, or the lien will expire.

Answer: D. The answer is the mason contractor must now file suit against the general contractor within the statutory period, or the lien will expire. The mason contractor must file suit against the general contractor within the statutory period, or the lien will expire. The mason must file suit against the contractor within one year.

Reference: State Laws and Rules > Substantive Regulations

105. A retiree who lives in a condominium development offers to provide the owners' association with management services for a nominal fee. Under Georgia license law, which statement is TRUE?:

A. The retiree's management duties will have to be overseen by a licensed broker.

B. The retiree will not need a real estate license.

C. The retiree will have to acquire a community association management (CAM) license.

D. The retiree can perform the duties without a license but only if no compensation is paid.

Answer: B. The answer is the retiree will not need a real estate license. Under Georgia license law, the retiree will not need any license. Georgia permits an exception to licensure for a member of a community association that provides management services for only that association. The exception will not apply if the retiree holds a real estate license.

Reference: State Laws and Rules > Required Licensure

106. An owner tells a listing broker that his property is connected to the city sewer system, when in fact it is not. A buyer purchases the property relying on that information, and shortly after the closing, discovers that the sewer connection does not exist. Who may be subject to legal action by the buyer?:

A. Neither the owner nor the broker is liable for legal action since it is the buyer's responsibility to discover the material facts about a property.

B. Only the owner is liable, because the seller lied to the broker.

C. Only the broker is liable, because the law holds the broker ultimately responsible for stating the truth about a property.

D. Both the owner and the broker may be subject to legal action.

Answer: D. The answer is both the owner and the broker may be subject to legal action. In this situation, both the owner and the broker may be subject to legal action by the buyer because of misrepresentation about the sewer connection. The owner is guilty of not disclosing the property's lack of a sewer connection. The broker relied on the owner's information without verifying accuracy of the owner's statements about the sewer connection.

Reference: State Laws and Rules > Substantive Regulations

107. A broker manages three properties for the same owner. One property is in need of emergency repairs, but there is not enough money in the management account to cover the cost. The broker borrows money from the trust account of one of the other properties to make the repairs. Which statement is TRUE?:

A. The broker must use personal funds for repairs if there is not enough money in the management account.

B. Such action is proper when the same person owns all properties.

C. The broker has violated regulations by improperly handling escrow funds.

D. The broker has acted properly by safeguarding the client's interest.

Answer: C. The answer is the broker has violated regulations by improperly handling escrow funds. The broker has violated Georgia law by using funds from one property to make repairs on another property. There must be enough money credited to a property owner's account to pay bills for that property, including funds for any repairs to be made on the property.

Reference: State Laws and Rules > Substantive Regulations

108. If a broker establishes an account to hold money belonging to others, which of the following is TRUE?:

A. The account must be reconciled at least quarterly.

B. A separate account is opened for each transaction.

C. The broker may delegate the responsibility for receiving and depositing checks into the trust account.

D. The account cannot be in the same bank in which the broker has a business or personal account.

Answer: C. The answer is the broker may delegate the responsibility for receiving and depositing checks into the trust account. The broker may delegate the responsibility for receiving and depositing checks into the trust account. Georgia law requires that a licensee's trust account must be reconciled monthly; it is not necessary to open an account for each transaction. Brokers may open and keep a trust account in the bank where the brokers keep their business or personal accounts.

Reference: State Laws and Rules > Substantive Regulations

109. A salesperson has been found guilty of several serious infractions of the license law as well as of the federal fair housing law. In order for her broker to not to be held accountable for the actions of the salesperson, the broker must show all of the following EXCEPT:

A. the broker was not a party to the misdeeds and was not aware of them.

B. there was a reasonable degree of management oversight in the office.

C. the company provided affective training for its affiliates.

D. the broker was out of town and had another broker acting on his behalf when the infractions occurred.

Answer: D. The answer is the broker was out of town and had another broker acting on his behalf when the infractions occurred. The broker would not have to prove that he was out of town when the infractions occurred. A Commission investigation will usually find the broker to be innocent of the salesperson's illegal activities if there was training and oversight and if the broker was unaware of the infractions.

Reference: State Laws and Rules > Fair Housing Laws

110. Which person must have a Georgia real estate license in order to negotiate the sale or lease of real estate in Georgia?:

A. An attorney in fact acting under a properly executed power of attorney

B. General partner of a limited partnership negotiating the sale of the partnership's property

C. Person who negotiates the sales of entire businesses, including their stock equipment and buildings, for a promised fee

D. Owner of a six-plex residential property who personally manages the building, collects rents, and shows the apartments to prospective tenants

Answer: C. The answer is person who negotiates the sales of entire businesses, including their stock equipment and buildings, for a promised fee. A person who negotiates the sale of another person's property for a fee as part of the sale of a business must have a real estate license. The license law exempts general partners of a limited partnership in the sale of partnership's property, apartment owners in the leasing of their own property, and attorneys in fact acting under proper legal authority.

Reference: State Laws and Rules > Required Licensure

111. Which is NOT a protected class under the Georgia fair housing law?:

A. Race

B. Handicap

C. Sexual preference

D. National Origin

Answer: C. The answer is sexual preference. Sexual preference is not a protected class under Georgia's fair housing law. The protected classes under Georgia's fair housing law are those protected under the federal fair housing laws: race, color, national origin, sex (male or female, not sexual preference), religion, handicap, and familial status.

Reference: State Laws and Rules > Fair Housing Laws

FINANCE AND CLOSING

1. The use of the security deed in Georgia:

A. does not allow for any right of redemption by the borrower.

B. creates a statutory right of redemption for the borrower.

C. requires a process of judicial foreclosure.

D. allows lenders to foreclose without going to court.

Answer: D. The answer is allows lenders to foreclose without going to court. Through the security deed, the borrower conveys legal title to a property to the lender, allowing for a non-judicial foreclosure process in which the lender does not have to go to court to foreclose on a property. Georgia does not have a statutory right of redemption for a borrower. However, a security deed usually includes the right of equitable redemption, which is the right of the borrower to reinstate a defaulted loan after acceleration but before foreclosure under certain conditions specified in the security deed.

Reference: Finance and Closing > Finance

2. Twenty-one years ago, a homeowner acquired a conventional 30-year fixed-rate loan to purchase her current home. She now wants to pay off her loan early, before the end of the 30-year term. Does Georgia allow for her to repay her loan early?:

A. Twenty-one years ago, a homeowner acquired a conventional 30-year fixed-rate loan to purchase her current home. She now wants to pay off her loan early, before the end of the 30-year term. Does Georgia allow for her to repay her loan early?

B. The original loan documents will state whether prepayment of this loan is possible and if there is any financial penalty for early repayment.

C. The homeowner may prepay the balance of the loan only if the loan has not been refinanced.

D. Georgia law permits the homeowner to prepay the loan with a penalty set by law.

Answer: B. The answer is the original loan documents will state whether prepayment of this loan is possible and if there is any financial penalty for early repayment. There are no laws or rules in Georgia stating that a borrower may prepay any loan. The original loan documents will determine if prepayment is an option for the homeowner, and if so, if the homeowner will owe any penalties for prepayment.

Reference: Finance and Closing > Finance

3. VA loans in Georgia may be made by:

A. a local mortgage banker or lending institution.

B. Fannie Mae.

C. the Veterans Administration.

D. HUD.

Answer: A. The answer is a local mortgage banker or lending institution. In Georgia, any private local mortgage lender or lending institution approved by the VA may make a VA loan.

Reference: Finance and Closing > Finance

4. A homebuyer financing a purchase in Georgia with a conventional loan that will close on September 1 will make the first monthly payment to the lender on:

A. September 1.

B. November 1.

C. the date negotiated between the seller and the buyer in the purchase contract.

D. October 1.

Answer: D. The answer is October 1. When a loan closes on the first day of the month, the borrower's first mortgage payment will be due on the 1st of the next month. If the loan closes on any other day of the month, the buyer's first mortgage payment will not be due in the next month, but on the first day of the following month. The mortgage due date is not negotiated between the buyer and the seller.

Reference: Finance and Closing > Finance

5. How soon must deeds of conveyance be recorded after closing?:

A. Three business days

B. One business day

C. A reasonable time

D. One month

Answer: C. The answer is a reasonable time. Deeds must be recorded within a reasonable time. Recording a deed is not required for the deed to be valid between the parties, but recording the deed provides constructive notice of the owner's interest in the property.

Reference: Finance and Closing > Closing Procedures

6. What is the redemption period after a foreclosure sale is complete?:

A. Three years

B. No redemption period

C. One year

D. Six months

Answer: B. The answer is no redemption period. The equity of redemption on a loan foreclosure ends when the property is sold. The borrower has a right of redemption anytime between delinquency on the loan and the actual foreclosure sale. If no redemption is made at the time of the sale, the redemption period ends.

Reference: Finance and Closing > Finance

7. A buyer purchases a home in Georgia for $260,000. The sales contract states that the buyer will assume the existing seller's home loan of $58,000. How much is the Georgia transfer tax in this transaction?:

A. $606

B. $546

C. $245

D. $202

Answer: D. The answer is $202. The transfer tax in Georgia is a state tax paid in the county in which the property is located when title is transferred. The tax is charged at a rate of ten cents (0.10) per $100 of the sales price or portion thereof of the property, minus the amount of any assumed loan (divide the sales price, minus any assumption amount, by 100, and multiply by .10). Calculation: $260,000 (sales price) – $58,000 (the assumed loan) = $202,000; $202,000 ÷ 100 = 2,020 × 0.10 = $202.

Reference: Finance and Closing > Closing Procedures

8. At a closing in Georgia, all of the following would appear as a debit on the seller's closing statement EXCEPT:

A. accrued mortgage interest.

B. rent prorations.

C. prepaid property taxes.

D. listing broker's commission.

Answer: C. The answer is prepaid property taxes. The seller would receive a refund or credit from the buyer at closing for the buyer's share of the year's property taxes since the seller has already paid the taxes for the entire year. Rent prorations are paid by the seller to the buyer. The listing broker's commissions are paid by the seller to the broker. Accrued interest on the existing home loan is paid by the seller to the lender at closing.

Reference: Finance and Closing > Closing Procedures

9. A lender in Georgia requires borrowers to prepay funds for property taxes into an escrow account. At closing, the lender estimates how many months have accrued since the last tax bill on the property was paid. How many months will the lender add to that total to determine how much money the borrower is required to prepay into the account at closing?:

A. Six months

B. Four months

C. Two months

D. Eight months

Answer: C. The answer is two months. A lender in Georgia may add two months to the number of months since the tax bill was paid to arrive at a total required for the tax escrow account. The lender may require the borrower at closing to prepay into that account funds sufficient to pay taxes for that total of months.

Reference: Finance and Closing > Closing Procedures

10. The right of a borrower to reclaim a property by reimbursing an investor from a foreclosure sale:

A. is never recognized in any state.

B. is not recognized in Georgia.

C. may be permitted if allowed in a security deed.

D. is always permitted in Georgia.

Answer: B. The answer is is not recognized in Georgia. Once a foreclosure sale is final, some states allow a borrower to reclaim a property after a foreclosure sale by reimbursing the investor who purchased the property at the sale. This right is known as the right of statutory redemption and is not recognized in Georgia.

Reference: Finance and Closing > Finance

11. In Georgia, the closing costs for a real estate transaction include an intangibles tax in the amount of:

A. $2.50 per $500 of the value of personal property accompanying the transaction.

B. $1.50 per 500 square feet of land.

C. $1.50 per $500 or part thereof of the new loan amount.

D. $1.00 per $1,000 or part thereof of the sales price.

Answer: C. The answer is $1.50 per $500 or part thereof of the new loan amount. In Georgia, the closing costs for a real estate transaction include an intangibles tax in the amount of $1.50 per

$500 or part thereof of the new loan amount. If there is no new loan involved in the transaction, there is no intangibles tax.

Reference: Finance and Closing > Closing Procedures

12. In Georgia, when a mortgagor is in default, the lender must do which of the following in order to foreclose?:

A. Advertise before holding a sale of the property

B. Seize the property

C. Sue the defaulting borrower in circuit court

D. Notify junior lien holders

Answer: A. The answer is advertise before holding a sale of the property. The lender must advertise before holding a sale of the property. Most residential foreclosures in Georgia are non-judicial, provided a power of sale clause is included in the security deed. The foreclosure sale must be advertised in the official county newspaper where the property is located once a week for four weeks prior to the date of the sale.

Reference: Finance and Closing > Finance

13. When a buyer is financing the purchase of a home in Georgia, the note that will be signed at the closing is accompanied by what document?:

A. Security deed, conveying title to the lender

B. Security agreement

C. Trust deed, conveying title to a trustee

D. Mortgage contract, conveying a lien to the lender

Answer: A. The answer is security deed, conveying title to the lender. A security deed is the most common form for securing a housing loan in Georgia. A security deed conveys title to the lender to secure the debt. The borrower retains equitable title to the property and a right of redemption, the right to pay off the debt and secure legal title to the property.

Reference: Finance and Closing > Finance

14. The alienation clause in a security deed:

A. requires a lender to cancel a security instrument when the borrower pays the debt in full.

B. requires the borrower to acquire mortgage insurance on behalf of the lender.

C. permits a lender to call the entire debt payable when a borrower sells a property without the lenders consent.

D. provides the borrower with the right to reinstate a defaulted loan before foreclosure.

Answer: C. The answer is permits a lender to call the entire debt payable when a borrower sells a property without the lenders consent. When a borrower sells or conveys a property without the lender's consent, a lender may call for full payment as permitted in the alienation or "due on sale" clause of a security deed. The right of equitable redemption allows a borrower to reinstate a defaulted loan by paying off the loan before foreclosure. The defeasance clause in a security deed requires a lender to cancel the security deed when the borrower makes full payment for the debt. Most lenders require borrowers to pay mortgage insurance on behalf of the lender.

Reference: Finance and Closing > Finance

15. A closing takes place in Georgia on August 22 and the property taxes of $2,900 have already been paid by the seller for the calendar year of January 1 through December 31. How much will the buyer owe the seller for taxes paid on the property? (Use the exact days of the month and the standard calendar year of 365 days in your calculations.):

A. $1,032.87

B. $1,040.82

C. $1,024.93

D. $1,048.88

Answer: B. The answer is $1,040.82. Since the seller has already paid the full year's taxes, the buyer at closing will refund the seller the property taxes paid from the day after closing through December 31. The seller does not receive a refund for the day of closing. The days from August 23 through December 31 total 131 days. Calculation: $2,900 (taxes paid) ÷ 365 (days in calendar year) = $7.9452 per day × 131 = $1,040.82, the prorated taxes due to the seller.

Reference: Finance and Closing > Closing Procedures

16. A buyer acquires an 80%, 30-year loan to purchase a home in Georgia for $275,000. At closing, what is the cost of the intangibles tax?:

A. $660

B. $525

C. $725

D. $825

Answer: A. The answer is $660. The intangibles tax in Georgia is assessed against any new loan of more than $1,500 that will require more than three years to repay. The rate is $1.50 per $500 or any portion thereof (divide the new loan amount by 500, rounding up any fraction, and multiply that amount by $1.50).

Calculation: .80 (80%) x $275,000 (sale price) = $220,000 (the new loan amount); $220,000 ÷ 500 = 440; 440 x $1.50 = $660.

Reference: Finance and Closing > Closing Procedures

17. In Georgia, the closing of a real estate transaction may be conducted by a:

A. salesperson.

B. lender.

C. licensed attorney.

D. broker.

Answer: C. The answer is licensed attorney. In Georgia, only a licensed attorney may conduct a closing. The closing attorney represents the lender. A broker or salesperson may attend the closing but may not conduct the closing.

Reference: Finance and Closing > Closing Procedures

18. Twenty years ago, a homeowner obtained a 30-year mortgage loan to purchase a home. The interest rate on the loan was 9.275%. Today, the homeowner is prepared to pay off the loan early. Based on these facts, which statement is TRUE in Georgia?:

A. The homeowner has a right to prepay the loan only if the property has been sold.

B. The loan documents will determine if prepayment is possible and whether a penalty can be imposed.

C. Prepayment penalties are always imposed, although the rates may be negotiable.

D. The homeowner's lender is entitled by statute to charge the homeowner a prepayment penalty equal to one year's interest on the current balance of the loan.

Answer: B. The answer is the loan documents will determine if prepayment is possible and whether a penalty can be imposed. The loan documents will determine if prepayment is possible and whether a penalty can be imposed. Lenders typically permit prepayment of a loan but may impose a penalty for early repayment.

Reference: Finance and Closing > Finance

19. The transfer tax stamp for a recently sold property indicates that $192.50 was paid for the county transfer tax. What was the sales price of the property?:

A. $175,000

B. $211,750

C. $200,000

D. $192,500

Answer: D. The answer is $192,500. The Georgia transfer tax is $.10 per $100 of the property's sales price. The property sold for $192,500. ($192.50 ÷ $0.10 × 100 = $192,500).

Reference: Finance and Closing > Closing Procedures

20. In Georgia, the transfer tax is paid at the rate of:

A. $0.10 per $100 on any assumed loan.

B. $0.50 per $100 on the sales price of the property.

C. $0.10 per $100 on the sales price of the property.

D. $0.50 per $100 on any assumed loan.

Answer: C. The answer is $0.10 per $100 on the sales price of the property. The transfer tax is a state tax charged at a rate of $.10 per $100 or portion thereof of the sales price of a property. The tax is usually charged to the seller, and the amount of any assumed loan is deducted from the sales price. A new loan is not deducted.

Reference: Finance and Closing > Closing Procedures

21. A closing in Georgia takes place on August 10, and the seller has already paid the annual property taxes of $3,500 for the calendar year of January 1 through December 31. How much will the buyer owe the seller at closing for the buyer's share of the property taxes? (Use the exact days of

the month and the standard calendar year of 365 days in your calculations.):

A. $2,128.76

B. $1,380.82

C. $1,371.23

D. $1,361.64

Answer: C. The answer is $1,371.23. Since the seller has already paid the full year's taxes, the buyer at closing will refund the seller the property taxes paid from the day after closing through December 31. The seller does not receive a refund for the day of closing. The days from August 11 through December 31 total 143 days. Calculation: $3,500 (yearly taxes) ÷ 365 (days in a calendar year) = $9.5890 per day × 143 days = $1,371.23, the prorated taxes due to the seller.

Reference: Finance and Closing > Closing Procedures

22. In Georgia, the responsibility for ensuring the accuracy of any promissory notes involved in a closing belongs to the:

A. buyer or buyer's broker.

B. closing attorney as a representative of the lender.

C. closing attorney as representative of the buyer.

D. seller's broker.

Answer: B. The answer is closing attorney as a representative of the lender. The responsibility for making sure any promissory note involved in a closing is accurate belongs to the closing attorney as a representative of the lender. The closing attorney represents the lender, not the buyer.

Reference: Finance and Closing > Closing Procedures

23. A closing in Georgia involving rental property takes place on December 15. Tenants pay rent on the first day of each month. At the closing, the:

A. seller will owe the buyer 16 days' rent.

B. buyer will owe the seller for 17 days' rent.

C. buyer will owe the seller for 16 days' rent.

D. seller will owe the buyer for 17 days' rent.

Answer: A. The answer is seller will owe the buyer 16 days' rent. As rent is paid at the first of the month, the seller has received rent payments for the entire month of December. The seller may keep the prorated rent from the first through and including the day of closing, December 15 (15 days rent). Rent for the day after closing through the last day of the month belongs to the buyer. As December has 31 days, the seller will owe the buyer the rent for the remaining 16 days of December, from December 16 through December 31.

Reference: Finance and Closing > Closing Procedures

24. The Georgia transfer tax is:

A. $0.10 per $50 of the mortgage amount.

B. $5 per $100 of the mortgage amount.

C. $0.10 per $100 of the sales price.

D. $10 per $100 of the mortgage amount.

Answer: C. The answer is $0.10 per $100 of the sales price. Georgia does have a transfer tax in addition to an intangibles tax. It is usually paid by the seller, but like all closing costs, it is negotiable. It is calculated as $0.10 per $100 or fraction thereof of the purchase price, not including the amount of any loan assumption. The deed may not be recorded without paying the tax.

Reference: Finance and Closing > Closing Procedures

25. In Georgia, a buyer who is getting a mortgage loan will be signing which document at the closing?:

A. Note and mortgage

B. Warranty deed

C. Security deed and note

D. Limited warranty deed

Answer: C. The answer is security deed and note. In Georgia, a borrower will sign a promissory note, which establishes the amount of the debt, the terms of repayment, and the interest rate for the loan. The security deed provides collateral for the loan. With the security deed, the borrower empowers the lender to foreclose on the property in a non-judicial process in the event the borrower defaults on the loan.

Reference: Finance and Closing > Closing Procedures

26. In Georgia, deeds and other documents are recorded:

A. at the Georgia Bureau of Recordation.

B. in the county court.

C. in the offices of the local tax assessor.

D. in the city clerk's office of the city where the property is located.

Answer: B. The answer is in the county court. In Georgia, deeds and other documents are recorded in the court of the county where the property is located.

27. Spouses have transferred from another state and purchased a home in Georgia. At the closing, the closing attorney gives the couple documents for the transference of the title to the buyers. Who must sign the deed?:

A. Whoever the seller's deed indicates as title holder to the property

B. Either spouses

C. Both spouses

D. Both spouses and the seller

Answer: A. The answer is whoever the seller's deed indicates as title holder to the property. In Georgia, only the party indicated as the title holder on the seller's deed need sign the deed to transfer the title. The buyer is never required to sign the deed.

Reference: Finance and Closing > Closing Procedures

28. In calculating PMI, a lender in Georgia would consider a home purchased at $220,000 with a down payment of $28,600 as a(n):

A. 80% loan.

B. 90% loan.

C. 87% loan.

D. 85% loan.

Answer: B. The answer is 90% loan. For PMI calculations, a lender would classify loans as 90% or 95% of the purchase price. Any loan made between 80.1% and 90% of the purchase price would be classified as a 90% loan; any loan with an LTV between 90% and 95% would be classified as a 95% loan. In this case, the borrower's LTV is 87% ($28,600 is 13% of $220,000); the lender would consider the loan as a 90% loan.

Reference: Finance and Closing > Finance

29. If a loan amount is $210,000, the interest rate is 6%, and the closing date is March 17, what would be the buyer's adjusted interest for March? (Use the correct days of the month and a mortgage banker's calendar year of 360 days for your calculations in prorating days.):

A. $500.00

B. $475.00

C. $505.00

D. $525.00

Answer: D. The answer is $525.00. The interest on a mortgage loan is paid in arrears rather than in advance. The buyer will owe interest for March 17 through March 31, 15 days. Calculation: $210,000 (the loan amount) x 6% (.06) interest rate = $12,600 (yearly interest), ÷ 360 days = $35.00 per day, x 15 days = $525.00.

Reference: Finance and Closing > Closing Procedures

30. A security deed usually requires that the:

A. lender purchase hazard insurance on the property.

B. borrower maintain hazard insurance to cover the amount of the debt.

C. borrower maintain hazard insurance for at least one year.

D. lender waive any requirement for hazard insurance.

Answer: B. The answer is borrower maintain hazard insurance to cover the amount of the debt. A security deed usually requires the borrower to maintain hazard insurance as dictated by the lender, usually in an amount to cover any debt on the property. The hazard insurance must name the lender as the loss payee on the policy.

Reference: Finance and Closing > Finance

31. The written opinion of title identifying the fee owner of a property and naming anyone with a legitimate right or interest in the property is a(n):

A. abstract of title.

B. lender's title insurance policy.

C. buyer's title insurance policy.

D. certificate of title.

Answer: D. The answer is certificate of title. The certificate of title is a written opinion, signed by an attorney, and attached to an abstract of title. The certificate names the fee owner of a property and any other persons with legitimate interests in the property. Title insurance ensures lenders and buyers against defects in the title or errors in the abstract of title.

Reference: Finance and Closing > Closing Procedures

32. A Georgia lender will typically assess private mortgage insurance (PMI) for:

A. VA loans.

B. 98% FHA loans.

C. promissory notes with an LTV of 79% or less.

D. a 95% conventional loan.

Answer: D. The answer is a 95% conventional loan. PMI insurance will apply to conventional loans with less than 20% equity. VA loans require no mortgage insurance. FHA loans require a mortgage insurance premium called MIP.

Reference: Finance and Closing > Finance

33. In Georgia, as long as payments are being made on a loan, the certificate of title is held by the:

A. closing attorney.

B. title company.

C. lender.

D. borrower.

Answer: C. The answer is lender. The certificate of title for a property is held by the lender while loan payments are being made, as the lender receives legal title to the property through the security deed. The borrower retains equitable title to the property, but does not receive the certificate of title until the loan is fully paid.

Reference: Finance and Closing > Finance

34. The attorney who conducts real estate closings in Georgia represents the:

A. broker(s) involved in the transaction.

B. the seller.

C. mortgage lender.

D. the buyer.

Answer: C. The answer is mortgage lender. The closing attorney customarily represents the mortgage lender in Georgia. If no loan is involved in the transaction, the attorney may represent the seller, the buyer, or neither party.

35. When a real estate sale closed on November 30, the sellers had paid their yearly hazard insurance premium at a cost of $1,500 a year, and the policy anniversary date was May 10. At the closing, the sellers would receive a refund for the unused portion of their homeowner's yearly premium for what amount? (In your calculations, use the actual days of the month and a standard calendar year of 365 days for daily proration of the policy.):

A. $657.53

B. $653.33

C. $661.55

D. $665.75

Answer: A. The answer is $657.53. Policy days refunded to the seller will be counted from the day after closing, December 1, to and including the last day of the policy, May 9, for a total of 160 days. The amount of the policy, $1,500, ÷ 365 days = $4.1095 per day, x 160 days, = a total refund of $657.53. The other answers would be correct only if the total number of days used to calculate the refund were 159, 161, or 162 days.

Reference: Finance and Closing > Closing Procedures

36. A borrower signs a security deed on a residential property. The deed requires the borrower to occupy the property for at least one year as her primary residence. The borrower, however, intends to use the property as an investment and rent it as soon as possible. In this situation, the borrower:

A. may only rent the property after 60 days from the day of closing.

B. has the right to use the property in any way she chooses.

C. has committed fraud and may be subject to prosecution.

D. may only rent the property after six months from the day of closing.

Answer: C. The answer is has committed fraud and may be subject to prosecution. A security deed for a residential property in Georgia usually requires the borrower to occupy the property within 60 days after closing, and to occupy the property for at least one year as the borrower's primary residence. A borrower who signs the deed and does not reside on the property but uses the property as an investment property has committed loan fraud and may be subject to prosecution.

Reference: Finance and Closing > Finance

37. If a closing in Georgia occurs on March 12 and the loan balance as of the March 1 payment was $210,400 with an interest rate of 5%, how much accrued interest does the seller owe at closing? (Use the correct days of the month and a mortgage banker's calendar year of 360 days for your calculations in prorating days.):

A. $350.67

B. $321.42

C. $292.22

D. $379.89

Answer: A. The answer $350.67. The interest on a mortgage loan is paid in arrears. The seller's March 1 loan payment paid for interest due in the month of February, but the seller still owes interest for March, including for the day of closing, March 12. The seller owes interest for 12 days. Calculation: $210,400 (the loan amount) × 5% (.05) interest rate = $10,520 (yearly interest) ÷ 360 days = $29.222 per day, × 12 days = $350.67.

Reference: Finance and Closing > Closing Procedures

38. The security deed in Georgia provides that:

A. payments received from the borrower will be first applied to the principal and then to interest owed.

B. the borrower may make partial payments on the monthly payment due date.

C. the property must be occupied as a principal residence for a minimum of two years.

D. payments received from the borrower will be first applied to interest owed and then to principal.

Answer: D. The answer is payments received from the borrower will be first applied to interest owed and then to principal. The security deed in Georgia provides that the borrower's payments are applied first to interest owed, and then to principal. The deed does not permit partial monthly payments to the lender. The deed requires that the borrower occupy the property as a principal residence for at least one year unless the lender agrees otherwise in writing.

Reference: Finance and Closing > Finance

39. A broker or salesperson may perform all of the following in preparation for the closing EXCEPT:

A. explain closing procedures to both buyer and seller and anticipate decision-making alternatives.

B. provide approximate closing expenses for either the buyer or the seller.

C. coordinate inspections and deliver documents and escrow monies to the appropriate attorney.

D. conduct any title searches that might be required.

Answer: D. The answer is conduct any title searches that might be required. Conducting a title search may lead to charges of practicing law without a license. The broker can, however, provide approximate closing expenses, explain closing procedures to both parties, and coordinate inspections and deliver documents and escrow monies.

Reference: Finance and Closing > Closing Procedures

40. A house was purchased for $203,000 in cash. How much will the transfer tax cost?:

A. $203.00

B. $900.00

C. $545.00

D. $945.56

Answer: A. The answer is $203.00. The Georgia transfer tax is $.10 per $100 of the property's sales price. The transfer tax will cost $203.00. ($203,000 ÷ 100 × $0.10 = $203.00).

Reference: Finance and Closing > Closing Procedures

41. The grantor of a security deed in Georgia is the:

A. title company.

B. lender.

C. borrower.

D. seller.

Answer: C. The answer is borrower. The grantor is the party giving the deed, the borrower, who transfers the interest in the property to the lender with the right to non-judicial foreclosure in the event of a default. The lender is the grantee, the party receiving the deed and accepting an interest in the property as security for the debt. The seller is not a party to the new security deed in a real estate transaction. The title company issues title insurance to the lender and/or the borrower.

42. A security deed in Georgia conveys:

A. legal title to the borrower.

B. lien rights to the lender.

C. lien rights to the seller.

D. legal title to the lender.

Answer: D. The answer is legal title to the lender. A security deed (or deed to secure debt) conveys legal title to the lender. The borrower empowers the lender to act as an attorney in fact. The security deed permits the lender to foreclose on the property in a non-judicial foreclosure. The borrower retains equitable title to the property and a right to redemption in a foreclosure proceeding. A mortgage instrument conveys lien rights to a lender.

Reference: Finance and Closing > Finance

43. A mortgage lender in Georgia makes a loan at 5 1/4 percent. If the lender's yield on the loan is actually 6%, how many loan discount points are being charged on this loan?:

A. Three discount points

B. Five discount points

C. Four discount points

D. Six discount points

Answer: D. The answer is six discount points. Points charged to raise a lender's monetary return on a loan are known as discount points. Each discount point affects the lender's yield by 1/8 of 1 percentage point. If the lender's yield increases from the interest rate of 5 1/4 % (= 5 2/8) to 6 % (= 5 8/8), six discount points would be required (5 8/8 minus 5 2/8 = 5 6/8, or 6 discount points).

Reference: Finance and Closing > Finance

44. The acceleration clause in a security deed:

A. requires the borrower to reinstate a defaulted loan before foreclosure.

B. requires the lender to cancel a security instrument upon full payment of the loan.

C. permits a lender to demand an immediate payment of the debt in the event of default.

D. allows the borrower to convey the property to another without the lender's consent.

Answer: C. The answer is permits a lender to demand an immediate payment of the debt in the event of default. The acceleration clause in a security deed allows a lender to demand immediate payment of the debt in the event of the borrower's default. An alienation clause permits the lender to demand immediate payment of the full debt if the borrower conveys interest in the property to another without the lender's consent. The right to equitable redemption permits a borrower under certain circumstances to reinstate a defaulted loan after acceleration but before foreclosure. The defeasance clause in a security deed requires a lender to cancel the security deed upon full payment of the debt.

Reference: Finance and Closing > Finance

45. When a borrower in default on a loan has not made payments after being contacted by the lender, the lender:

A. may advertise the property in the appropriate county newspaper for an upcoming foreclosure sale.

B. must allow the borrower to reclaim the property after a foreclosure sale.

C. sues the borrower in municipal court to force payment on the loan.

D. sues the borrower in district court to force payment on the loan.

Answer: A. The answer is may advertise the property in the appropriate county newspaper for an upcoming foreclosure sale. The use of the security deed in Georgia permits a lender to foreclose without going to court. The lender advertises the property in the appropriate county newspaper for four weeks before a foreclosure sale. Georgia does not have a statutory right to redemption, which allows a borrower to reclaim a property after a property has been sold in a foreclosure sale.

Reference: Finance and Closing > Finance

46. The Georgia intangibles tax is assessed at a rate of:

A. $1.50 per $500 on a new loan.

B. $3.00 per $1,000 on the sales price of the property.

C. $3.00 per $500 on the sales prices of the property.

D. $1.00 per $500 on a new loan.

Answer: A. The answer is $1.50 per $500 on a new loan. The intangibles tax is assessed against any new loan of more than $1,500 with a repayment period of more than three years. The tax is paid by either the seller or the buyer at a rate of $1.50 per $500 or portion thereof of any new loan.

Reference: Finance and Closing > Closing Procedures

AMP REAL ESTATE EXAMS

These are the LATEST and most COMPREHENSIVE questions and answers available to help you prepare for the AMP Real Estate Exam. Features topics related to, and in the order of, the latest AMP Examination Content Outline with rationales to help you improve your ability to pass on the first try.

1. A broker may act as a dual agent and represent both the seller and the buyer in the same transaction if:

A. the seller and the buyer are related by blood or marriage.

B. both parties are represented by attorneys.

C. the broker informs either the buyer or the seller that the broker is representing both parties to the transaction.

D. both the seller and the buyer give their informed consent, usually in writing.

Answer: D. The answer is both the seller and the buyer give their informed consent, usually in writing. When a broker represents both the seller and the buyer in the same transaction, the broker is practicing dual agency. State laws, where dual agency is allowed, require both parties give written consent of dual agency. Informing only one party of the dual agency does not meet the requirements for practicing dual agency.

Reference: Agency Relationships and Contracts > Agency Relationships

2. A real estate professional has found a buyer for a seller's home. The buyer has indicated in writing a willingness to buy the property for $1,000 less than the asking price and has deposited $5,000 in earnest money with the real estate professional. The seller is out of town for the weekend, and the real estate professional has been unable to inform the seller of the signed document. At this point, the buyer has a(n):

A. executory contract.

B. offer.

C. voidable contract.

D. implied contract.

Answer: B. The answer is offer. Until the seller accepts the offer and the buyer is notified of the acceptance there is no contract only an offer.

Reference: Agency Relationships and Contracts > Purchase Contracts (contracts between seller and buyer)

3. Under an exclusive-agency listing, the listing broker would be entitled to a commission EXCEPT:

A. if another co-op broker secures a qualified buyer for the property.

B. if a salesperson from a cooperating brokerage secures a qualified buyer for the property.

C. if the broker sells the property himself.

D. if the seller sells the property himself to a relative moving from out-of-town.

Answer: D. The answer is if the seller sells the property himself to a relative moving from out-of-town. An exclusive-agency listing authorizes the listing brokerage or co-op broker to sell and receive a commission, but the seller retains the right to sell the property without obligation to the broker. A seller who sells the property himself to a relative is not required under an exclusive-agency listing to pay the listing broker a commission. The seller is obligated to pay a commission to the listing broker when that broker, another broker, or a salesperson from a cooperating brokerage firm sells the property.

Reference: Agency Relationships and Contracts > Service/Listing Buyer Contracts (contracts between licensee and seller or buyer)

4. A real estate broker lists a home as agent for the seller. Later that same day, a buyer comes into the office and asks for general information about homes for sale in the area. Based on these facts, which statement is TRUE?:

A. If the buyer later asks for buyer representation by the firm, he cannot have it because the firm is an agent of the seller only.

B. The seller is the broker's client; the buyer is a consumer.

C. Both seller and buyer have no relationship with the brokerage except as consumers.

D. The brokerage firm owes fiduciary duties to both seller and buyer.

Answer: B. The answer is the seller is the broker's client; the buyer is a consumer. The listing contract creates the agency relationship and obligations between the seller and the broker. A prospective purchaser who asks for general information is not represented by the broker but a consumer. Consumers are not owed fiduciary duties but may later contract with the broker for buyer representation.

Reference: Agency Relationships and Contracts > Agency Relationships

5. A principal broker hires a salesperson as an employee of the brokerage firm. The employment contract between the broker and the salesperson will most likely include all of the following EXCEPT:

A. the salesperson is entitled to the firm's health insurance plan.

B. the broker will withhold federal income taxes and Social Security taxes from the salesperson's paycheck.

C. the salesperson attend weekly sales meeting.

D. the salesperson is responsible for direct payment of all income taxes and Social Security payments from each paycheck.

Answer: D. The answer is that the salesperson is responsible for direct payment of all income taxes and Social Security payments from each paycheck. A broker is responsible for withholding federal income taxes and Social Security payments from an employee's paycheck. The broker may require that the employee attend sales meeting and may include the employee in the firm's benefits, including a health insurance plan. A salesperson employed as an independent contractor is responsible for direct payment of all federal taxes and any required state taxes.

Reference: Agency Relationships and Contracts > Service/Listing Buyer Contracts (contracts between licensee and seller or buyer))

6. A purchase agreement would likely be voidable under all of these circumstances EXCEPT:

A. the purchaser is a minor.

B. the buyer didn't read or understand the contract.

C. the seller signed under duress.

D. the seller made a material misrepresentation to the buyer.

Answer: B. The answer is the buyer didn't read or understand the contract. Part of due diligence on the part of a buyer or seller is to fully read and understand all legal documents they are signing or consult an attorney or other advisor for help. Duress, fraud, misrepresentation, and minors always make contracts voidable.

Reference: Agency Relationships and Contracts > General Legal Principles, Theory and Concepts about Contracts

7. It is the duty of an agent to disclose to the principal every material step taken in the transaction of the principal's business. This duty exists because the:

A. state license laws have this requirement.

B. commission can be adjusted up or down according to the agent's efforts.

C. agent has fiduciary obligations to the principal.

D. terms of the purchase contract require the agent to do so.

Answer: C. The answer is agent has fiduciary obligations to the principal. One of the duties of a fiduciary is that of disclosure, keeping the principal informed of all facts or information related to the transaction. The duty exists because of the law of agency, not because of the terms of any contract. An agent's commission is established under a contract between the agent's broker and the principal and is based on the successful completion of a transaction.

Reference: Agency Relationships and Contracts > Agency Relationships

8. In regard to an offer and acceptance all the following are true EXCEPT:

A. an offer can be revoked at any time before acceptance.

B. in real estate, an oral acceptance creates a binding contract.

C. to offer means to put forward for acceptance or rejection.

D. a counter offer reverses the legal positions of the offeror and offeree.

Answer: B. The answer is in real estate, an oral acceptance creates a binding contract. The oral acceptance of an offer does not create a binding contract. The offer must be signed followed with communication of acceptance to become a binding contract.

Reference: Agency Relationships and Contracts > Purchase Contracts (contracts between seller and buyer)

9. A broker has an exclusive-right-to-sell listing on a building. The owner is out of town when the broker gets an offer from a buyer to purchase the building. The buyer must have an answer from the seller before the seller is scheduled to return to the city. Under these circumstances, the:

A. buyer is obligated to keep the offer open until the seller returns.

B. broker may enter into a binding agreement on behalf of the seller.

C. broker may collect a commission even if the transaction falls through because of the seller's absence from the city.

D. broker must obtain the signature of the seller to effect a contract.

Answer: D. The answer is broker must obtain the signature of the seller to effect a contract. A real estate broker is usually a special agent who when representing the seller is limited to finding a ready, willing, and able buyer for the property. As a special agent, the broker may not bind the principal to any contract. The broker may collect a commission only upon completion of the transaction. A buyer may write an offer requiring a response before the seller returns and is not obligated to keep the offer open past the time period the buyer states in the offer.

Reference: Agency Relationships and Contracts > Service/Listing Buyer Contracts (contracts between licensee and seller or buyer)

10. By executing an agency listing contract with a seller, a real estate brokerage firm becomes:

A. the agent of the seller.

B. a procuring cause.

C. responsible for sharing the commission.

D. obligated to open a special trust account.

Answer: A. The answer is the agent of the seller. An agency listing contract is an employment agreement whereby a brokerage agrees to represent the seller as the seller's agent in the sale of the seller's property. The brokerage firm or one of the firm's licensees may be a procuring cause if they produce a willing, ready and able buyer. The brokerage firm is obligated to open a special trust account only when receiving escrow funds from a prospective buyer. The brokerage firm is responsible for sharing the commission only with a salesperson or associate broker working for the brokerage firm.

Reference: Agency Relationships and Contracts > Service/Listing Buyer Contracts (contracts between licensee and seller or buyer)

11. The broker receives an earnest money deposit with a written offer to purchase that includes a 10-day acceptance clause. On the fifth day, before the offer is accepted, the buyer notifies the broker that she is withdrawing the offer

and requests the return of her earnest money deposit. In this situation, the:

A. seller and broker have the right to each retain one-half of the deposit.

B. buyer cannot withdraw the offer because it must be held open for the full 10 days.

C. buyer may revoke the offer but will not have the earnest money returned since the buyer failed to give the seller the full acceptance time.

D. buyer has the right to revoke the offer at any time until it is accepted and recover the earnest money.

Answer: D. The answer is buyer has the right to revoke the offer at any time until it is accepted and recover the earnest money. The offeror (the buyer) may revoke the offer at any time before the offer is accepted, even if the person making the offer agreed to keep the offer open for a set period of time. At that point, the earnest money deposit should be refunded to the buyer.

Reference: Agency Relationships and Contracts > Purchase Contracts (contracts between seller and buyer)

12. A salesperson representing a seller suggests to a buyer that the seller might accept less than the listing price. The salesperson in this situation:

A. is simply performing a ministerial act for the buyer.

B. may have unintentionally created an undisclosed dual agency by suggesting that the buyer offer less than the listing price.

C. no longer represents the seller since he has given advice to the buyer.

D. is fulfilling his fiduciary responsibilities to the seller by encouraging a buyer to purchase the property.

Answer: B. The answer is may have unintentionally created an undisclosed dual agency by suggesting that the buyer offer less than the listing price. The salesperson in giving advice to the buyer may lead the buyer to believe that the salesperson represents the buyer's interests and is acting as the buyer's advocate. The agent may have created an implied agency with the buyer and violated the duties of loyalty and confidentiality to the principal, the seller. The agent's fiduciary responsibilities to the seller continue even with his actions. Performing ministerial acts involves granting services that do not require any discretion or advice.

Reference: Agency Relationships and Contracts > Agency Relationships

13. An option to purchase binds which of the following parties?:

A. Neither buyer nor seller

B. Buyer only

C. Both buyer and seller

D. Seller only

Answer: D. The answer is seller only. An option contract is a unilateral contract in which the seller agrees to sell the property at a set price in the future if the buyer decides to buy.

Reference: Agency Relationships and Contracts > Purchase Contracts (contracts between seller and buyer)

14. The broker protection clause in a real estate listing contract provides:

A. the property owner will pay the listing broker a commission if, within a specified time after the listing expires, the owner transfers the property to someone the broker originally introduced to the owner.

B. the seller may not file a lawsuit against the broker for lack of performance.

C. the seller may not file a complaint against the broker with the state regulatory commission.

D. how the broker will be compensated.

Answer: A. The answer is the property owner will pay the listing broker a commission if, within a specified time after the listing expires, the owner transfers the property to someone the broker originally introduced to the owner. The listing contract must also state the circumstances under which the broker will be paid. Nothing in the listing contract prohibits a seller from taking action through the courts or a real estate commission if the broker does not perform according to the terms of the listing contract.

Reference: Agency Relationships and Contracts > Service/Listing Buyer Contracts (contracts between licensee and seller or buyer)

15. Every enforceable contract for the sale of real estate must be in writing and signed by all parties, in accordance with the:

A. Truth in Lending Act.

B. Real Estate License Act.

C. statute of frauds.

D. Uniform Commercial Code.

Answer: C. The answer is statute of frauds. Contracts for the sale of real estate must be in writing to be enforceable, according to the statute of frauds.

Reference: Agency Relationships and Contracts > General Legal Principles, Theory and Concepts about Contracts

16. A sales contract or land contract would give the buyer a(n):

A. cloud on the title.

B. equitable title.

C. quiet title.

D. legal title.

Answer: B. The answer is equitable title. The sales contract, land contract, or trust deed would give the buyer an equitable title. Legal title is transferred from the seller to the buyer via deed at closing of a sales contract and upon last payment to the seller from the buyer in a land contract.

Reference: Agency Relationships and Contracts > Purchase Contracts (contracts between seller and buyer)

17. After a particularly challenging transaction finally closes, a client gives the salesperson a check for $500 "for all your extra work." Which of the following statements isTRUE?:

A. The salesperson may accept the check, but the salesperson's broker is entitled to 80% of the check.

B. The salesperson may receive compensation only from her broker.

C. While such compensation is irregular, it is appropriate for the salesperson to accept the check.

D. The salesperson may accept the check if she deposits it immediately in a special escrow account.

Answer: B. The answer is the salesperson may receive compensation only from her broker. Most state statutes require that compensation for real estate brokerage activities be paid to licensed salespersons only by their own broker for work on any given transaction. The salesperson in this case may not receive a check directly from the client.

Reference: Agency Relationships and Contracts >

Service/Listing Buyer Contracts (contracts between licensee and seller or buyer)

18. In a real estate sales contract, the seller is typically required to:

A. check for material defects in the property.

B. convey title to the property at closing.

C. obtain a mortgage for the buyer.

D. have the property appraised.

Answer: B. The answer is convey title to the property at closing. The seller is required to deliver a deed at closing that transfers title to the buyer.
Reference: Agency Relationships and Contracts > Purchase Contracts (contracts between seller and buyer)

19. A seller agreed to list his home for $220,000, but the listing agent did not tell him that the fair market value of the home was $245,000. The listing agent purchased the property the next day. The agent has violated which of the following duties to the seller?:

A. Accounting

B. Disclosure

C. Loyalty

D. Care

Answer: C. The answer is loyalty. The fiduciary duty of loyalty means that the agent must place the client's interests above all others, including the agent's own self-interest. The duty of accounting requires agents to be accountable for money and the property of others that come into their possession in the performance of the agent's duties. The duty of care requires that agents use her skill and experience to the client's benefit. The duty of disclosure includes keeping the client informed of all relevant facts related to the transaction.

Reference: Agency Relationships and Contracts > Agency Relationships

20. A couple enter a real estate office asking to see a property listed with another brokerage office. A real estate salesperson calls the listing agent and makes an appointment to show the property. Without having the couple sign a written buyer agency contract, the salesperson drives the couple to the house, and even recommends that before they buy the house they secure an independent property inspection. He also confides to the couple that he knows the owners are getting a divorce and want to sell the house quickly. In this case, the salesperson has created a(n):

A. express agency relationship with the buyers.

B. implied agency relationship with the buyers.

C. universal agency relationship with the buyers.

D. general agency relationship with the buyers.

Answer: B. The answer is implied agency relationship with the buyers. The salesperson has unintentionally created an agency relationship with the buyers. There is no formal oral or written agency contract with the buyers. Express agency occurs when two parties enter into an oral or written formal agency agreement. Universal agency empowers the agent to do anything the principal could do personally, such as authorized by a power of attorney. General agency allows the agent to act for the principal in a wide range of matters, as authorized, for example, in a property management contract.

Reference: Agency Relationships and Contracts > Agency Relationships

21. Which statement is TRUE of a real estate broker acting as the agent of the seller?:

A. The broker can disclose confidential information about the seller to a buyer if the buyer is also represented by the broker.

B. The broker can accept a commission from the buyer without the seller's approval.

C. The broker can agree to a change in price without the seller's approval.

D. The broker has a fiduciary obligation of loyalty to the seller.

Answer: D. The answer is the broker has a fiduciary obligation of loyalty to the seller. Loyalty to the client-seller requires confidentiality—not revealing confidential information; it involves obedience—not publishing a price different from the one set by the client; and it requires disclosure. Dual agents have duties of confidentiality to both of the parties they represent.

Reference: Agency Relationships and Contracts > Agency Relationships

22. Which of the following does NOT create an agency relationship?:

A. A buyer agency contract

B. The payment of money or commissions

C. A property management contract

D. A listing contract

Answer: B. The answer is the payment of money or commissions. The payment of money or commissions does not create an agency relationship. A written contract or actions of the parties create agency. In real estate, a listing contract, buyer agency contract, or property management contract create an agency relationship between the broker and the principal to the contract.

Reference: Agency Relationships and Contracts > Agency Relationships

23. To assign a contract for the sale of real estate means to:

A. allow the seller and the buyer to exchange positions.

B. permit another broker to act as agent for the principal.

C. record the contract with the county recorder's office.

D. transfer one's rights under the contract.

Answer: D. The answer is transfer one's rights under the contract. An assignment is a transfer of the interest of one person to another. In an assignment, rights are assigned to a third party, but the original party remains primarily liable unless specifically released. Assignment of a contract does not change the broker/agent relationship.

Reference: Agency Relationships and Contracts > Purchase
Contracts (contracts between seller and buyer)

**24. Two salespeople working for the same broker obtained
offers on a property listed with their firm. The first offer
was obtained early in the day. A second offer for a higher
purchase price was obtained later in the afternoon. The
broker presented the first offer to the seller that evening.
The broker did not inform the seller about the second offer
so that the seller could make an informed decision about the
first offer. Which of the following statements is TRUE?:**

A. The broker's actions are permissible provided the
commission is split between the two salespeople.

B. After the first offer was received, the broker should have told
the salespeople that no additional offers would be accepted until
the seller decided on the offer.

C. The broker was smart to protect the seller from getting into a
negotiating battle over two offers.

D. The broker has no authority to withhold any offers from the
seller.

Answer: D. The answer is the broker has no authority to withhold any offers from the seller. It is the broker's duty to keep the principal informed of all facts or information that could affect a transaction. A broker for the seller has a duty to disclose all offers. A commission split does not affect the broker's responsibilities to submit all offers to the seller.

Reference: Agency Relationships and Contracts > Service/Listing Buyer Contracts (contracts between licensee and seller or buyer)

25. A contract that secures a brokerage firm to assist a buyer in finding a suitable property to buy is a(n):

A. escrow contract.

B. buyer agency contract.

C. option contract.

D. sales contract.

Answer: B. The answer is buyer agency contract. A buyer agency contract is an employment contract in which the broker is employed as the buyer's agent in finding a suitable property. A sales contract is a contract between a buyer and seller for purchase of a property. An escrow contract is an agreement between a buyer, seller, and escrow holder (such as a broker) defining the responsibilities of each. An option contract is a contract by which the optionor (usually an owner) gives an optionee the right to buy or lease a property at a fixed price within a certain period of time.

Reference: Agency Relationships and Contracts > Service/Listing Buyer Contracts (contracts between licensee and seller or buyer)

26. All of the following reasons are valid bases for terminating a listing contract EXCEPT:

A. agreement of the parties.

B. destruction of the premises.

C. the sale of the property.

D. the death of the salesperson.

Answer: D. The answer is the death of the salesperson. Since the listing contract is a contract with the broker, and not with the salesperson, the death of the salesperson does not terminate the listing. The broker may assign another salesperson to the listing. The sale of the property, an agreement by the seller and the broker, and the destruction of the property are all valid bases for terminating a listing contract.

Reference: Agency Relationships and Contracts > Service/Listing Buyer Contracts (contracts between licensee and seller or buyer)

27. An option to purchase binds which of the following parties?:

A. Neither buyer nor seller

B. Both buyer and seller

C. Buyer only

D. Seller only

Answer: D. The answer is seller only. In an option the seller has agreed to not sell the property to anyone else and to give the buyer the right to sell during the option period. The potential buyer (optionee) who purchases an option to purchase is not bound to purchase the property. However, should the buyer decide to exercise the option, the seller is bound to proceed with the sale in keeping with all the details contained in the option. Once the option is accepted the buyer and seller move forward with a bilateral purchase contract.

Reference: Agency Relationships and Contracts > Purchase Contracts (contracts between seller and buyer)

28. During a job interview, a principal broker tells a salesperson that she will work for the brokerage firm as an independent contractor. As an independent contractor, what can the salesperson expect from her work with the broker?:

A. She may participate in the firm's health insurance plan.

B. She will be required to work a minimum of 40 hours per week.

C. She must attend weekly sales meetings.

D. At least 90% of her income will be based on sales production.

Answer: D. The answer is that at least 90% of her income will be based on sales production. To be considered an independent contractor under Internal Revenue Service rules, at least 90% of the salesperson's income must be based on sales production. A broker may not require a minimum number of weekly hours or mandate sales meetings for independent contractors but may make such requirements for employees of the firm.

Reference: Agency Relationships and Contracts > Service/Listing Buyer Contracts (contracts between licensee and seller or buyer)

29. A buyer signed a purchase agreement, but then the seller decided not to sell. The buyer sued the seller successfully and was able to purchase the house. What was the contract remedy if the seller was in default?:

A. Mutual agreement

B. Unilateral rescission

C. Liquidated damages

D. Specific performance

Answer: D. The answer is specific performance. The buyer does not have the option of liquidated damages since the seller has not brought any earnest money to the contract. Mutual agreement is when the parties terminate and return all items of value to each party as if the contract did not exist. Unilateral rescission is one party terminating.

Reference: Agency Relationships and Contracts > Purchase Contracts (contracts between seller and buyer)

30. When the buyer is in default and the seller keeps the earnest money, the contract MOST likely provided for:

A. executed damages.

B. specific performance.

C. actual damages.

D. liquidated damages.

Answer: D. The answer is liquidated damages. Earnest money is not consideration; it is the seller's remedy in a liquated damages contract if the buyer defaults.

Reference: Agency Relationships and Contracts > Purchase Contracts (contracts between seller and buyer)

31. To be an independent contractor the requirements for the salesperson and principle broker would include all of the following EXCEPT:

A. the salesperson has signed an independent contractor agreement with the principal broker.

B. the principal broker withhold taxes from the salesperson's compensation.

C. the majority of the salespersons income be based on sales production.

D. the salesperson has a current real estate license.

Answer: B. The answer is the principal broker withhold from the salesperson's compensation. A broker does not withhold federal taxes or Social Security from an independent contractor's commissions. A principal broker is required to make those withholdings for all employees. An independent contractor situation must include the other three requirements to meet the conditions for independent contractor status established by the IRS.

Reference: Agency Relationships and Contracts > Service/Listing Buyer Contracts (contracts between licensee and seller or buyer)

32. A broker tells a prospective buyer that a lake property has a spectacular view of the lake. In fact, the view from the property also includes several large trees that block the view of parts of the lake. Which of the following statements is TRUE?:

A. The broker has committed fraud.

B. The broker is merely puffing, which is legal as long as there is no misrepresentation.

C. The broker is guilty of negligent misrepresentation.

D. The broker is guilty of intentional misrepresentation.

Answer: B. The answer is the broker is merely puffing, which is legal as long as there is no misrepresentation. The broker is exaggerating the benefits of the property, in this case, the view of the lake. In this situation the broker is not guilty of fraud or misrepresentation. Fraud is a deceitful practice or a misstatement of a material fact, known to be false.

Reference: Agency Relationships and Contracts > Purchase Contracts (contracts between seller and buyer)

33. The MLS lists a number of personal property items the seller was willing to include in the sale including the commercial stove and refrigerator along with all other appliances. The buyer and seller have gone back and forth over a number of items including price and the appliances, which were included in the first offer. The final contract did not included any appliances, in this case the appliances:

A. will belong to the buyer since they were listed in MLS and the seller is obligated to include all items listed in MLS as part of good faith in contracting.

B. will have to be paid for out of closing by the buyer in order to meet the requirements of the original contact.

C. belong to the seller who may take them upon closing the property.

D. if removed by the seller after closing would be a breach of contract by the seller and listing broker.

Answer: C. The answer is belong to the seller who may take them upon closing the property. The final contract is what is used to determine what is to be conveyed, and since no mention of the appliances was made, they belong to the seller who may take them.

Reference: Agency Relationships and Contracts > Purchase Contracts (contracts between seller and buyer)

34. A broker received a 6% commission from the sale of a property. The broker gave the salesperson $3,500, which was 30% of the firm's commission. What was the selling price of the property?:

A. $75,000

B. $83,333

C. $194,450

D. $196,000

Answer: C. The answer is $194,450. To find the broker's total commission, divide the salesperson's commission by the percentage of the salesperson's commission: $3500 ÷ .30 (30%) = $11,667. The broker's commission is 6% of the sales price. To find the sales price, divide the broker's commission by the percentage of the broker's commission: $11,667 ÷ .06 (6%) = $194,450.

Reference: Agency Relationships and Contracts > Service/Listing Buyer Contracts (contracts between licensee and seller or buyer)

35. A contract entered into without duress, menace, misrepresentation, or fraud means that it meets the legal requirement of the:

A. proper legal form.

B. meeting of the minds.

C. valuable consideration.

D. full consent.

Answer: D. The answer is full consent. Full consent means a contract was entered into without duress, menace, misrepresentation, or fraud.

Reference: Agency Relationships and Contracts > Purchase Contracts (contracts between seller and buyer)

36. An owner who is interested in selling his house is usually concerned about how much money he can get when it sells. A competitive market analysis (CMA) may help the seller determine a realistic listing price. Which of the following statements is TRUE?:

A. A broker, but not a salesperson, is permitted to prepare a competitive market analysis.

B. A competitive market analysis is the same as an appraisal.

C. A competitive market analysis is what is prepared by a certified real estate appraiser.

D. A competitive market analysis contains a compilation of facts about similar properties that have recently sold.

Answer: D. The answer is a competitive market analysis contains a compilation of facts about similar properties that have recently sold. A competitive market analysis (CMA) is a comparison of the prices of properties recently sold, properties currently on the market, and properties that did not sell. It is an analysis of the market activity among comparable properties designed to arrive at a fair market value for a subject property. Any real estate competent broker or salesperson may prepare a CMA. The CMA is not an appraisal, which may only be prepared by a state licensed or certified real estate appraiser.

Reference: Agency Relationships and Contracts > Service/Listing Buyer Contracts (contracts between licensee and seller or buyer)

37. A person approaches an owner and says, "I'd like to buy your house." The owner says, "Sure," and they agree on a price. What kind of contract is this?:

A. Unenforceable

B. No contract

C. Implied

D. Void

Answer: A. The answer is unenforceable. Until the parties put the agreement into writing it is unenforceable, since under the statute of frauds all transfers of real estate must be in writing.

Reference: Agency Relationships and Contracts > General Legal Principles, Theory and Concepts about Contracts

38. A buyer and a seller sign a contract for the sale of real property. A few days later they decide to change many terms of the contract, while retaining the basic intent to buy and sell. The process by which the new contract replaces the old one is called:

A. assemblage.

B. rescission.

C. assignment.

D. novation.

Answer: D. The answer is novation. When a new contract replaces an old one, the process is novation. The new contract may be between the same parties or between one of the original parties and a new party. In any event, the parties' obligations under the old contract are terminated.

Reference: Agency Relationships and Contracts > Purchase Contracts (contracts between seller and buyer)

39. A listing contract will usually include all of the following information EXCEPT:

A. the broker's authority and responsibilities.

B. the MLS standard commission rate.

C. unusual deed conditions or restrictions.

D. termination and default provisions.

Answer: B. The answer is the MLS standard commission rate. A listing contract will include the broker's commission. Commission rates are determined by the individual listing broker, not by an MLS. A listing contract will usually state the broker's responsibilities, reasons for termination or default of the contract, and any unusual deed conditions or restrictions.

Reference: Agency Relationships and Contracts > Service/Listing Buyer Contracts (contracts between licensee and seller or buyer)

40. A property manager is typically a(n):

A. designated agent.

B. universal agent.

C. special agent.

D. general agent.

Answer: D. The answer is general agent. A general agent represents a principal in a broad range of matters related to a particular business or activity. A broker has a property management contract with a property owner and may bind the owner to contracts or agreements related to management of the property. A universal agent is a person empowered to do anything the principal could do personally, authorized by a general power of attorney. A special agent may represent the principal in a specific transaction only and has no power to bind the principal; a real estate broker is typically a special agent. A designated agent is an individual licensee authorized by a broker to represent one party in a transaction in which the other party is also represented by the broker.

Reference: Agency Relationships and Contracts > Agency Relationships

41. Which of the following would be considered dual agency?:

A. A broker's representing more than one seller.

B. Two brokerage companies cooperating with each other.

C. A broker's acting for both the landlord and tenant in the same transaction.

D. A broker's listing and then selling the same property.

Answer: C. The answer is a broker's acting for both the landlord and tenant in the same transaction. In dual agency, the agent represents two principals in the same transaction. Because the agency originates with the broker, dual agency arises when the broker is the agent of the tenant or buyer and either the agent or subagent of the landlord or seller. Brokerage companies cooperate with each other through multiple listing services and other agreements. Brokerage companies represent many sellers through different listing agreements in which the broker agrees to represent the sellers in selling their properties.

Reference: Agency Relationships and Contracts > Agency Relationships

42. A new salesperson lists a unit in a condominium building for sale. In this transaction, the salesperson:

A. acts on behalf of the brokerage firm.

B. has a direct agency relationship with the owners of the unit.

C. must personally find a buyer for the unit to obtain a share of the commission.

D. acts on behalf of the condominium association as well as the seller.

Answer: A. The answer is acts on behalf of the brokerage firm. Salespersons or associate brokers act as an agent of their broker. Only the broker has a direct agency relationship with the owners of the unit but not with the condominium association. Under the terms of most listing agreements, the broker, and in turn the salesperson, is entitled to a share of the commission even if the broker or salesperson does not personally find a buyer for the unit.

Reference: Agency Relationships and Contracts > Agency Relationships

43. A seller has listed a property under an exclusive-agency listing with a broker. If the seller sells the property personally during the term of the listing to someone who learns about the property through the seller, the seller will owe the broker:

A. only reimbursement for the broker's costs.

B. no commission.

C. a partial commission.

D. the full commission.

Answer: B. The answer is no commission. In an exclusive-agency listing, if the property is sold by the seller the brokerage will receive no commission. Only the exclusive-right-to-sell listing earns the listing broker any commission if someone else sells the property during the term of the agreement.

Reference: Agency Relationships and Contracts > Service/Listing Buyer Contracts (contracts between licensee and seller or buyer)

44. The amount of commission that is paid to a salesperson is determined by:

A. the local real estate board.

B. mutual agreement with the client.

C. state law.

D. mutual agreement with her broker.

Answer: D. The answer is mutual agreement with her broker. All commissions must be paid through the broker, and the amount the salesperson receives is set by mutual agreement between these two parties. The local board and state law do not dictate the amount of commissions paid. A client must agree to the amount of commission paid to a broker but is not involved in the split of the commission between the broker and a salesperson.

Reference: Agency Relationships and Contracts > Service/Listing Buyer Contracts (contracts between licensee and seller or buyer)

45. Upon acceptance and communication of acceptance, an offer is considered:

A. a contract.

B. unilateral.

C. valid.

D. a counteroffer.

Answer: A. The answer is a contract. An offer lacks acceptance, once acceptance is communicated to all parties the offer, if a purchase contract becomes an executory contract. A unilateral contract exchanges a promise for performance. Valid contracts are binding and enforceable. Counteroffers terminate the original offer.

Reference: Agency Relationships and Contracts > General Legal Principles, Theory and Concepts about Contracts

46. Mutual rescission is BEST defined as the:

A. ability of one party to sue a defaulting party.

B. agreement of both sides to allow one party to prevail and keep any funds.

C. agreement that the party in default will make payment to the nondefaulting party.

D. dissolution of a contract with the return of all funds or things of value to both sides.

Answer: D. The answer is dissolution of a contract with the return of all funds or things of value to both sides. Mutual rescission is when both parties agree to terminate any agreement and return all funds, property, or things of value to the respective parties.

Reference: Agency Relationships and Contracts > Purchase Contracts (contracts between seller and buyer)

47. A real estate broker hired by an owner to sell a parcel of real estate must comply with:

A. all dual agency requirements.

B. the concept of caveat emptor.

C. the common law of agency, even if a state statute exists.

D. all lawful instructions of the owner.

Answer: D. The answer is all lawful instructions of the owner. Under the law of agency, a broker serving as agent for an owner must obey all lawful instructions of the owner. Unless the broker also represents a buyer in the same transaction, the broker is not subject to the requirements of dual agency. Caveat emptor, meaning "let the buyer beware," applies in some states but is not a responsibility of a broker representing a seller. If a state agency statute exists, it must be followed by the broker.

Reference: Agency Relationships and Contracts > Agency Relationships

48. When a buyer and a seller enter into a purchase agreement (contract of sale), the legal remedy that each has to force the other party to perform the terms of the agreement is:

A. actual damages.

B. specific performance.

C. liquidated damages.

D. unilateral rescission.

Answer: B. The answer is specific performance. Specific performance is defined as suing to perform if this is the remedy being used as the default when the suing party wants the other party to complete the terms of the transaction. In a purchase agreement, this is available to both the buyer and seller. Actual damages is a suit to receive money in return for damages not necessarily requiring the performance of the contract. Liquidated damages is where the buyer's earnest money is kept, and unilateral recession is a one-sided terminate when that party feels the other party has failed to complete their side of the agreement.

Reference: Agency Relationships and Contracts > Purchase Contracts (contracts between seller and buyer)

49. The buyer and the seller have entered into a binding contract for sale. However, before closing the law changes and the buyer's intended use of the property becomes illegal. Which is TRUE?:

A. The contract is void due to impossibility of performance.

B. The contract is valid, but the price must be renegotiated.

C. The contract is valid and enforceable under the rules of risk.

D. The contract is terminated due to fraud by the seller.

Answer: A. The answer is the contract is void due to impossibility of performance. An essential element of a contract is the lawful objective or purpose; if this is no longer part of the contract then the contract is void. In this case the seller did not commit fraud and no contract requires the price to be renegotiated if it becomes void.

Reference: Agency Relationships and Contracts > General Legal Principles, Theory and Concepts about Contracts

50. A buyer who owns the property in equity has a(n):

A. lease.

B. liquidated damages contract.

C. option contract.

D. executory contract.

Answer: D. The answer is executory contract. During any point in the executory contract (time period between signed offer to title transfer), the buyer has equitable title (also called the owner in equity). An executory purchase contract can be liquidated damages or specific performance. In an option contract only one party is bound and there is no equity of title.

Reference: Agency Relationships and Contracts > General Legal Principles, Theory and Concepts about Contracts

51. What action returns a contract's parties to their positions before the contract, including return of any deposit?:

A. Cancellation

B. Subordination

C. Substitution

D. Rescission

Answer: D. The answer is rescission. A rescission occurs when one party cancels or terminates the contract as if it had never been made. Cancellation terminates the contract without a return to the original position. Substitution is an appraisal principle of value. Subordination is used as place holder and indicates a mortgage or other interest will not move in front of a newer recording.

Reference: Agency Relationships and Contracts > Purchase Contracts (contracts between seller and buyer)

52. The amount of earnest money deposit is determined by:

A. listing broker's office policy on such matters.

B. agreement between the parties.

C. meeting the acceptable minimum of 5% of the purchase price.

D. real estate licensing statutes.

Answer: B. The answer is agreement between the parties. The amount of earnest money deposit is determined by agreement of the parties. Under the terms of most listing agreements, a real estate broker is required to accept a "reasonable amount" as earnest money. Brokerage firms and license law may not set the amount of earnest money required. The amount is set by the seller and negotiated by the buyer.

Reference: Agency Relationships and Contracts > Purchase Contracts (contracts between seller and buyer)

53. The buyer's offer stipulates that the closing must take place by April 15 or the contract is null and void. The buyer may refuse to purchase on April 16 if the contract contained a:

A. contingency clause.

B. transfer clause.

C. settlement clause.

D. time is of the essence clause.

Answer: D. The answer is time is of the essence clause. Time is of the essence means that if the requirement is not met, the contract has been breached.

Reference: Agency Relationships and Contracts > Purchase Contracts (contracts between seller and buyer)

54. All of the following are true of an open listing and an exclusive-agency listing EXCEPT:

A. under each, the broker earns a commission regardless of who sells the property, as long as it is sold within the listing period.

B. each must contain a definite termination date defining the period in which a commission may be paid.

C. each grants a commission to any brokerage who procures a buyer for the seller's property.

D. under each, the seller avoids paying the broker a commission if the seller sells the property to someone the broker did not procure.

Answer: A. The answer is under each, the broker earns a commission regardless of who sells the property, as long as it is sold within the listing period. Both open and exclusive-agency listings allow the owner to sell without broker aid and thus avoid the seller having to pay a commission. Each require the broker to be the procuring cause or in an exclusive-agency tied to the procuring broker through the MLS agreements. All listings must have a definite termination date.

Reference: Agency Relationships and Contracts > Service/Listing Buyer Contracts (contracts between licensee and seller or buyer)

55. Salespersons working as an employee for a principal broker can be required to:

A. deposit all earnest money into their personal escrow account.

B. decline to have their federal income tax withheld by the broker.

C. work specific hours each day as assigned by the broker.

D. advertise properties only in their name.

Answer: C. The answer is work specific hours each day as assigned by the broker. A broker who hires a salesperson as an employee may expect the salesperson to follow rules governing such activities as working hours, office hours, and attendance at meetings. A broker is required to withhold federal income taxes and Social Security taxes from the payroll of any employee. A salesperson hired as an employee or as an independent contractor must advertise properties in the name of the brokerage firm and deposit earnest money into the broker's designated escrow account.

Reference: Agency Relationships and Contracts > Service/Listing Buyer Contracts (contracts between licensee and seller or buyer)

56. Under the statute of frauds, all contracts for the sale of real estate must be:

A. in writing to be enforceable.

B. on preprinted forms.

C. originated by a real estate professional.

D. accompanied by earnest money deposits.

Answer: A. The answer is in writing to be enforceable. The statue of frauds requires all documents for the transfer of real estate be in writing; the exception is leases of 12 months or less.

Reference: Agency Relationships and Contracts > General Legal Principles, Theory and Concepts about Contracts

57. A buyer signs a buyer agency contract with a broker agreeing to pay commission to the buyer broker but with the expectation that the seller will actually pay the commission. However, the buyer learns that the seller has not agreed to a sharing of the commission with the buyer agent. The buyer refuses to pay any commission to the broker. In this case, the:

A. buyer has breached the agency contract with the broker and will be held liable for the broker's commission.

B. listing broker is liable for payment of the buyer broker's commission.

C. seller is liable for payment of the buyer broker's commission.

D. buyer broker is unable to collect a commission.

Answer: A. The answer is buyer has breached the agency contract with the broker and will be held liable for the broker's commission. If the buyer is unwilling to pay the buyer broker a commission according to the terms of the buyer agency contract, the broker may sue the buyer to recover the broker's commission. The buyer is liable for the commission according to the terms of the contract.

Reference: Agency Relationships and Contracts > Service/Listing Buyer Contracts (contracts between licensee and seller or buyer)

58. A broker who represents a seller under an exclusive-agency listing receives two offers for the property at the same time, one from one of his salespeople and one from the salesperson of a cooperating broker. What should the broker do?:

A. Submit the higher offer first.

B. Submit both offers at the same time.

C. Submit the offer from the other salesperson first.

D. Submit the offer from his salesperson first.

Answer: B. The answer is submit both offers at the same time. An agent for the seller has a duty to disclose all offers, unless directed by the seller to not present an offer after one has been accepted. The broker may not prioritize offers made at the same time by salespersons from competing companies. The broker must submit both low and high offers on the property no matter when the offers are received.

Reference: Agency Relationships and Contracts > Service/Listing Buyer Contracts (contracts between licensee and seller or buyer)

59. A listing broker presents an offer to her client, a seller, with a selling price much lower than what the seller is asking for the property. The offer allows the seller 24 hours to accept. The broker recommends the seller counter the offer and leaves a blank counter with the seller. The seller emails the broker in the morning saying that based on the wishes of

her children, who are not on the title, she has accepted the offer. It this case the offer:

A. may be a voidable contract due to duress.

B. is void due to undue influence by the children.

C. gives the buyer possession until closing.

D. is a valid contract which may be voidable due to fraud.

Answer: A. The answer is may be a voidable contract due to duress. The seller would have to claim her children forced her to accept the buyer's offer under duress in order to terminate the contract or make it voidable. Void contracts lack one or all of the essential elements of a contract. A contract must be entered into freely and voluntarily by each party, without undue influence. Duress, undue influence, misrepresentation, fraud, or a minor party entering into a contract are all circumstances that may create a contract that is voidable by the injured party.

Reference: Agency Relationships and Contracts > General Legal Principles, Theory and Concepts about Contracts

60. A salesperson lists a residence. The owner confides to the salesperson that a lower price would be acceptable. The salesperson tells a prospective buyer that the seller will accept up to $5,000 less than the asking price for the property. Based on these facts, which statement is TRUE?:

A. The relationship between the salesperson and the seller ends automatically if the purchaser submits an offer.

B. The salesperson should have disclosed this information, regardless of its accuracy.

C. The salesperson has not violated any agency responsibilities to the seller.

D. The disclosure is improper-and possibly illegal-regardless of the salesperson's motive.

Answer: D. The answer is the disclosure is improper-and possibly illegal-regardless of the salesperson's motives. Such action is an example of the salespersons failure to obey the seller and maintain confidentiality-both breaches of fiduciary duties. The salesperson may not disclose such information without the seller's written permission. Such an action does not terminate the agency relationship upon the submission of an offer.

61. A buyer makes an offer on a property and gives the listing agent a check for $1,000 for earnest money. The listing agent deposits the check into his personal account, and a week later, wrote the broker a check from his account to deposit into the broker's trust account. Has the agent fulfilled his fiduciary duty to the client?:

A. Yes, if the buyer has given him permission to follow that procedure.

B. No, because he has commingled funds.

C. Yes, if he has followed procedures provided by the broker.

D. No, because he has embezzled the funds.

Answer: B. The answer is no, because he has commingled funds. Under the fiduciary duty of accountability, the agent must account for funds received on behalf of the seller. His action violates not only his fiduciary duty, but most license laws require that earnest money deposits be deposited immediately (or within a specific time limit) into the brokerage firm's trust account. Depositing the money into the agent's own checking account is commingling, and it is illegal.

Reference: Agency Relationships and Contracts > Agency Relationships

62. Which of the following is an essential element of a contract?:

A. Competent parties

B. Words of conveyance

C. Competent grantor

D. Signature of the grantee

Answer: A. The answer is competent parties. One of the five essential elements of a contract is competent parties. Words of conveyance and competent grantor are elements of a deed. The grantor, not grantee, signs the deed.

Reference: Agency Relationships and Contracts > Purchase Contracts (contracts between seller and buyer)

63. Which statement is TRUE of a listing contract?:

A. It automatically binds the owner, broker, and MLS to its agreed-on provisions.

B. It obligates the seller to convey the property if the broker procures a ready, willing, and able buyer.

C. It obligates the broker to work diligently for both the seller and the buyer.

D. It is an employment contract for the professional services of the brokerage.

Answer: D. The answer is it is an employment contract for the professional services of the brokerage. The listing is the brokerage firm's contract of employment with the seller. It is not a contract between the seller and any buyer and so cannot be enforced on the seller by a buyer, even though the buyer makes an offer that is the "mirror image" of the terms of the listing. However, in such an event, the seller may owe the brokerage a full commission for having produced the result the listing called for: an able buyer who is ready and willing to buy on the terms of the listing. The listing contract obligates the broker to work diligently only for the seller.

Reference: Agency Relationships and Contracts > Service/Listing Buyer Contracts (contracts between licensee and seller or buyer)

64. A buyer's broker whose commission is shared via the MLS with the commission paid by the seller to the listing broker in a real estate purchase:

A. becomes a designated agent for the buyer.

B. remains the agent of the buyer.

C. becomes the agent of the seller.

D. must disclose the dual agency to the buyer.

Answer: B. The answer is remains the agent of the buyer. The source of compensation for a broker is not the factor that determines agency relationship. A buyer's broker whose commission is shared with the listing broker remains the agent of the buyer. A buyer's agent may be compensated by either the buyer or the seller.

Reference: Agency Relationships and Contracts > Service/Listing Buyer Contracts (contracts between licensee and seller or buyer)

65. The legal proceeding or legal action brought by either the buyer or the seller under a purchase contract to enforce the terms of the contract is known as:

A. a lis pendens.

B. an attachment.

C. liquidated damages.

D. suit for specific performance.

Answer: D. The answer is suit for specific performance. In a suit for specific performance, the court may force the buyer or seller to go through with the sale and convert the property as previously agreed. Lis pendens is a recorded legal document giving constructive notice of an action filed in court. An attachment is the legal process in which a defendant in a lawsuit seizes property by judicial order or levy, holding the property as security for satisfaction of a judgment. Liquidated damages is the seller's remedy if the buyer is in default, which is keeping the earnest money.

Reference: Agency Relationships and Contracts > Purchase Contracts (contracts between seller and buyer)

66. One contract was substituted for another contract, and there was a release of liability from the original contract. The term that defines the release is:

A. alienation.

B. assignment.

C. novation.

D. exchange.

Answer: C. The answer is novation. Novation is a new contract replacing the old with the full release of liability. The transfer of rights duties, but not the liabilities from one person to another person, is an assignment. Alienation is the process of transferring ownership via a deed.

Reference: Agency Relationships and Contracts > Purchase Contracts (contracts between seller and buyer)

67. A buyer makes an offer on a seller's house and the seller accepts. Both parties sign the sales contract. At this point, the buyer has what type of title to the property?:

A. Equitable

B. Escrow

C. Voidable

D. Contract

Answer: A. The answer is equitable. The seller holds legal title until closing and the buyer's interest in the property is recognized in the buyer holding equitable title.

Reference: Agency Relationships and Contracts > Purchase Contracts (contracts between seller and buyer)

68. In an executory contract, the:

A. seller grants the buyer possessory rights.

B. buyer may take posse

C. buyer receives legal title to the property.

D. buyer receives equitable title to the property.

Answer: D. The answer is buyer receives equitable title to the property. Equitable title occurs when the buyer and the seller have an accepted offer, which creates an executory contract, at which time the buyer acquires equitable title without yet holding legal title. Legal title will not pass until the deed is passed at closing. The buyer has no right to take possession of the property until all requirements of the contract have been met, usually at the day of closing.

Reference: Agency Relationships and Contracts > General Legal Principles, Theory and Concepts about Contracts

69. A contract that conveys the right to the possess the real property of another, but does not convey title, is a:

A. quitclaim deed.

B. dedication.

C. bill of sale.

D. lease.

Answer: D. The answer is lease. The lessor (landlord) grants the right of possession to the lessee (tenant); the lessor retains title.

Reference: Agency Relationships and Contracts > Purchase Contracts (contracts between seller and buyer)

70. Under the statute of frauds, all contracts for the sale of real estate must be:

A. on preprinted forms.

B. originated by a real estate broker.

C. in writing to be enforceable.

D. accompanied by earnest money deposits.

Answer: C. The answer is in writing to be enforceable. Statutes of frauds call for real estate sales contracts to be in writing. The law does not address who writes the agreements or on what forms they are written. Earnest money is not consideration and is not an essential element of a contract of sale, although it is often mistakenly said to be.

Reference: Agency Relationships and Contracts > General Legal Principles, Theory and Concepts about Contracts

71. A listing agent does not disclose to his client that he has agreed to manage a duplex for the buyer once it has been sold. The agent's action:

A. terminates the agency contract with the seller.

B. is legal under dual agency.

C. violates his duty of disclosing material facts to the seller.

D. is legal and ethical as his managing the property after the sale does not affect the seller.

Answer: C. The answer is violates his duty of disclosing material facts to the seller. The agent has a fiduciary duty to keep the seller, his client, informed of all facts that could affect the transaction. The agent's future contract with the buyer may affect his ability to properly represent his seller's interest in his eagerness to have the property sold. Dual agency requires full disclosure of material facts. He may accidentally create an implied agency by acting in the buyer's interest. The action does not in itself terminate the contract with the seller.

Reference: Agency Relationships and Contracts > Agency Relationships

72. The type of agency that exists when a broker represents the seller or buyer in a transaction, but not both, is:

A. designated agency.

B. single agency.

C. dual agency.

D. facilitator or transaction broker.

Answer: B. The answer is single agency. When a broker is representing only the seller or buyer in a transaction, the agency is single agency. Dual agency exists when an agent represents two principals in the same transaction. Designated agency is created when an agent is appointed by a broker to act for a specific principal or client when the brokerage firm represents both parties in the same transaction. A transaction broker does not have the fiduciary obligations to either party in a transaction.

Reference: Agency Relationships and Contracts > Agency Relationships

73. The law of agency is a common-law concept. As common-law, it is:

A. a legal doctrine that is formed from common sense and usual practices.

B. enacted by a legislatures and other governing bodies.

C. part of a body of law established by tradition and court decisions.

D. may not be superseded by statutory law.

Answer: C. The answer is part of a body of law established by tradition and court decisions. The law of agency is law from judgments and decrees as opposed to law established by legislatures or other governing bodies. In many states, statutes have been enacted to further define agency representation with laws and regulations that set forth the responsibilities of real estate licensees to clients and customers.

Reference: Agency Relationships and Contracts > Agency Relationships

74. A woman tells her neighbor, a real estate broker, that she is thinking about selling her home. The broker contacts several prospective buyers to whom she has shown her firm's listings in the past month. One of the buyers makes an

attractive offer on the woman's home without even seeing the property. The broker goes to the woman's house and presents the offer, which the homeowner accepts. What is the agency relationship between the homeowner and the broker?:

A. Implied agency

B. Express agency

C. General agency

D. Universal agency

Answer: A. The answer is implied agency. The homeowner and the broker did not have an oral or written agency contract, but the broker's actions implied to prospective buyers that the broker was acting as the homeowner's agent. Express agency occurs when two parties enter into an oral or written formal agency agreement. Universal agency empowers the agent to do anything the principal could do personally, such as authorized by a power of attorney. General agency allows the agent to act for the principal in a wide range of matters, as authorized, for example, in a property management contract.

Reference: Agency Relationships and Contracts > Agency Relationships

75. A contract is said to be bilateral if:

A. if there is a contingency that has not been met.

B. all parties to the contract exchange binding promise

C. the contract has yet to be fully performed.

D. only one party to the contract is bound to act.

Answer: B. The answer is all parties to the contract exchange binding promises. When all parties to a contract are bound by its provisions, the contract is said to be bilateral. A contract yet to be performed is executory. A contract that binds only one party to act is unilateral. A contingency can be in both bilateral and unilateral contracts.

Reference: Agency Relationships and Contracts > General Legal Principles, Theory and Concepts about Contracts

76. An agent for a brokerage firm has six listings. Another agent for the same firm represents a buyer who wants to purchase one of the six listings. The firm's broker appoints the listing agent as an agent for the seller, while appointing the other agent to represent the buyer in the same transaction. The broker has both the seller and the buyer sign a statement acknowledging that arrangement. The arrangement that results is:

A. single agency.

B. undisclosed agency.

C. implied agency.

D. designated agency.

Answer: D. The answer is designated agency. The brokerage firm represents both parties to the transaction as a dual agent, and the broker designates two salespersons from the company to represent opposite sides in the same transaction. Implied agency occurs when an agency relationship is accidental. In single agency, a broker represents only one party to a transaction. The broker in this case has disclosed the firm's dual agency and the designated agent to each party in the transaction.

77. Each of two brokerage companies claimed full commission for the sale of a property that was listed by both of the firms under an open listing agreement. The broker who is entitled to the commission is the one who:

A. was the procuring cause of the sale.

B. listed the property.

C. advertised the property.

D. obtained the first offer.

Answer: A. The answer is was the procuring cause of the sale. In an open listing, the seller retains the right to employ any number of brokers as agents. The brokers can act simultaneously, and the seller is obligated to pay a commission only to that broker who successfully procures a ready, willing, and able buyer. The broker who can prove that the sale resulted from that broker's efforts will be considered the procuring cause of the sale and be entitled to the commission.

Reference: Agency Relationships and Contracts >
Service/Listing Buyer Contracts (contracts between licensee and
seller or buyer)

**78. A real estate broker learns that her neighbor wishes to
sell his house. The broker knows the property well and is
able to persuade a buyer to make an offer for the property.
The broker then asks the neighbor if she can present the
offer, and the neighbor agrees. At this point, which
statement is TRUE?:**

A. The buyer is obligated to pay the broker for locating the
property.

B. The broker may not be considered the procuring cause
without a written contract.

C. The neighbor is obligated to pay the broker a commission for
producing an offer to purchase.

D. The neighbor is not obligated to pay the broker a
commission.

Answer: D. The answer is the neighbor is not obligated to pay the broker a commission. The broker procured a buyer for the property on the basis of an oral agreement with her neighbor, the seller. State real estate commissions generally require a commission agreement to be in writing and signed by both parties, the broker and the client. The broker in this case has no written contract for her services with either the seller or the buyer and is not entitled to a commission from either even if she is the procuring cause of the sale.

Reference: Agency Relationships and Contracts > Service/Listing Buyer Contracts (contracts between licensee and seller or buyer)

79. A broker took a listing and later discovered that the client had been declared legally incompetent before signing the listing. The listing is now:

A. voidable by the broker.

B. void.

C. voidable by the incompetent client.

D. valid.

Answer: B. The answer is void. A contract made by a person who has been adjudicated incompetent is void because the judgment of sanity is a matter of public record. The contract is not valid or voidable as it is missing the essential element of competency or competent parties.

Reference: Agency Relationships and Contracts > General Legal Principles, Theory and Concepts about Contracts

80. A contract for the sale of real estate that does not state the consideration and provides no basis on which the consideration could be determined is considered:

A. voidable.

B. executory.

C. enforceable.

D. void.

Answer: D. The answer is void. Consideration is an essential element of a real estate contract along with competent parties, meeting of the minds, lawful objective, and in writing. Without all the elements a contract is void and cannot be voidable, executory, or enforceable.

Reference: Agency Relationships and Contracts > General Legal Principles, Theory and Concepts about Contracts

81. A listing agent loses the seller's house keys. The agent has breached her fiduciary duty of:

A. accounting.

B. disclosure.

C. care.

D. loyalty.

Answer: A. The answer is accounting. The fiduciary duty of accounting requires real estate professionals to be accountable for money and the property of others that come into their possession in the performance of the agent's duties. The duty of care requires that agents use their skill and experience to the client's benefit. The duty of disclosure includes keeping the client informed of all relevant facts related to the transaction. The duty of loyalty means that the agent must place the client's interests above all others, including the agent's own self-interest.

Reference: Agency Relationships and Contracts > Agency Relationships

82. The provision in a listing contract that gives additional authority to the broker and obligates the broker to distribute the listing to other brokers is a(n):

A. net listing clause.

B. multiple listing clause.

C. joint listing clause.

D. open listing clause.

Answer: B. The answer is multiple listing clause. Listing agreements usually include clauses that give authority to a broker to distribute the listing to other brokers. A multiple listing service (MLS) is a marketing organization whose broker members make their own exclusive listings available through other brokers. A net listing clause would permit a broker to receive as commission all excess monies over and above the minimum sales price agreed to in the listing agreement. Net listings are not only discouraged but illegal in many states. An open listing clause states that any number of brokers may work simultaneously to sell the property, with the commission going to the broker who secures a buyer able to purchase the property.

Reference: Agency Relationships and Contracts > Service/Listing Buyer Contracts (contracts between licensee and seller or buyer)

83. An attorney was discussing an investment with a buyer who will be attending a foreclosure sale. The attorney said "caveat emptor." This means let the:

A. buyer beware.

B. bank beware.

C. seller beware.

D. neighbors beware.

Answer: A. The answer is buyer beware. Caveat emptor means "let the buyer beware."

Reference: Agency Relationships and Contracts > Purchase Contracts (contracts between seller and buyer)

84. A contract that has no legal force or effect is:

A. void.

B. voidable.

C. valid.

D. unenforceable.

Answer: A. The answer is void. When a contract has no legal force or effect, it is void and unenforceable. When a contract meets all of the essential elements and is enforceable, it is a valid contract. Duress, fraud, misrepresentation, and minors always make contracts voidable.

**85. The transfer of rights and duties, but not liabilities from
one contract to another contract or from one person to
another person, is an:**

A. addendum.

B. assignment.

C. amendment.

D. acknowledgment.

Answer: B. The answer is assignment. The transfer of rights
and duties, but not the liabilities from one person to another
person, is an assignment. Acknowledgement is a notarized
signature. Addendums are items added to offers and an
amendment modifies an executory contract.

Reference: Agency Relationships and Contracts > Purchase
Contracts (contracts between seller and buyer)

86. A buyer makes an offer on a house, and the seller accepts the offer. At this point, the buyer has what type of title to the property?:

A. Voidable

B. Legal

C. Possessionary

D. Equitable

Answer: D. The answer is equitable. On formation of the contract between both parties, the contract is now an executory contract with the buyer having equitable title. Voidable is a term used to describe a contract that is able to be voided because of duress, fraud, misrepresentation, or because one party to the contract is a minor. In the executory stage the seller holds legal title and possession until closing, unless a different time of possession is negotiated.

Reference: Agency Relationships and Contracts > Purchase Contracts (contracts between seller and buyer)

87. A buyer agrees to buy a property, and then changes his mind. The seller in this agreement has no recourse against the buyer. The contract was:

A. an option.

B. voidable.

C. a purchase agreement.

D. a lease.

Answer: A. The answer is an option. In an option contract, the seller's only recourse is to retain the option money. A seller may sue a buyer for specific performance if a buyer does not perform according to the provisions of a purchase agreement. A lease is a contract to rent a property, not to buy that property. A voidable contract appears to be valid but may be rescinded on some legal principle, as in the case of a contract entered into by a minor.

Reference: Agency Relationships and Contracts > Purchase Contracts (contracts between seller and buyer)

88. The mixing of trust funds with a broker's personal funds is:

A. legal in most states.

B. permitted in offices with fewer than three agents.

C. conversion.

D. commingling.

Answer: D. The answer is commingling. Commingling, or mixing of funds, is illegal regardless of the size of an office. Conversion occurs when brokers use escrow funds for their own use.

Reference: Agency Relationships and Contracts > Purchase Contracts (contracts between seller and buyer)

89. The typical relationship between a listing broker and a seller represents what type of agency?:

A. Universal

B. Implied

C. Special

D. General

Answer: C. The answer is special. The broker serves the client—either a buyer or a seller—usually by performing the specific brokerage acts spelled out in the employment contract (listing or buyer brokerage agreement). Specific assignments create a special agency. In a general agency relationship, the agent is authorized by a principal to perform any and all acts associated with a particular job or business. Implied agency arises out of the words or conducts of the parties. A universal agent is a person empowered to do anything that a principal could do personally, and is a general agent. Reference: Agency Relationships and Contracts > Agency Relationships

90. The remedy available only to the seller as compensation if a buyer is in default is known as:

A. actual damages.

B. consideration.

C. liquidated damages.

D. rescission.

Answer: C. The answer is liquidated damages. When parties agree that a certain amount of money will compensate the non-breaching party in the event one party defaults on a contract, that money is called liquidated damages. Earnest money typically serves as liquidated damages in a purchase contract in case the buyer defaults. Actual damages refer to monies awarded by a court to a plaintiff for a wrong committed against the plaintiff. Rescission is the mutual agreement of the parties to return to their original state. Consideration is an essential element of a contract, something of value offered by one party and accepted by the other.

Reference: Agency Relationships and Contracts > Purchase Contracts (contracts between seller and buyer)

91. A couple offers to purchase a house for $120,000, including its draperies, with the offer to expire on Saturday at noon. The sellers reply in writing on Thursday accepting the $120,000 offer but excluding the draperies. On Friday,

while the buyers consider this counteroffer, the sellers decide to accept the original offer; draperies included, and state that in writing. At this point, the buyers:

A. must buy the house but may deduct the value of the draperies from the $120,000.

B. are legally bound to buy the house, although they have the right to insist that the draperies be included.

C. are not bound to buy.

D. must buy the house and are not entitled to the draperies.

Answer: C. The answer is are not bound to buy. The sellers' counteroffer is regarded in law as a new offer. They have rejected or terminated the buyers' original offer by changing something in it and thereby releasing the buyers from the original offer. At this point, the sellers can keep both their draperies and their house, and the buyers are not bound by any agreement to buy the property.

Reference: Agency Relationships and Contracts > Purchase Contracts (contracts between seller and buyer)

92. A buyer's agent knows that a property has been on the market for a time longer than normal for the neighborhood and type of house. Her buyer decides to write an offer above the listed price of the home because the buyer is in a hurry to find a home and move in. The buyer's agent does not mention to the buyer the length of time the home has been on the market. Has the buyer's agent violated any duties to the buyer?:

A. No, because the agent has served the buyer's interest in finding a suitable home that the buyer wants to purchase.

B. Yes, because the license law requires agents to disclose the length of time on the market to all parties in a transaction.

C. Yes, the agent should disclose the time on the market as that fact creates a more favorable opportunity for the buyer to offer a lower price.

D. No, because the agent is not required to disclose that information to any party in the transaction.

Answer: C. The answer is yes, the agent should disclose the time on the market as that fact creates a more favorable opportunity for the buyer to offer a lower price. The buyer's agent has a duty to disclose any material information to the buyer. The extended time the home has been on the market provides the buyer with the possibility that the seller's will accept an offer lower than the listed price for the home. The license law does not prohibit or require disclosing information about how long a property has been on the market. The license laws of most states do require agents to disclose any material facts to clients and customers.

Reference: Agency Relationships and Contracts > Agency Relationships

93. A seller listed his residence with a broker with a contract that agreed to pay the broker a 5% commission. Within several weeks the broker brought an offer at full listing price and the terms of the listing from buyers ready, willing, and able to pay cash for the property. However, the seller rejected the buyers offer. In this situation, the seller:

A. is liable to the buyers for compensatory damages.

B. must sell his property.

C. owes a commission to the broker.

D. is liable to the buyers for specific performance.

Answer: C. The answer is owes a commission to the broker. The listing contract is a binding agreement on both the seller and the broker. While the seller may refuse to sell the home to the buyer, he owes a commission to the broker according to the listing contract. The seller is not liable to the buyers as the seller has not signed any agreement with the buyers.

Reference: Agency Relationships and Contracts > Service/Listing Buyer Contracts (contracts between licensee and seller or buyer)

94. A listing agent brings an offer from his separated spouse to his seller. The agent and his spouse, though separated, still own the property. The agent does not tell the seller, his client, that the buyer is his spouse, as she has retained her maiden name throughout the marriage. The agent's action:

A. violates his duty of disclosing material facts to the seller.

B. creates an express agency with the buyer.

C. is legal and ethical as the agent's relationship to the buyer does not affect the seller.

D. terminates the agency contract with the seller.

Answer: A. The answer is violates his duty of disclosing material facts to the seller. The agent has a fiduciary duty to keep the seller, his client, informed of all facts that could affect the transaction. The agent's relationship with the buyer and interest in the property may affect his ability to properly represent his seller's interest in his eagerness to have the property sold. The agent does not have an express agency contract with the buyer at this point. He may accidentally create an implied agency by acting in the buyer's interest. The action does not in itself terminate the contract with the seller.

Reference: Agency Relationships and Contracts > Agency Relationships

95. The multiple listing service clause in a listing contract provides that:

A. the broker agrees to the standard commission rate set by the MLS.

B. the seller grants permission for the broker to make the listing available through an MLS (multiple listing service).

C. the seller enter the listing into the MLS.

D. a buyer broker may not represent a purchaser in the transaction.

Answer: B. The answer is the seller grants permission for the broker to make the listing available through an MLS (multiple listing service). The multiple listing service clause grants authority for brokers to share the listing with other brokers through an MLS. Brokers enter the listing into the MLS within a time period stated in their contract with the MLS. The sellers do not enter the information with the MLS. Brokers negotiate their own commission rate with the sellers, and buyer brokers may represent buyers for properties listed in an MLS.

Reference: Agency Relationships and Contracts > Service/Listing Buyer Contracts (contracts between licensee and seller or buyer)

96. Which of the following BEST defines the common law of agency?:

A. The principles that govern one's conduct in business

B. The selling of another's property by an authorized agency

C. The rules and regulations of the state licensing agency

D. The rules of law that apply to the responsibilities and obligations of a person who acts for another

Answer: D. The answer is the rules of law that apply to the responsibilities and obligations of a person who acts for another. The common law of agency is formed by the judgments and decrees of courts regarding the responsibilities of a person who acts for another. Many states have enacted specific agency statutes to replace the common law of agency. A code of ethics encompasses the principles that govern one's conduct in business. Regulations of the state licensing agency may include specific mandates and responsibilities related to agency.

Reference: Agency Relationships and Contracts > Agency Relationships

97. A buyer defaults on a purchase agreement, and the seller goes to court to force the buyer to buy. The seller's remedy is:

A. specific performance.

B. partial performance.

C. liquidated damages.

D. money damages.

Answer: A. The answer is specific performance. An action in court to have the defaulting party perform on the contract is called a suit for specific performance.

Reference: Agency Relationships and Contracts > Purchase Contracts (contracts between seller and buyer)

98. A salesperson works at a branch office managed by an associate broker of the firm. The salesperson makes a change in the listing price of a listing contract without the

knowledge or consent of the seller. The ultimate responsibility for the salesperson's actions rests with the:

A. associate broker managing the office.

B. firm's principal broker.

C. associate broker and the salesperson.

D. salesperson.

Answer: B. The answer is firm's principal broker. The principal broker of a real estate brokerage firm holds ultimate responsibility for the actions of associate brokers and salespersons employed by the firm. The broker's responsibility extends to both employees and independent contractors working for the firm. While a real estate regulatory agency may find the principal broker ultimately responsible for the salesperson's actions, the agency may also hold the managing associate broker and the salesperson responsible.

Reference: Agency Relationships and Contracts > Service/Listing Buyer Contracts (contracts between licensee and seller or buyer)

99. A contract that may be rescinded by one party due to duress, fraud, misrepresentation, or because one party is a minor, is also known as a(n):

A. voidable contract.

B. void contract.

C. valid.

D. novation.

Answer: A. The answer is voidable contract. A contract is voidable if only one party may enforce or rescind it against the other party. Valid contracts contain all the essential elements and are binding and enforceable. Void contracts lack an essential element and are not binding. Novation is a new contact replacing an old one.

Reference: Agency Relationships and Contracts > General Legal Principles, Theory and Concepts about Contracts

100. Fiduciary means that there is a(n):

A. legal relationship between parties that creates a position of trust and confidence.

B. oral agreement between the parties that does not create an agency agreement.

C. written agreement between the parties to pay a real estate commission.

D. legal relationship in which only the duties of honesty and good faith are owed to the parties.

Answer: A. The answer is legal relationship between parties that creates a position of trust and confidence. The term fiduciary refers to the relationship in which the agent (the real estate broker) is held in a position of special trust and confidence by the principal (the client). An agent owes the duties of honesty and good faith to the customer, the third party or non-represented consumer in the transaction. The payment of compensation in the form of a commission does not determine or define an agency relationship.

Reference: Agency Relationships and Contracts > Agency Relationships

101. All of the following documents would create an agency relationship EXCEPT:

A. a listing contract.

B. a property management contract.

C. a buyer agency contract.

D. a sales contract.

Answer: D. The answer is a sales contract. A sales contract is a contract between an owner and a buyer to purchase a property. It does not create a relationship in which a person acts on behalf of another. The other contracts create agency relationships establishing the duties of a brokerage firm on behalf of a principal.

Reference: Agency Relationships and Contracts > Agency Relationships

102. A contract that secures the employment of a brokerage firm to find a ready, willing, and able buyer for a seller is a(n):

A. option contract.

B. listing contract.

C. escrow contract.

D. sales contract.

Answer: B. The answer is listing contract. A listing contract is a personal service contract securing the employment of a brokerage firm to find a ready, willing, and able buyer for a seller. A sales contract is a contract between a buyer and seller for purchase of a property. An escrow contract is an agreement between a buyer, seller, and escrow holder (such as a broker) defining the responsibilities of each. An option contract is a contract by which the optionor (usually an owner) gives an optionee the right to buy or lease a property at a fixed price within a certain period of time.

Reference: Agency Relationships and Contracts > Service/Listing Buyer Contracts (contracts between licensee and seller or buyer)

103. Contracts that transfer interests in real estate should be express:

A. implied contracts.

B. bilateral contracts.

C. written contracts.

D. oral or written contracts.

Answer: C. The answer is written contracts. Documents transferring an interest in real estate, per the statute of frauds, must be in an express written form. The contract could be unilateral or bilateral, but it cannot be implied or oral.

Reference: Agency Relationships and Contracts > Purchase Contracts (contracts between seller and buyer)

104. A seller has listed her home with a broker for $190,000. The listing broker tells a prospective buyer to submit a low

offer because the seller is desperate to sell. The buyer offers $185,000 and the seller accepts it. In this situation:

A. the broker's action was unethical but not illegal.

B. any broker is authorized by the listing contract to encourage such bids for the property.

C. he broker acted properly to obtain a quick offer on the property.

D. the broker has violated his fiduciary relationship with the seller.

Answer: D. The answer is the broker has violated his fiduciary relationship with the seller. The agent has a fiduciary responsibility to respect the confidentiality of his client. Agents may not reveal confidential items such as the principal's willingness to accept less than the list price or the seller's anxiousness to sell unless the principal has authorized the disclosure. In this case, the broker's actions might be considered illegal under some state laws and by a court of law. Under the common law of agency a broker is not authorized to encourage an offer lower than the listing price without specific instructions from the seller, even if to do so would obtain a quicker offer on the property.

**105. A principal broker has hired three new salespeople all
with new licenses. In working with the new people the
principal broker's most important obligation is to make sure
the new salespeople are:**

A. supervised.

B. mentored.

C. given a regular schedule.

D. trained.

Answer: A. The answer is supervised. The number one
requirement for a principal broker is to assure all licensees of the
firm are properly supervised.

Reference: Agency Relationships and Contracts >
Service/Listing Buyer Contracts (contracts between licensee and
seller or buyer)

106. A salesperson's written contract with her broker specifies that she is not an employee. In the last year, just less than half of the salesperson's income from real estate activity came from sales commissions. The remainder was based on an hourly wage paid by the broker. Using these facts, it is MOST likely that the Internal Revenue Service (IRS) would classify the salesperson as which of the following for federal income tax purposes?:

A. Self-employed

B. Employee

C. Independent contractor

D. Part-time real estate salesperson

Answer: B. The answer is employee. Because her earnings were more than half in non-commissions, the IRS would not see her as a self-employed independent contractor and could treat her as an employee.

Reference: Agency Relationships and Contracts >

Service/Listing Buyer Contracts (contracts between licensee and seller or buyer)

107. A contract in which one party purchases the right to buy at a fixed price within a specified period is a(n):

A. listing contract.

B. purchase contract.

C. lease contract.

D. option contract.

Answer: D. The answer is option contract. An option is a unilateral contract binding on the seller with an obligation to sell for a set price if the buyer decides to buy. Typically, if the buyer does not buy the seller will keep the option fee, which the amount of was set by the option contract. A listing, lease, and purchase contract are all bilateral contracts.

Reference: Agency Relationships and Contracts > Purchase Contracts (contracts between seller and buyer)

108. An option:

A. makes the seller liable for a commission.

B. requires the optionee to complete the purchase.

C. gives the optionee an easement on the property.

D. binds the optionor for a specified time.

Answer: D. The answer is binds the optionor for a specified time. An option obligates an owner (the optionor) to sell at a fixed price within a certain period of time but does not obligate the optionee (the proposed buyer) to exercise the option. The option gives the optionee no rights to the property and does not require the optionee to complete the purchase. The seller is only liable for a commission to a broker when the option is exercised, that is, when the buyer actually purchases the property from the seller.

Reference: Agency Relationships and Contracts > Purchase Contracts (contracts between seller and buyer)

109. Whether or not state law requires the time when an agent must disclose his firm's agency alternatives, good business practice requires that an agent make a disclosure about agency:

A. before any confidential information is disclosed about an individual's motivation or financial situation.

B. when performing ministerial acts for a customer.

C. at the closing of a real estate transaction.

D. at the closing of a real estate transaction.

Answer: A. The answer is before any confidential information is disclosed about an individual's motivation or financial situation. Many states have mandatory agency disclosure laws. Whatever the law requires, agents should disclose her firm's agency alternatives and any agency relationship by which the agent is bound before any confidential information is provided about an individual's motivation or financial situation.

Reference: Agency Relationships and Contracts > Agency Relationships

110. In order for a purchase agreement to be binding on all parties it must contain certain essential elements. Of the following, which is essential for a purchase agreement to be valid?:

A. Recordation

B. Notarization

C. Lawful objective

D. Lawful objective

Answer: C. The answer is lawful objective. The essential elements of a contract are competent parties, mutual agreement, lawful objective, consideration, and the document in writing. To be valid, a contract does not need to be recorded or notarized. Competent grantor is a requirement of a valid deed.

Reference: Agency Relationships and Contracts > Purchase Contracts (contracts between seller and buyer)

111. A lease agreement is signed by a lessee who is 16 years of age. Which of the following is TRUE?:

A. A 16-year-old person cannot sign a lease.

B. The lease agreement is voidable by the minor.

C. The lease agreement is void.

D. The lease agreement is valid provided the security deposit is increased.

Answer: B. The answer is the lease agreement is voidable by the minor. A 16-year-old person can sign a contract. However, it was incumbent on an adult who is the other party to the contract to stop the minor from signing the contract. If this does not occur because the lessee is a minor, the lease is voidable by the minor. The amount of the security deposit does not affect the validity of a lease contract. The 16-year-old may in fact decide to enforce the lease contract, in which case the lease is valid.

Reference: Agency Relationships and Contracts > General Legal Principles, Theory and Concepts about Contracts

112. A buyer under an executory contract has found numerous inspection issues the seller is unwilling to repair. The seller and the buyer agree to terminate the contract with all things of value returned to each party. This is known as:

A. liquidated damages.

B. mutual rescission.

C. specific performance.

D. mutual performance.

Answer: B. The answer is mutual rescission. When both parties to a contract are returned to their original position, it is known as mutual rescission. Liquidated damages and specific performance are types of purchase contracts chosen for the remedy for default by one of the parties. Mutual performance is when both parties complete the contract.

Reference: Agency Relationships and Contracts > Purchase Contracts (contracts between seller and buyer)

113. To be classified by the Internal Revenue Service as an independent contractor, a real estate salesperson may receive:

A. a company-provided automobile if negotiated with the broker.

B. company-provided health insurance if negotiated with the broker.

C. commissions on transactions as negotiated with the broker.

D. a monthly salary or hourly wage as negotiated with the broker.

Answer: C. The answer is commissions on transactions as negotiated with the broker. An independent contractor may not receive any employee benefits, such as health insurance or a company-provided automobile. An independent contractor must not be treated as an employee for federal tax purposes by receiving a monthly salary or hourly wage.

Reference: Agency Relationships and Contracts > Service/Listing Buyer Contracts (contracts between licensee and seller or buyer)

114. A seller has received an offer. The seller crossed out a number of items, wrote in the changes the seller wanted, initialed them, and returned the document to the buyer. The original offer the offeror gave the seller is considered to be:

A. a partial termination with conditional acceptance of the offer.

B. binding only on the original offeror.

C. a partial acceptance of the original offer.

D. terminated and countered.

Answer: D. he answer is terminated and countered. The counteroffer effectively terminates the original offer and creates a new offer. Therefore, the original offer is not valid, accepted, or binding.

Reference: Agency Relationships and Contracts > Purchase Contracts (contracts between seller and buyer)

115. The relationship of agents to their principal is that of a(n):

A. attorney-in-fact.

B. fiduciary.

C. trustee.

D. subagent.

Answer: B. The answer is fiduciary. The principal is the party to whom the agent gives advice and counsel. The agent's fiduciary relationship of trust and confidence with the principal means that the broker owes the principal certain specific duties. A trustee holds property for another as a fiduciary, but an agent does not hold the principal's property. A subagent, though working in the principal's interest, is an agent of the brokerage firm/principal broker who is already acting as agent for the principal. An attorney-in-fact is a competent third-party authorized by the principal to act in the principal's place through a written and recorded power of attorney.

Reference: Agency Relationships and Contracts > Agency Relationships

116. A salesperson representing a buyer is told that the buyer plans to operate a dog-grooming business out of any house he buys. The salesperson does tell the buyer to verify local zoning ordinances to determine in which parts of town such a business can be conducted. Which duty does the salesperson violate?:

A. Care

B. Obedience

C. Loyalty

D. Disclosure

Answer: A. The answer is care. Salespersons must use their skills and knowledge to protect the client's interests in purchasing. In this case the salesperson should have told the buyer to verify local zoning ordinances might prohibit a buyer conducting a business from a home. All salespersons and broker's owe this duty and the disclosure of material facts to the consumer. An agent would owe obedience and loyalty to the principal.

117. When neither party can sue the other to force performance, the real estate contract is said to be:

A. voidable.

B. valid.

C. unenforceable.

D. void.

Answer: C. The answer is unenforceable. When neither party can sue the other to force performance, the contract is said to be unenforceable. When a contract meets all of the essential elements and is enforceable, it is a valid contract. Duress, fraud, misrepresentation, and minors always make contracts voidable. Void real estate contracts lack an essential element and are unenforceable.

Reference: Agency Relationships and Contracts > General Legal Principles, Theory and Concepts about Contracts

118. A listing contract in which payment of the commission is contingent on the broker's being able to produce a buyer before the property is sold by the owner or another broker is called a(n):

A. net listing.

B. exclusive-right-to-sell listing.

C. exclusive-agency listing.

D. open listing.

Answer: D. The answer is open listing. In an open listing, the seller retains the right to employ any number of brokers to sell the property. The brokers can act simultaneously, and the seller is obligated to pay a commission only to that broker who successfully procures a ready, willing, and able buyer. A net listing clause would permit a broker to receive as commission all excess monies over and above the minimum sales price agreed to in the listing agreement. Net listings are not only discouraged but illegal in many states. In an exclusive-right-to-sell listing, if the property is sold while the listing is in effect, the seller must pay the broker a commission regardless of who sells the property. An exclusive-agency listing provides the brokerage firm and co-op broker will be paid unless the seller sells the property on their own.

Reference: Agency Relationships and Contracts > Service/Listing Buyer Contracts (contracts between licensee and seller or buyer)

119. The principal to whom a real estate broker provides professional opinions and counsel is a(n):

A. customer.

B. subagent.

C. fiduciary.

D. client.

Answer: D. The answer is client. The person with whom a broker has a service contract to provide professional opinions and advise is a client. A customer is another party to a real estate contract with whom a broker has no contract. A subagent is an agent of a person who is already acting as an agent for a client. The term fiduciary describes the relationship owed by an attorney or broker to a client

Reference: Agency Relationships and Contracts > Service/Listing Buyer Contracts (contracts between licensee and seller or buyer)

120. As an agent for the seller, a real estate broker can:

A. guarantee a prospective buyer that the seller will accept an offer at the price and terms offered.

B. advise a prospective buyer as to the best manner of taking title to the property.

C. change the terms of the listing contract on behalf of the seller.

D. solicit an offer to purchase the property from a prospective buyer.

Answer: D. The answer is solicit an offer to purchase the property from a prospective buyer. An agent representing the seller has a fiduciary responsibility to exercise skill and care to market the property to secure a buyer. The agent is a special agent for the seller, and as such is not authorized to make a decision for the seller or to change the listing contract. The agent cannot guarantee that the seller will accept an offer and must present the offer to the seller. The agent must not provide advice to the prospective buyer as doing so might create an agency relationship with the buyer.

Reference: Agency Relationships and Contracts > Service/Listing Buyer Contracts (contracts between licensee and seller or buyer)

121. In a standard sales contract, several words were crossed out or inserted by the parties. To eliminate future controversy as to whether the changes were made before or after the contract was signed, the usual procedure is to:

A. have each party write a letter to the other approving the changes.

B. redraw the entire contract.

C. write a letter to each party listing the changes.

D. have both parties initial or sign in the margin near each change.

Answer: D. The answer is have both parties initial or sign in the margin near each change. All parties must initial or sign the changes. If negotiations had gone back and forth a number of times it might merit redrawing the contract for clarity, in this case initialing is sufficient. Letters approving all changes might be treated as part of the contract but such a cumbersome procedure is seldom seen. More often changes are done with pre-printed standard or approved addendum forms.

Reference: Agency Relationships and Contracts > Purchase Contracts (contracts between seller and buyer)

122. In an executory purchase contract, the buyer's interest is described as:

A. ownership in equity.

B. possessionary interest.

C. free and clear title.

D. legal title.

Answer: A. The answer is ownership in equity. Once an executory contract is created the buyers interest is called ownership in equity, the seller retains legal ownership until the deed is passed. Free and clear title is free from liens. A possessionary interest gives the hold the right to possess the property, which is not part of a purchase contract.

Reference: Agency Relationships and Contracts > General Legal Principles, Theory and Concepts about Contracts

123. A buyer entered into a buyer agency agreement that gave him the right to purchase property on his own and not pay the buyer's agent. This BEST describes a(n):

A. designated buyer agency contract.

B. exclusive-agency buyer agency contract.

C. exclusive-right-to-buy buyer agency contract.

D. open buyer agency contract.

Answer: B. The answer is exclusive-agency buyer agency contract. Exclusive buyer or seller agency contracts allow the buyer find a property and buy it without owing the buyer's agent a commission. A seller under these agreements is allowed to sell the property on her own without paying a commission.
Reference: Agency Relationships and Contracts > Service/Listing Buyer Contracts (contracts between licensee and seller or buyer)

124. A seller has told the listing agent that the agent must only represent the seller in the sale of the property. In this case the first guide for the agent is to obey:

A. any state dual agency requirements.

B. the concept of caveat emptor.

C. all lawful instructions of the owner.

D. the common law of agency, even if a state agency statute exists.

Answer: C. The answer is all lawful instructions of the owner. A real estate broker hired by a seller must obey all lawful instructions of the owner. A state's agency statute may modify aspects of the common law of agency, in which case the broker must comply with the agency statute. A selling broker is not required to engage in dual agency. Caveat emptor is a warning to purchasers, not to brokers.

Reference: Agency Relationships and Contracts > Agency Relationships

125. When a party is in default in a contract due to missing a payment deadline, the contract is considered:

A. unilateral.

B. illegal.

C. breached.

D. executed.

Answer: C. The answer is breached. Anytime one of the parties misses a deadline or payment that party is in breach of the contract.

Reference: Agency Relationships and Contracts > Purchase Contracts (contracts between seller and buyer)

126. Which statement BEST identifies the meaning of the term novation?:

A. A rejection of a contract by all parties

B. Substitution of a new contract for an existing one

C. A recorded notice of lis pendens

D. A return of all parties to their condition before the contract was executed

Answer: B. The answer is a substitution of a new contract for an existing one. Novation is a new contract that replaces the original. Rescission is the return of all parties to their condition prior to the contract, and lis pendens is a notice of a pending lawsuit.

Reference: Agency Relationships and Contracts > Purchase Contracts (contracts between seller and buyer)

127. A buyer's agent would NOT recommend the buyer seek expert advice if the buyer asked:

A. "Would you recommend a radon test?"

B. "Does this crack in the foundation mean there is structural damage?"

C. "How should I take title to the property?"

D. "How long has the property been on the market?"

Answer: D. The answer is "How long has the property been on the market?" This is not a question that would require the buyer to seek expert advice.

Reference: Agency Relationships and Contracts > Service/Listing Buyer Contracts (contracts between licensee and seller or buyer)

128. In a preprinted sales contract, several words were crossed out or inserted by the parties. To eliminate future controversy as to whether the changes were made before or after the contract was signed, the usual procedure is to:

A. have each party write a letter to the other approving the changes.

B. write a letter to each party listing the changes.

C. redraw the entire contract.

D. have both parties initial or sign in the margin near each change.

Answer: D. The answer is have both parties initial or sign in the margin near each change. If there are minor changes in a contract the initialing or signature at the changes notes the party saw and agreed to the change. The best course of action if there are many or major changes to a contract is to draft a new one with all the agreed to changes.

Reference: Agency Relationships and Contracts > Purchase Contracts (contracts between seller and buyer)

129. In an offer, a buyer requested the freestanding bookcase and the installed hot tub with the property. Negotiations went back and forth, and the buyer's agent finally wrote a new offer that failed to mention either item. At closing, the buyer should expect to have:

A. the seller remove both items because they were not in the final contract.

B. the bookcase left and the hot tub removed by the seller.

C. the hot tub remain and the bookcase removed by the seller.

D. both items left with the property because they were mentioned in the first offer.

Answer: C. The answer is the hot tub remain and the bookcase removed by the seller. The hot tub, which is a fixture, would have to be excluded from the contract if the seller was going to keep it. However, the bookcase is personal property and can be removed by the seller because it was not included in the contract.

Reference: Agency Relationships and Contracts > Purchase
Contracts (contracts between seller and buyer)

**130. In the purchase agreement, the buyer and seller agreed
to liquidated damages as a remedy for default. If the buyer
defaults, this means the seller:**

A. needs to notify the buyer of the intent to sue for liquidated
damages.

B. keeps only the buyer's earnest money.

C. sues the buyer and keeps the earnest money.

D. sues the buyer to buy the property.

Answer: B. The answer is keeps only the buyer's earnest
money. Liquidated damages as a remedy allows the seller to
keep the earnest money and nothing more. Specific performance
is a lawsuit to have the buyer perform the terms of the contract.

Reference: Agency Relationships and Contracts > Purchase
Contracts (contracts between seller and buyer)

131. A buyer signs a contract under which he is given the right to purchase a property for $130,000 anytime in the next six months. The buyer pays the current owner $500 at the time that contract is signed. Which of the following BEST describes this agreement?:

A. A unilateral option contract binding the seller

B. An installment land contract binding both parties

C. A bilateral executory sales contract

D. A bilateral contingency contract

Answer: A. The answer is a unilateral option contract binding the seller. The buyer has the right to buy in the future but is not bound to buy, which creates an option contract.

Reference: Agency Relationships and Contracts > Purchase Contracts (contracts between seller and buyer)

132. A real estate broker lists her neighbor's home for $212,000. Later that same day a buyer to the community comes into her office and asks for information on houses for sale in the $180,000 - $225,000 price range. The broker offers to represent the buyer as a buyer's agent, but the newcomer refuses representation by her company at this time. Based on these facts, which of the following statements is TRUE?:

A. Both the neighbor and the buyer are the broker's customers.

B. The neighbor is the broker's client, and the buyer is her customer.

C. The real estate broker owes fiduciary duties to both her neighbor and the buyer.

D. If the buyer later asks for buyer representation from the broker's firm, the broker cannot offer buyer representation because of her listing contract with the neighbor.

Answer: B. The answer is the neighbor is the broker's client, and the buyer is her customer. The listing contract with the neighbor establishes an agency relationship with the neighbor, who becomes the client of the broker. Without representation, the buyer remains a customer of the broker, a non-represented consumer who is entitled to fairness and honesty. The broker owes fiduciary duties only to the neighbor, her client. The broker may offer buyer representation to the buyer at a later date if the broker's company policy permits dual agency in a situation in which the buyer may want to purchase one of the company's own listings.

Reference: Agency Relationships and Contracts > Agency Relationships

133. A broker who has done a proper CMA (competitive market analysis) discusses the probable market value of the property with the seller, and the seller wants an unrealistic price on the property. The broker may do all of the following EXCEPT:

A. take the listing at the seller's proposed price planning on reducing the price himself in the future when the seller is more realistic.

B. take the listing with the understanding from the seller that price reductions may be needed to sell the property.

C. suggest the seller have a formal appraisal done.

D. decline to take the listing at the high price.

Answer: A. The answer is take the listing at the seller's proposed price planning on reducing the price himself in the future when the seller is more realistic. Whether a CMA or a formal appraisal is conducted, the value sought is the property's market value. While it is the property owner's privilege to set whatever listing price they choose, a broker should consider rejecting any listing that is severely out of line. If the broker chooses to accept the listing at the seller's proposed price, the broker should advise the seller that the price may have to be reduced in the future in order to sell the house.

Reference: Agency Relationships and Contracts > Service/Listing Buyer Contracts (contracts between licensee and seller or buyer)

134. A person approaches an owner and says, "I'd like to buy your house." The owner says, "Sure," and they agree on a price and write it down on a piece of note paper and sign it. What kind of contract is this?:

A. Valid

B. Unenforceable

C. Voidable

D. Void

Answer: A. The answer is valid. Anytime a buyer and seller agree in writing with notice and acceptance a valid contract is formed. If the offer is missing an essential element it is void and unenforceable. Duress, fraud, misrepresentation, and minors always make contracts voidable.

Reference: Agency Relationships and Contracts > Purchase Contracts (contracts between seller and buyer)

135. To create an executory contract, the offeree must accept the offer:

A. only after it has been approved by an attorney.

B. within twenty-four hours of receiving the offer.

C. without any changes to the offer.

D. before the end of the business day of receiving it.

Answer: C. The answer is without any changes to the offer. An offer must be accepted without any changes. Time frames for acceptance are created in the offer and can vary. Contracts do not have to be written or approved by an attorney to be valid.

Reference: Agency Relationships and Contracts > Purchase Contracts (contracts between seller and buyer)

136. A brokerage represents the owner in the sale of the owner's property, which has a salesperson acting as the listing agent. Which of the following events will terminate that agency relationship?:

A. The owner abandons the property.

B. During the listing, the salesperson dies.

C. The broker engages other brokers to help sell the property.

D. During the listing, the owner of the property dies.

Answer: D. The answer is during the listing, the owner of the property dies. When a property owner dies during a listing period, the agency relationship with a broker is terminated. The agency relationship remains in effect with any of the other events including the death of a salesperson since the contract belongs to the firm not the salesperson.

Reference: Agency Relationships and Contracts > Agency Relationships

137. A real estate contract with a minor is:

A. void.

B. unilateral.

C. voidable.

D. illegal.

Answer: C. The answer is voidable. Duress, fraud, misrepresentation, and minors always make contracts voidable. A promise exchanged for performance is a unilateral contract. A void contract lacks an essential element an illegal contract lacks a lawful purpose so is also void.

138. The buyer has made an offer to the seller who has countered and given the buyer 24 hours to accept the counter. In this case the original offer is considered to be:

A. executory.

B. terminated.

C. voidable.

D. void.

Answer: B. The answer is terminated. A counter offer terminates the original offer and creates a new offer. Since there is not a contract, the terms are executory. An offer is not a contract, and cannot be considered voidable or void.

Reference: Agency Relationships and Contracts > Purchase Contracts (contracts between seller and buyer)

139. A minor entered into a contract to sell the house she had inherited to a buyer. This contract is MOST likely:

A. voidable by the minor.

B. valid.

C. voidable by the buyer.

D. void.

Answer: A. e answer is voidable by the minor. Contracts with minors are always voidable. In this case the contract is not voidable by the buyer since the buyer is the adult.

Reference: Agency Relationships and Contracts > General Legal Principles, Theory and Concepts about Contracts

140. A broker assigns a salesperson to work open houses in a new subdivision for a developer that the firm represents. After two months, the salesperson's work has resulted in sales above the developer's expectations, and he offers to pay

the salesperson a $1000 bonus. The salesperson may receive the bonus payment:

A. only if paid after the salesperson's assignment to the subdivision ends.

B. only if paid from her principal broker.

C. from the developer if permission is granted from the state regulatory agency.

D. from the developer if the bonus is placed in the broker's trust account.

Answer: B. The answer is only if paid from her principal broker. Salespersons may not receive commissions or bonus payments from anyone other than their principal broker. The salesperson may receive the bonus payment if the developer pays it directly to the broker, who then gives all or part of the bonus to the salesperson, depending on the salesperson's employment agreement with the broker. Payments of this type would be deposited into the firms operations account not put into a trust account.

Reference: Agency Relationships and Contracts > Service/Listing Buyer Contracts (contracts between licensee and seller or buyer)

141. Which of the following BEST defines the law of agency?:

A. The principles that govern one's conduct in business

B. The rules of law that apply to the responsibilities of a person who acts as agent for another

C. The selling of another's property by a properly licensed brokerage

D. The rules and regulations of the state's licensing agency

Answer: B. The answer is the rules of law that apply to the responsibilities of a person who acts as agent for another. The law of agency determines how an agent is authorized to act on behalf of another and the responsibilities of that agent. The selling of another's property by a licensed brokerage is determined by a listing or brokerage agreement. Principles that govern one's conduct in business are often stated in a business code of ethics. Rules and regulations of a state's licensing agency state the requirements for real estate licensing for persons and firms.

Reference: Agency Relationships and Contracts > Agency Relationships

142. A real estate broker was responsible for a chain of events that resulted in the sale of one of his client's properties. The broker's efforts are referred to as:

A. procuring cause.

B. private offering.

C. pro forma.

D. proffered offer.

Answer: A. The answer is procuring cause. The procuring cause in a real estate transaction is the effort and work that brings about the result stated in a brokerage agreement. A broker who starts a chain of events that results in a sale and does so without abandoning the transaction may be considered the procuring cause of sale. Pro forma is a term meaning "for form only," in other words, not official. A private offering is the offering of a real estate security that is not required to be registered with any state or federal agency because it is not a public offering. The word "proffer" means the same as "offer," although a "proffered offer" is a term used to describe an informal, oral offer made before the start of any formal negotiations.

Reference: Agency Relationships and Contracts > Service/Listing Buyer Contracts (contracts between licensee and seller or buyer)

143. In a real estate transaction, the term fiduciary typically refers to the:

A. principal's relationship to the agent.

B. agent's relationship to the principal.

C. person who has legal power to act on behalf of another.

D. set of obligations owed by the principal to the agent and vice versa.

Answer: B. The answer is agent's relationship to the principal. An agent's relationship to a principal involves care, obedience, accounting, loyalty, and disclosure—a fiduciary relationship.

Principals do not owe fiduciary obligations to agents. Persons with legal power to act for another are created by a power of attorney; most real estate brokers do not have such powers.

Reference: Agency Relationships and Contracts > Agency Relationships

144. A legally enforceable contract in which two parties exchange promises to do something for each other is known as a(n):

A. option contract.

B. bilateral contract.

C. unilateral contract.

D. void contract.

Answer: B. The answer is bilateral contract. A bilateral contract is one in which both parties make a promise to the other. A unilateral contract is a one-sided contract in which one party makes a promise to induce a second party to do something. A void contract lacks one or all of the essential elements of a contract. An option contract is a unilateral contract in which only one party makes a promise to perform, in this case to hold open the right for a buyer to purchase a property in the future.

Reference: Agency Relationships and Contracts > General Legal Principles, Theory and Concepts about Contracts

145. A legally enforceable agreement under which both parties promise to do something for each other is called a(n):

A. escrow agreement.

B. legal pledge.

C. option agreement.

D. bilateral contract.

Answer: D. The answer is bilateral contract. Bilateral contracts are created by the parties both making promises. Escrow agreements set the terms for closing. An option is a unilateral contract.

**146. A contract entered into while someone is under duress
is considered to be:**

A. voidable.

B. fully valid and enforceable.

C. executory.

D. void.

Answer: A. The answer is voidable. Duress, fraud,
misrepresentation, and contracts entered into by minors create
voidable contracts. Such contracts are neither valid nor
enforceable. A void contract has no legal force and is not
enforceable due to its lacking an essential element, such as one
made for an illegal purpose. An executory contract is a valid
contract that has been signed but not fully fulfilled.

Reference: Agency Relationships and Contracts > General Legal
Principles, Theory and Concepts about Contracts

147. A bilateral contract is one in which:

A. a restriction is placed in the contract by one party to limit the performance by the other.

B. only one of the parties is obligated to act.

C. something is to be done by one party only.

D. the promise of one party is given in exchange for the promise of the other party.

Answer: D. The answer is the promise of one party is given in exchange for the promise of the other party. In a bilateral contract, both parties agree to do something, and promises are exchanged. A unilateral contract is a one-sided agreement that does not obligate a second party.

Reference: Agency Relationships and Contracts > General Legal Principles, Theory and Concepts about Contracts

148. After a long period of negotiation, the seller and the buyer are under contract. The buyer's lender has some issues with getting the final numbers, so the buyer asks to postpone the closing by three days. The seller agrees to the change. To make the change binding and enforceable, the seller and the buyer should sign an:

A. amendment

B. addendum

C. ad valorem

D. attachment

Answer: A. The answer is amendment. The document that modifies a contract is an amendment. Attachments are items that explain and are added to offers, such as an addendum for a long legal description. Ad valorem is used in property taxes.

Reference: Agency Relationships and Contracts > General Legal Principles, Theory and Concepts about Contracts

149. A contract between two or more parties, each making a promise to perform certain acts, is called:

A. an implied contract.

B. a unilateral contract.

C. a voidable contract.

D. a bilateral contract.

Answer: D. The answer is a bilateral contract. Promises exchanged for promises define bilateral contracts. A promise exchanged for performance is a unilateral contract. Implied contracts are created by actions.

Reference: Agency Relationships and Contracts > General Legal Principles, Theory and Concepts about Contracts

150. Earnest money:

A. is required as part of all purchase agreements.

B. may become the seller's if the buyer defaults.

C. is considered to be consideration and is required in a purchase offer.

D. will be a credit to the seller and a debit to the buyer at closing.

Answer: B. The answer is may become the seller's if the buyer defaults. Earnest money is not consideration. Therefore, it is not an essential element of a contract or required; it is a show of good faith on the part of the buyer and liquidated damages for the seller, if the buyer defaults.

Reference: Agency Relationships and Contracts > Purchase Contracts (contracts between seller and buyer)

151. A broker lists a property for sale at $100,000 with a 5% commission. He later obtains an oral offer from a prospective buyer to purchase the property. The seller indicates to the broker that the offer would be acceptable if it were submitted in writing. Before it can be put in writing, the buyer backs out and revokes the oral offer. In this situation, the broker would be entitled to:

A. no commission.

B. a commission of $5,000.

C. only a partial commission.

D. the standard rate of commission for the area.

Answer: A. The answer is no commission. The broker only earns a commission with the procuring of a ready, willing, and able buyer who purchases the property on the seller's terms. There is no standard rate of commission for a locality, as commission rates are determined by individual agreements between a broker and client. Reference: Agency Relationships and Contracts > Service/Listing Buyer Contracts (contracts between licensee and seller or buyer)

152. A listing salesperson schedules an open house with the sellers. Before the open house, she advises the sellers to place valuable jewelry that is visible in the bedroom into a safe or another secure place. The sellers ignore the salesperson's advice. The morning after the open house, the sellers call the salesperson to inform her that some of their jewelry is

missing from the bedroom. Will the salesperson likely be held accountable for the missing jewelry?:

A. No, because the sellers should have watched over their valuables during the open house.

B. Yes, because the salesperson should have checked every visitor leaving the open house for any stolen valuables.

C. No, because the salesperson advised the sellers to remove or hide all valuables before the open house.

D. Yes, because the salesperson is accountable for the money or property of her clients.

Answer: C. The answer is no, because the salesperson advised the sellers to remove or hide all valuables before the open house. The salesperson has a duty to account for any money or possessions given to her by her clients, and to exercise care in her actions on their behalf. Because she advised them to remove the jewelry, she has fulfilled her duty to them. In most cases, sellers will not be present during an open house. It is not reasonable and may not be lawful for the salesperson to search visitors leaving the open house.

Reference: Agency Relationships and Contracts > Agency Relationships

153. A property owner individually signed a 90-day listing contract with a brokerage. The owner was killed in an accident before the listing expired. Now the listing is:

A. binding on the owner's spouse for the remainder of the 90 days.

B. terminated automatically because of the death of the principal.

C. binding only if the broker can produce offers to purchase the property.

D. still in effect as the owner's intention was clearly defined.

Answer: B. The answer is terminated automatically because of the death of the principal. A listing contract may be terminated if either party dies or becomes incapacitated. Neither the dead owner's intention nor the 90-day listing period keeps the listing in effect.

Reference: Agency Relationships and Contracts >

Service/Listing Buyer Contracts (contracts between licensee and seller or buyer)

154. The remedy for parties in default that is available to both the buyer and the seller in a purchase contract is:

A. liquidated damages.

B. specific performance.

C. lis pendens.

D. actual damages.

Answer: C. The answer is specific performance. If the purchase contract gives both parties the remedy of suing if the other party defaults the contract is specific performance. A liquidated damages contract allows the seller to keep the earnest money if the buyer defaults and gives the buyer specific performance remedies if the seller defaults.

Reference: Agency Relationships and Contracts > Purchase Contracts (contracts between seller and buyer)

155. A buyer signed a listing contract and agreed to pay the buyer's brokerage firm when the buyer purchased any property. The buyer signed a(n):

A. open buyer contract.

B. buyer agency disclosure form.

C. exclusive buyer agency contract.

D. exclusive-agency buyer contract.

Answer: C. The answer is exclusive buyer agency contract. The buyer signed an exclusive buyer agency contract, which states that whenever the buyer purchases the property described in the contract, the buyer's brokerage firm will be paid. An exclusive-agency and open listing would let the buyer purchase properties the broker had not shown them, and the buyer would not be obligated to pay the brokerage firm.

Reference: Agency Relationships and Contracts > Service/Listing Buyer Contracts (contracts between licensee and seller or buyer)

156. The clause in a contract that makes timely performance a condition of the contract is called the:

A. unity of time clause.

B. time is of the essence clau

C. within a reasonable time clause.

D. drop dead clause.

Answer: B. The answer is time is of the essence clause. Time is of the essence means that timely performance is a condition of the contract.

Reference: Agency Relationships and Contracts > Purchase Contracts (contracts between seller and buyer)

157. The most typical contingency in a real estate contract is for:

A. inspections.

B. the buyer to sell a current home.

C. appraisal.

D. financing.

Answer: D. The answer is financing. Most buyers must use some form of financing and typically the contract is contingent on the buyer receiving the financing. Other common contingencies include sale of a property, inspections, and appraisals.

Reference: Agency Relationships and Contracts > Purchase Contracts (contracts between seller and buyer)

158. A broker is hired as a buyer's agent. The buyer confides he filed for bankruptcy two years ago. The buyer would like to find a seller who is willing to carry the loan. In this situation, a correct statement about the broker's responsibility regarding disclosure of the bankruptcy when presenting the offer to purchase is that the broker is:

A. not required to disclose the bankruptcy because the seller might reject the offer.

B. not required to disclose the bankruptcy because the broker has no agency relationship with the seller.

C. required to disclose the bankruptcy because it is a material fact-information important to the seller's evaluation of the offer.

D. required to disclose the bankruptcy under ECOA.

Answer: C. The answer is required to disclose the bankruptcy because it is a material fact-information important to the seller's evaluation of the offer. The broker is obligated to disclose any material fact-something that might make a party to the transaction change their mind, regardless of the agency or non-agency relationship the broker has with the seller. The ECOA is a federal law prohibiting discrimination in the granting of credit and does not regulate disclosures required by in a real estate transaction.

Reference: Agency Relationships and Contracts > Agency Relationships

159. A buyer and seller are both represented by the same real estate brokerage firm acting as an agent in the same transaction. In this transaction, the firm is practicing:

A. single agency.

B. implied agency.

C. universal agency.

D. dual agency.

Answer: D. The answer is dual agency. When the firm represents both principals in the same transaction, the broker practices dual agency. Single agency exists when the broker represents only one party, the buyer or the seller. Implied agency is created accidentally by the actions of one of the parties. Universal agency empowers an agent to do anything the principal could do personally and would not apply in this instance.

Reference: Agency Relationships and Contracts > Agency Relationships

160. A listing taken by a real estate salesperson is an employment contract between the seller and:

A. local multiple listing service.

B. brokerage firm.

C. salesperson.

D. both the salesperson and the broker.

Answer: B. The answer is brokerage firm. The parties to a listing contract are the seller and the broker. The brokerage firm and principal broker represent the seller to list and sell the property. The salesperson does so in the name and under the supervision of the brokerage firm and principal broker.

Reference: Agency Relationships and Contracts > Service/Listing Buyer Contracts (contracts between licensee and seller or buyer)

161. A seller may keep the buyer's earnest money as liquidated damages if:

A. that is stated in the listing agreement as a remedy for the seller.

B. the seller failed to perform an essential element of the contract.

C. the buyer defaults and the purchase agreement stipulates liquidated damages as a remedy.

D. the seller and the broker agree that the buyer defaulted and the contract calls for specific performance.

Answer: C. The answer is the buyer defaults and the purchase agreement stipulates liquidated damages as a remedy. A liquidated damages purchase contract allows the seller to keep the earnest money if the buyer defaults. Typically the buyer will have specific performance remedies if the seller is in default.

Reference: Agency Relationships and Contracts > Purchase Contracts (contracts between seller and buyer)

162. Which statement BEST explains the meaning of this sentence: To enforce a commission for brokerage services, a broker must be employed as the agent of the client?:

A. The broker must work in a real estate office.

B. The broker must have a salesperson employed in the office.

C. The broker must express an interest in representing the client.

D. The broker must have a written contract to provide brokerage services for the client.

Answer: D. The answer is the broker must have a written contract to provide brokerage services for the client. A broker's contract of employment by a client is the brokerage services agreement (a listing or buyer representation contract) signed by the parties. A valid expressed written listing is one of the usual requirements in a suit for a brokerage commission; it is proof of employment.

Reference: Agency Relationships and Contracts > Service/Listing Buyer Contracts (contracts between licensee and seller or buyer)

163. Upon notice that an offer has been accepted, what should the listing broker do with the earnest money deposit?:

A. Give the earnest money to the seller to hold until closing

B. Have the buyer's broker who typically holds the funds deposit them into the listing brokers trust account

C. Deposit the earnest money into the brokerage or title company's trust account

D. Hold the earnest money until all the contingencies have been met and then deposit it into a trust account

Answer: C. The answer is deposit the earnest money into the brokerage or title company's trust account. Upon acceptance of the offer, which creates an executory contract, the earnest money is deposited into the brokerage or a title company's trust account. The money may not be held by the buyer's broker or seller or until the contingencies are completed.

Reference: Agency Relationships and Contracts > Purchase Contracts (contracts between seller and buyer)

164. When showing a property, an agent exaggerates the property's benefits. This practice is:

A. an illegal ministerial act.

B. puffing, which is legal as long as there is no misrepresentation.

C. fraud on the part of the agent.

D. an illegal misrepresentation of the property.

Answer: B. The answer is puffing, which is legal as long as there is no misrepresentation. The broker is exaggerating the benefits of the property. In this situation the broker is not guilty of fraud or misrepresentation. Fraud is a deceitful practice or a misstatement of a material fact, known to be false. A ministerial act is a routine act performed for a customer that does not involve judgment, discretion, or advice.

Reference: Agency Relationships and Contracts > Purchase Contracts (contracts between seller and buyer)

165. The type of listing contract that provides the LEAST protection for the listing broker is the:

A. net listing.

B. open listing.

C. exclusive-right-to-sell listing.

D. exclusive-agency listing.

Answer: B. The answer is open listing. In an open listing, the seller retains the right to employ any number of brokers to sell the property. The brokers can act simultaneously, and the seller is obligated to pay a commission only to that broker who successfully procures a ready, willing, and able buyer. A broker entering into an open listing should negotiate terms in writing that specify a commission due the broker if the broker is the procuring cause of a sale. An exclusive-agency listing authorizes a broker to act as sole agent of the seller, but the seller may sell the property without the broker and without paying the broker a commission. In an exclusive-right-to-sell listing, if the property is sold while the listing is in effect, the seller must pay the broker a commission regardless of who sells the property. A net listing clause would permit a broker to receive as commission all excess monies over and above the minimum sales price agreed to in the listing agreement. Net listings are not only discouraged but illegal in many states.

Reference: Agency Relationships and Contracts > Service/Listing Buyer Contracts (contracts between licensee and seller or buyer)

166. A listing agreement states that the broker will receive a 6% commission. The broker produces a buyer who purchases the home for $210,000. What is the net amount that the seller will receive from the sale?:

A. $197,400

B. $203,000

C. $196,000

D. $147,000

Answer: A. The answer is $197,400. To find the seller's net from the sale, subtract the amount of the broker's commission from the selling price of the home. First, calculate the amount of the commission: 6% (.06) x $210,000 (selling price) = $12,600. $210,000 - $12,600 = $197,400. Or take $210,000 X .94 = $197,400.

167. Whose signature is necessary for a signed offer to purchase real estate to become a contract?:

A. Buyer's only

B. Seller's and seller's broker

C. Seller's only

D. Buyer's and seller's

Answer: D. The answer is buyer's and seller's. A signed offer already has the buyer's signature, but to be a ratified contract, both the buyer's and the seller's signatures are necessary.

Reference: Agency Relationships and Contracts > Purchase Contracts (contracts between seller and buyer)

168. A purchase contract contains several personal property items and fixtures that will be transferred upon sale of the property. Which of the following is TRUE?:

A. All fixtures must be listed in the deed to convey to the buyer.

B. There is no need to list the personal property in the contract because it will automatically convey unless it is excluded by the seller.

C. The fixtures and personal property will need to be itemized in the bill of sale.

D. All personal property must be listed in the bill of sale to convey to the buyer.

Answer: D. The answer is all personal property must be listed in the bill of sale to convey to the buyer. Fixtures are appurtenant, attached to the property, and automatically conveyed with the deed without being listed. Personal property must be listed in the bill of sale in order to be included in the sale.

Reference: Agency Relationships and Contracts > Purchase Contracts (contracts between seller and buyer)

169. Which of the following events will terminate the agency relationship between the brokerage and seller?:

A. The broker appoints other salespeople to help sell the property.

B. The broker discovers that the market value of the property is such that the broker will not make an adequate commission.

C. The owner dies.

D. The owner abandons the property.

Answer: C. The answer is the owner dies. The common law of agency holds that the death of either the broker or the seller ends the agency relationship created by the listing. The market value of the property does not affect the agency relationship, and the broker may assign other agents to help sell listed property. An owner abandoning property does not terminate an agency relationship but could result in termination if the property is taken over by a third party, such as a lending institution in the event of the owner's bankruptcy or a foreclosure proceeding.

Reference: Agency Relationships and Contracts >

Service/Listing Buyer Contracts (contracts between licensee and seller or buyer)

170. A listing contract must be signed by:

A. only the broker.

B. only the seller.

C. both the seller and the listing broker.

D. an attorney.

Answer: C. The answer is both the seller and the listing broker. All parties identified in the listing contract must sign it, including all individuals who have a legal interest in the party. As the contract is between the seller and the listing broker, the listing broker or the broker's designated representative must sign the contract.

Reference: Agency Relationships and Contracts > Service/Listing Buyer Contracts (contracts between licensee and seller or buyer)

171. Before the buyer signs a buyer agency contract, a real estate professional must do all of the following EXCEPT:

A. explain the forms of agency available.

B. obtain financial information from the buyer.

C. describe specific services to be provided.

D. inform the buyer of the charges or compensation for services.

Answer: B. The answer is obtain financial information from the buyer. Once the buyer representation contract is signed, not before, the real estate professional should obtain detailed financial information from the buyer. State regulations require that real estate professionals inform the buyer of all types of agency available, the broker's compensation requirements, and the services that the broker will provide under the agreement.

Reference: Agency Relationships and Contracts > Service/Listing Buyer Contracts (contracts between licensee and seller or buyer)

172. A broker who is the agent of the buyer should do which of the following?:

A. Disclose to the seller the maximum price the buyer is willing to pay

B. Present to the seller only offers that are acceptable

C. Advise the buyer if the listing price of the seller's house is unrealistic

D. Disclose to the seller that the buyer is a minority person

Answer: C. The answer is advise the buyer if the listing price of the seller's house is unrealistic. Agents have the fiduciary duty of reasonable care to their client. Reasonable care requires that an agent for the buyer disclose to the buyer if the property is overpriced. Fair housing laws prohibit discrimination based on race or national origin and prohibit the real estate professionals from disclosing to the seller that the buyer is a minority person. The duty of confidentiality requires that the agent not disclose the maximum price the buyer is willing to pay. The agent is required to present to the seller all offers from the buyer, even if the agent believes the seller will not accept the offer.

Reference: Agency Relationships and Contracts > Agency
Relationships

**173. A buyer and a seller agree on a purchase price of
$200,000 for a house. The contract contains a clause stating
that "time is of the essence." Which statement isTRUE?:**

A. The closing date must be stated as a particular calendar date
and not simply as a formula, such as "two weeks after loan
approval."

B. A "time is of the essence" clause is not binding on either
party.

C. If the closing date passes and no closing takes place, the party
who failed to close is considered to in default.

D. The closing must take place within a reasonable period
before the stated date.

Answer: C. The answer is if the closing date passes and no
closing takes place, the party who failed to close is considered to
in default. The non-defaulting party may have remedies to retain
the earnest money (liquidated damages) or to sue the defaulting

party to perform the contract terms (specific performance).

Reference: Agency Relationships and Contracts > Purchase
Contracts (contracts between seller and buyer)

**174. A principal broker authorizes one agent in her firm to
represent the seller and another to represent the buyer in
the same real estate transaction. Each agent is a:**

A. single agent.

B. dual agent.

C. designated agent.

D. universal agent.

Answer: C. The answer is designated agent. A designated agent
or representative is a person authorized by a real estate
brokerage to act as the agent of a specific principal. The
designated agent has a fiduciary relationship toward the
principal, and the brokerage is a dual agent in the transaction. In
a single agent, a brokerage represents only the buyer or the
seller in a transaction. Universal agency empowers an agent to

do anything the principal could do personally.

Reference: Agency Relationships and Contracts > Agency Relationships

175. Which of the following statements regarding an executory purchase contract is TRUE?:

A. The contract terms must be identical to the terms in the listing agreement.

B. The contract is binding on both parties.

C. The contract conveys legal title when signed by both parties.

D. The contract may be oral.

Answer: B. The answer is the contract is binding on both parties. An executory purchase contract is one in which both parties have reached mutual agreement and are both bound to the complete the contract. A deed conveys legal title in the executory phase of a contract; the buyer has equitable title while the seller retains legal title.

Reference: Agency Relationships and Contracts > General Legal Principles, Theory and Concepts about Contracts

176. Which of the following requires that real estate sales contracts be in writing?:

A. Statute of limitations

B. Truth in Lending Act

C. Statute of frauds

D. Caveat emptor law

Answer: C. The answer is statute of frauds. The statute of frauds requires all transfers of interests in real estate be in writing, the exception is a lease of 12 months or less. The statute of limitations sets the amount of time law suits can be filed. Truth in Lending Act sets disclosure requirements for lender fees. Caveat emptor means buyer beware.

Reference: Agency Relationships and Contracts > Purchase Contracts (contracts between seller and buyer)

177. A promise, or something of value, made by one party to induce another party to enter into a contract is:

A. words of conveyance.

B. the authorization to perform.

C. the meeting of the minds.

D. legal consideration.

Answer: D. The answer is legal consideration. Legal consideration is a promise, or something of value, made by one party to induce another party to enter into a contract. In a purchase contract, consideration is the promise of the seller to sell and the buyer to buy. Words of conveyance are used in deeds to create the estate being transferred.

Reference: Agency Relationships and Contracts > Purchase Contracts (contracts between seller and buyer)

178. A listing contract is best described as a(n):

A. property management contract.

B. sales contract.

C. escrow contract.

D. personal service contract.

Answer: D. The answer is personal service contract. A listing is a personal employment contract between brokers and their clients setting forth the broker's responsibilities in finding for the seller a ready, willing, and able buyer. A property management contract establishes the responsibilities of a broker in managing a principal's property. A sales contract is a contract between a buyer and seller for purchase of a property. An escrow contract is an agreement between a buyer, seller, and escrow holder (such as a broker) defining the responsibilities of each.

Reference: Agency Relationships and Contracts > Service/Listing Buyer Contracts (contracts between licensee and seller or buyer)

179. Unless some other written agreement has been made, the brokerage will usually receive his brokerage commission when:

A. the seller lists the property with the broker.

B. the purchaser takes possession of the property.

C. the transaction is closed.

D. an offer, procured from a ready, willing, and able buyer, has been accepted by the seller.

Answer: C. The answer is the transaction is closed. Although a commission is usually earned when the buyer has been procured, it is usually payable when the sale is closed unless another arrangement for payment has been agreed to in writing.

Reference: Agency Relationships and Contracts > Service/Listing Buyer Contracts (contracts between licensee and seller or buyer)

180. According to its state's laws, a brokerage firm is allowed to have an agency relationship with only one party in the same transaction. This relationship is known as:

A. single agency.

B. exclusive-buyer agency.

C. designated agency.

D. disclosed dual agency.

Answer: A. The answer is single agency. In single agency, the agent represents only one party in any single transaction. Designated agency exists when a brokerage acting as a dual agent for both parties in a transaction assigns an individual agent to represent the seller and another agent to represent the buyer in the same real estate transaction; each agent is known as a designated agent. Dual agency exists when an agent represents both the buyer and the seller in the same transaction. In an exclusive-buyer agency relationship, the agent represents the buyer and is entitled to a commission regardless of whether or not the agent actually locates the property purchased by the buyer.

Reference: Agency Relationships and Contracts > Agency Relationships

181. At the time a buyer was negotiating the purchase of a lot on which to build a new home, the seller represented that the soil was firm enough to support the construction of a building when, in fact, the seller knew it was not. This contract is:

A. void because of the seller's misrepresentation.

B. voidable by the seller because of the mistake.

C. valid because no harm was done yet.

D. voidable by the buyer because of fraud.

Answer: D. The answer is voidable by the buyer because of fraud. The contract is voidable because it contains all the essential elements of a contract but could be rescinded due to fraud by the seller. A void contract lacks one of the essential elements of a contract. In this voidable contract the buyer has the right to terminate but the seller does not. The contract is not valid since the seller has misrepresented the property.

**182. In a dual agency situation, a broker may represent both
the seller and the buyer if:**

A. the broker determines dual agency is the only option to sell
the property and get paid a full commission.

B. both parties give their informed consent, usually in writing,
to the dual agency.

C. both parties are represented by attorneys.

D. the broker informs either the buyer or the seller of this fact.

Answer: B. The answer is both parties give their informed
consent, usually in writing, to the dual agency. Dual agency, in
states that allow it, requires informed written consent from both
parties. The broker must have written consent from both parties;
consent from only one party will not permit dual agency. The
dual agency relationship does not determine payment of
commissions, and does not require attorney representation by
either party.

183. During the period of time after a real estate sales contract is signed, but before title actually passes, the status of the contract is:

A. unilateral.

B. executed.

C. voidable.

D. executory.

Answer: D. The answer is executory. A contract is in executory status when its terms of agreement have not yet been carried out. When it has been carried out, it is said to be executed. A unilateral contract binds only one party to act. A voidable contract is one that is able to be voided because of duress, fraud, misrepresentation, or because one party to the contract is a minor.

Reference: Agency Relationships and Contracts > General Legal Principles, Theory and Concepts about Contracts

184. An optionee has communicated to the optionor that the optionee will purchase the property. This option contract is now exercised and is BEST described as a(n):

A. executed bilateral purchase contract.

B. executory unilateral purchase contract.

C. executed unilateral purchase contract.

D. executory bilateral purchase contract.

Answer: D. The answer is executory bilateral purchase contract. When the buyer informs the seller that he is going to purchase the property, the option is exercised, and an executory bilateral purchase contract exists.

Reference: Agency Relationships and Contracts > Purchase Contracts (contracts between seller and buyer)

185. A broker was told by her principal not to advertise her property in a certain newspaper, which was out of the area. The broker complied because he:

A. must obey the lawful instructions of her principal.

B. is allowed to advertise only in local newspapers.

C. had never advertised in that newspaper anyway.

D. was not intending to advertise the property at all.

Answer: A. The answer is must obey the lawful instructions of her principal. The fiduciary relationship obligates the agent to act in good faith at all times, obeying the principal's instructions in accordance with the contract. The seller has a right to advertise in a newspaper of her choice, provided any advertisement does not violate fair housing laws.

Reference: Agency Relationships and Contracts > Service/Listing Buyer Contracts (contracts between licensee and seller or buyer)

186. A salesperson finally concluded some extremely difficult negotiations resulting in the sale of a listed parcel of land. For all of her extra efforts, she can legally receive a performance bonus directly from:

A. the seller.

B. no one.

C. the buyer.

D. her principal broker.

Answer: D. The answer is her principal broker. Bonus and commissions are paid directly to the broker, who then pays the salesperson. The salesperson may not receive commissions or bonus from anyone other than her principal broker.

Reference: Agency Relationships and Contracts > Service/Listing Buyer Contracts (contracts between licensee and seller or buyer)

187. In an appointment with a seller, a salesperson presents a competitive market analysis (CMA) that provides a

reasonable market value for the seller's property. The seller insists on pricing the property $15,000 higher than the salesperson's suggested price. Under these circumstances, the salesperson:

A. must hire an appraiser to conduct a formal appraisal.

B. may change the listing price in the contract once it is executed.

C. may choose to refuse the listing.

D. must accept the listing with the seller's higher listing price.

Answer: C. The answer is may choose to refuse the listing. An unrealistic listing price may make it difficult for the broker to properly market the property within the time period of the listing. The salesperson is not required to accept the listing with the higher listing price or to hire an appraiser for a formal appraisal. The salesperson may not change the listing price in a listing contract without the explicit permission of the seller.

Reference: Agency Relationships and Contracts > Service/Listing Buyer Contracts (contracts between licensee and seller or buyer)

188. The principal in a real estate transaction is:

A. the client of the brokerage.

B. the customer of the agent.

C. the subagent to the client.

D. a facilitator to the transaction.

Answer: A. The answer is the client of the brokerage. The principal in a real estate transaction is the individual who hires the brokerage and delegates to the firm the responsibility of representing the principal's interest in the transaction. The customer is the third party or non-represented consumer in the transaction. A facilitator is a middleman between a buyer and seller who assists one or both parties without fiduciary obligations to either. A subagent is an agent of the agent. Salespersons and broker associates who work for a brokerage are considered agents of the principal broker and subagents of the principal. Reference: Agency Relationships and Contracts > Agency Relationships

189. A principal broker uses earnest money placed in the company trust account to pay for the rent owed on the brokerage firm's office. Using escrow funds for this purpose is:

A. legal if the seller gives consent in writing.

B. illegal conversion.

C. legal if the trust account is reimbursed by the end of the calendar month.

D. illegal unless the client has approved the expenditure.

Answer: B. The answer is illegal conversion. Trust funds may not be deposited into an operations or personal account.

Reference: Agency Relationships and Contracts > Purchase Contracts (contracts between seller and buyer)

190. In order for contracts transferring real property to be valid they must include all of the following EXCEPT:

A. all parties must meet the legal definition of competency.

B. the objective of the offer/contract must have legal purpose with the ability to transfer title.

C. the parties must come to a mutual agreement as to all terms and conditions.

D. earnest money must be given from the buyer to the seller as consideration for selling.

Answer: D. The answer is earnest money must be given from the buyer to the seller as consideration for selling. Consideration is a required element of a valid contract but earnest money is not. The parties must be competent; come to a meeting of the minds; the contract must have a lawful objective or purpose; and if for the transfer of real estate (except for certain leases) it must be in writing and signed.

Reference: Agency Relationships and Contracts > Purchase Contracts (contracts between seller and buyer)

191. A listing broker is typically a(n):

A. universal agent.

B. special agent.

C. general agent.

D. designated agent.

Answer: B. The answer is special agent. A real estate broker is usually a special agent, an agent authorized to represent the principal (the seller) in one specific business transaction, with no power to bind the principal. The listing broker's authority is limited to finding a ready, willing, and able buyer for the property. A general agent represents the principal in a broad range of matters related to a particular business and has a limited power to bind the principal. A property manager is usually a general agent. A universal agent is a person empowered to fully bind the principal as authorized by a general power of attorney. A designated agent is an individual licensee authorized by a broker to represent one party in a transaction in which the other party is also represented by the broker.

Reference: Agency Relationships and Contracts > Agency Relationships

192. A broker has found a buyer for a seller's home. The buyer has indicated in writing a willingness to buy the property by signing a written agreement. The seller is out of town for the weekend, and the broker has been unable to inform the seller of the signed document. At this point, the buyer has signed a(n):

A. executory contract.

B. implied contract.

C. voidable contract.

D. offer.

Answer: D. The answer is offer. A form that offers to buy property but has not been seen or acted on by the property owner is simply an offer. Even if the offer had been for full price, no contract or agreement would yet exist, and the offeror (buyer) would have no claim on the offeree (seller).

Reference: Agency Relationships and Contracts > Purchase Contracts (contracts between seller and buyer)

193. A salesperson who works for ABC Realty was the buyer's agent for a property that was listed by XYZ Realty. The seller agreed to pay the commission. From whom will the salesperson receive her commission check?:

A. The principal broker of XYZ Realty.

B. The principal broker of ABC Realty.

C. Either principal broker may pay her.

D. Directly from the buyer.

Answer: B. The answer is the principal broker of ABC Realty. The salesperson may receive the commission check only from her broker. While the seller may pay the commission to the principal broker of XYZ, the listing broker, the salesperson may receive her share of the commission only from that part of the commission provided to her broker by the listing broker.

Reference: Agency Relationships and Contracts > Service/Listing Buyer Contracts (contracts between licensee and seller or buyer)

194. A real estate broker acting as the agent of the seller:

A. should present to the seller only the highest offer for the property.

B. must promote and safeguard the seller's best interest.

C. can disclose the seller's minimum price.

D. can accept an offer on behalf of the seller.

Answer: B. The answer is must promote and safeguard the seller's best interest. Real estate brokers must be loyal to their principal by promoting the principal's best interest. A broker acting as agent for a seller should present all offers on the property but may not accept an offer on behalf of the seller. Only the seller may accept an offer. The broker may not disclose any confidential information of the seller tied to price, term, or motivation without the seller's written permission.

Reference: Agency Relationships and Contracts > Agency Relationships

195. In a bilateral contract:

A. both parties to the contract have duties to be performed.

B. only one of the parties is bound to the contract.

C. a restriction is placed in the contract.

D. consideration is not an essential element.

Answer: A. The answer is both parties to the contract have duties to be performed. In a bilateral contract, both parties are obligated to perform what they have promised to do. Only one party is bound in a unilateral contract. Consideration is an essential element of all contracts.

Reference: Agency Relationships and Contracts > General Legal Principles, Theory and Concepts about Contracts

196. A broker sold a residence for $210,000 and received $10,500 as commission in accordance with the terms of the listing contract. What was the broker's commission rate?:

A. 5%

B. 7.50%

C. 6%

D. 8%

Answer: A. he answer is 5%. To find the commission rate, divide the selling price by the actual amount of the commission: $210,000 ÷ $10,500 = 5% (.05).

Reference: Agency Relationships and Contracts > Service/Listing Buyer Contracts (contracts between licensee and seller or buyer)

197. Under the common laws of agency, in a typical agency relationship between broker and client, the broker's commission is determined by:

A. the Sherman Antitrust Act.

B. local real estate boards.

C. the top three office producers.

D. negotiation in advance.

Answer: D. The answer is negotiation in advance. A broker and client negotiate and determine what commission schedule will apply to the transaction. Commissions are always negotiable. Each brokerage firm may determine its own commission guidelines and suggestions for its salespeople, but the actual commission is negotiated with the client. The Sherman Antitrust Act of 1980 makes it illegal to competing companies or real estate boards to set standard commission rates for brokerage firms.

Reference: Agency Relationships and Contracts > Service/Listing Buyer Contracts (contracts between licensee and seller or buyer)

198. After signing a listing contract with a homeowner, the owner tells the listing agent that because his home is in such good condition he does not want the home sold to any buyers with small children. The agent takes the listing, and obeys the owner's instructions by not showing the home to any buyers with small children. He discourages other agents from showing the home to families by telling them the home is not suitable for a family. Are the agent's actions legal?:

A. No, because refusing to show a property to buyers with families violates fair housing laws.

B. No, because fair housing laws do not exempt any property from being marketed to families.

C. Yes, because the agent has obeyed the owner's instructions.

D. Yes, because an agent may choose to whom to market a home she has listed.

Answer: A. The answer is no, because refusing to show a property to buyers with families violates fair housing laws. Federal and state fair housing laws prohibit discrimination against families in the marketing and selling of residential homes. Some residential properties are exempted if they meet specific requirements for senior housing. The agent's duty of obedience does not require agents to obey unlawful or unethical instructions from their client.

Reference: Agency Relationships and Contracts > Agency Relationships

199. A seller has sold property to a neighbor without the services of a real estate broker. However, the seller still owes the broker a commission because the seller signed a(n):

A. open listing.

B. exclusive-right-to-sell listing.

C. option listing.

D. exclusive-agency listing.

Answer: B. The answer is exclusive right-to-sell listing. In an exclusive-right-to-sell listing, a commission will be owed to a broker regardless of which party sells the house. In exclusive-agency and open listings, the seller retains the right to sell without obligation to the broker. An option listing permits the broker to retain an option to purchase the property for the broker's own account.

Reference: Agency Relationships and Contracts > Service/Listing Buyer Contracts (contracts between licensee and seller or buyer)

200. All of the following are typically found in a listing contract EXCEPT:

A. the price the seller is asking for the property.

B. the date the broker will schedule an open house.

C. the responsibilities of the broker and seller.

D. the commission rate to be paid to the listing broker.

Answer: B. The answer is the date the broker will schedule an open house. All listing contracts tend to require similar information: type of listing agreement, broker's authority and responsibilities, names of all parties to the contract, brokerage firm, list price, real and personal property, description of property, commission, termination of the contract, etc. They are not required to provide the dates of open houses.

Reference: Agency Relationships and Contracts > Service/Listing Buyer Contracts (contracts between licensee and seller or buyer)

201. The relationship between a broker and a seller is generally what type of agency?:

A. Special agency

B. Implied agency

C. Universal agency

D. General agency

Answer: A. The answer is special agency. A special (or limited) agent is authorized to represent the principal in a specific act or business transaction, under detailed instructions from the principal. The relationship between a brokerage and seller is usually a special agency, as is the agency between a brokerage and a buyer client. A general agent may represent the principal in a broad range of matters. A property manager is typically a general agent for the owner. A universal agent is a person empowered to do anything the principal could do personally, as is authorized in a power of attorney. An implied agency is usually created unintentionally or accidentally by the actions of the parties.

Reference: Agency Relationships and Contracts > Agency Relationships

202. The law that requires real estate contracts to be in writing to be enforceable is the:

A. probate requirement.

B. law of descent.

C. statute of limitations.

D. statute of frauds.

Answer: D. The answer is statute of frauds. The statute of frauds requires real estate contracts to be in writing to be enforceable. An oral contract, although unenforceable, is still valid between parties. The law of descent regulates the processes by which an heir acquires an intestate estate. Probate is used to distribute property in a will. The statute of limitations is law dictating a period of time within which actions regarding an alleged offense may be brought to court by an accuser.

Reference: Agency Relationships and Contracts > General Legal Principles, Theory and Concepts about Contracts

203. A new contract that transfers all rights and liabilities is a(n):

A. option.

B. assignment

C. subordination

D. novation

Answer: D. The answer is novation. In a novation a new contract is used to replace the original contract. Subordination is used in recording to keep liens in place. An assignment is the transfer of contract duties but not liabilities. An option is a contract that exchanges a promise for performance.

Reference: Agency Relationships and Contracts > General Legal Principles, Theory and Concepts about Contracts

204. An agent forgot to get the buyer to sign the offer. What is the status of the offer?:

A. Valid

B. Voidable

C. Voluntary

D. Void

Answer: D. The answer is void. The offer is missing an essential element and is void. Duress, fraud, misrepresentation, and minors always make contracts voidable. A contract that is binding and enforceable is valid.

Reference: Agency Relationships and Contracts > General Legal Principles, Theory and Concepts about Contracts

205. The buyer has made an offer that the seller has accepted and proper notice has been given to the buyer of the seller's acceptance. The offer is now considered an:

A. executory contract.

B. executed contract.

C. unilateral contract.

D. assignment.

Answer: A. The answer is executory contract. The period from when the contract is agreed to and signed by both parties until it is executed (closed) is called the executory period. Executed contracts have been closed. Unilateral contracts bind only one party such as an option. Assignments transfer the contract duties but not liabilities.

Reference: Agency Relationships and Contracts > General Legal Principles, Theory and Concepts about Contracts

206. To insert additional terms into the offer, the real estate professional would use a(n):

A. addendum

B. adaptation clause.

C. contingency clause.

D. amendment form.

Answer: A. The answer is addendum. The purpose of an addendum is to legally change any of the provisions of the offer or to insert new terms. Amendments modify executory contracts.

Reference: Agency Relationships and Contracts > General Legal Principles, Theory and Concepts about Contracts

207. A buyer and a seller have entered into a binding contract for the sale of real estate. During this phase and until closing, the buyer has which type of title?:

A. Escalating

B. Executory

C. Legal

D. Equitable

Answer: D. The answer is equitable. The buyer has equitable title, which recognizes that he has an interest but has not received legal title. Legal title will pass at closing when the seller gives the buyer the deed.

Reference: Agency Relationships and Contracts > Purchase Contracts (contracts between seller and buyer)

208. A buyer makes an offer to purchase a certain property listed with a real estate professional and leaves an earnest money deposit to show good faith. The offer is accepted. The real estate professional should:

A. put the deposit in the real estate professional's personal checking account.

B. immediately apply the deposit to the listing expenses.

C. give the deposit to the seller when the offer is presented.

D. put the deposit in a trust account, as provided by state law.

Answer: D. The answer is put the deposit in an account, as provided by state law. Once an offer becomes an accepted contract the earnest money must be deposited in a trust account per rules of the state law.

Reference: Agency Relationships and Contracts > Purchase
Contracts (contracts between seller and buyer)

**209. A buyer agency contract states that the contract expires
on April 30. Which event would NOT terminate the buyer
agency contract?:**

A. Death of the buyer

B. Mutual agreement to end the contract

C. The salesperson leaving the brokerage firm

D. Death of the broker

Answer: C. The answer is the salesperson leaving the brokerage
firm. The contract is with the buyer and the firm not the
salesperson. If the salesperson leaves the principal broker may
assign another salesperson to assist the buyer. The buyer and the
principal broker may come to a mutual agreement to terminate
the contract. The death of either party terminates the contract.

Reference: Agency Relationships and Contracts >

Service/Listing Buyer Contracts (contracts between licensee and seller or buyer)

210. An investor does not want to be obligated to purchase a property but would like to have the right to purchase a property within 60 days for $300,000. The investor should try to negotiate a(n):

A. purchase agreement.

B. contract for deed.

C. purchase-money mortgage.

D. option.

Answer: D. The answer is option. An option contract would allow the investor the time to determine if she wants to buy and has the advantage of locking the seller into selling at a price agreed to at the beginning of the process. Contract for deed and purchase-money mortgages are forms of seller financing and would not give this type of flexibility. Both require a purchase agreement to create the terms of the financing.

**211. A broker helps a buyer and a seller with paperwork but
does not represent either party. This arrangement is:**

A. a transaction brokerage.

B. prohibited in all states as a broker must always represent one
party.

C. dual agency.

D. designated agency.

Answer: D. The answer is a transaction brokerage. When a
broker does not represent either party in a transaction and acts as
a facilitator or non-agent, the arrangement is known as
transaction brokerage and is legal in some states. Dual agency
exists when an agent represents both the buyer and the seller in
the same transaction. Designated agency exists when a broker
acting as a dual agent for both parties in a transaction assigns an
individual agent to represent the seller and another agent to
represent the buyer in the same real estate transaction; each

agent is known as a designated agent.

Reference: Agency Relationships and Contracts > Agency Relationships

212. A brokerage represents the owner in the sale of the owner's property. Which of the following events will terminate that agency relationship?:

A. The broker engages other brokers to help sell the property.

B. The owner abandons the property.

C. The broker discovers that an adequate commission cannot be made due to the low market value of the property.

D. A fire destroys the owner's property.

Answer: D. The answer is a fire destroys the property. The destruction or condemnation of a property during a listing period terminates the listing. The agency relationship remains in effect with any of the other events.

213. In order for a listing contract to be enforceable, MOST states require that the contract be:

A. in writing.

B. an oral contract.

C. a form contract used by all licensees.

D. drafted by an attorney.

Answer: A. The answer is in writing. While in some states oral listings are legal, a listing contract must be in writing in order for either party to be able to enforce the provisions of the contract. Many licensees use form contracts drafted by a real estate association or real estate commission. Many states do not require all licensees to use the same contract form.

Reference: Agency Relationships and Contracts > Service/Listing Buyer Contracts (contracts between licensee and seller or buyer)

214. The seller has accepted monetary consideration and has agreed to sell his property for an agreed upon amount within a specified timeframe, if the buyer then chooses to purchase. This contract is called a(n):

A. land contract.

B. listing contract.

C. sales contract.

D. option contract.

Answer: D. The answer is option contract. In an option contract, the seller accepts option money and agrees to sell his property for a specified amount within a specified timeframe, if the buyer chooses to purchase in the future.

Reference: Agency Relationships and Contracts > Purchase Contracts (contracts between seller and buyer)

215. Legal action that may be taken to enforce the terms of the contract is:

A. suit for money damages.

B. suit for specific performance.

C. suit to quiet the title.

D. suit for possession.

Answer: B. The answer is suit for specific performance. Legal action that may be taken to enforce the terms of the contract is a suit for specific performance. A suit to quiet title is used if there is cloud on title.

Reference: Agency Relationships and Contracts > Purchase Contracts (contracts between seller and buyer)

216. A listing agent's duty of care to a seller includes all of the following EXCEPT:

A. making reasonable efforts to market the property.

B. helping the seller evaluate an offer to purchase and write a counter offer if needed.

C. helping the seller arrive at a realistic listing price and commission splits for the MLS entry.

D. sharing the seller's financial situation with a buyer in order to expedite a sale.

Answer: D. The answer is sharing the seller's financial situation with a buyer in order to expedite a sale. An agent representing a seller may not disclose confidential information to a buyer without the seller's explicit permission, even to expedite the sale of the property. All the other activities are examples of an agent exercising the duty of care for the seller.

Reference: Agency Relationships and Contracts > Agency Relationships

217. An individual who is authorized and who consents to represent the interests of another person above their own interests is a(n):

A. client

B. principal

C. agent

D. customer

Answer: C. The answer is agent. An individual authorized by a principal (client) to represent the interests of that person is an agent; the fiduciary obligations require the agent to put the interests of the principal above the agents. In real estate, a firm's principal broker is the agent. The principal is the individual who hires the brokerage firm to represent the individual's interests and act as an agent. The client is the principal. The customer is a third party or non-represented consumer who is entitled to fairness and honesty from the agent of the principal.

Reference: Agency Relationships and Contracts > Agency Relationships

218. The essential elements of a contract includes all of the following EXCEPT:

A. offer and acceptance.

B. consideration.

C. competent grantor.

D. lawful purpose.

Answer: C. The answer is competent grantor. Competent grantor is a requirement of a deed but not an essential element of a contract. Offer and acceptance, lawful purpose, consideration, voluntary consent, and legally competent parties are the essential elements of a contract.

Reference: Agency Relationships and Contracts > Purchase Contracts (contracts between seller and buyer)

219. A broker deposits earnest money into the company operations account. This action is:

A. commingling of funds and is illegal.

B. legal if both parties to a transaction give consent in writing.

C. legal if the seller gives consent in writing.

D. legal if the trust account is reimbursed by the end of the calendar month.

Answer: A. The answer is commingling of funds and is illegal. The mixing of trust funds with a broker's personal funds is commingling. Commingling is illegal regardless of any plan to later reimburse the account and is not legal even with written consent from any party in a transaction.

Reference: Agency Relationships and Contracts > Purchase Contracts (contracts between seller and buyer)

220. If an owner takes his property off the market for a definite period of time in exchange for some consideration, but he grants an individual the right to purchase the property within that period for a stated price, the contract is called a(n):

A. installment agreement.

B. option

C. contract of sale.

D. right of first refusal.

Answer: B. The answer is option. An option is granted when an owner (optionor) gives the potential purchaser (optionee) the right to purchase the property at a fixed price within a certain period of time. A contract of sale occurs when a seller and a buyer come to an agreement on the sale of a property. A right of first refusal is an agreement in which the holder of the right has the first opportunity to either purchase or lease real property once the owner offers the property for sale or lease. An installment agreement, also known as a contract for deed, is an agreement in which the seller becomes the lender and the buyer takes possession of the property, retaining equitable title to the property until the final payment to the seller is made.

Reference: Agency Relationships and Contracts > Purchase Contracts (contracts between seller and buyer)

221. A contract that has been fully performed is:

A. unenforceable.

B. executed.

C. executory.

D. voidable.

Answer: B. The answer is executed. Prior to execution, the contract is executory. Once the parties have performed, it is called executed.

Reference: Agency Relationships and Contracts > General Legal Principles, Theory and Concepts about Contracts

222. Consideration could be all of the following EXCEPT:

A. money

B. a promise.

C. earnest money.

D. something of value.

Answer: C. The answer is earnest money. Consideration is defined as a promise, money, or something of value. Earnest money is not consideration; it is the seller's remedy in a liquated damages contract.

Reference: Agency Relationships and Contracts > Purchase Contracts (contracts between seller and buyer)

223. A contract that has NOT yet been fully performed is:

A. voidable.

B. unenforceable.

C. executed.

D. executory.

Answer: D. The answer is executory. The phase from offer to a closed and executed/closed contract is called the executory period. Voidable contracts are binding on one party and not the other. An unenforceable contract is also void due to lack of an essential element.

Reference: Agency Relationships and Contracts > General Legal Principles, Theory and Concepts about Contracts

224. A buyer and a seller sign a contract to purchase. The seller backs out, and the buyer sues for specific performance. What is the buyer seeking in this lawsuit?:

A. Deficiency judgment

B. Money damages

C. New contract

D. Transfer of the property

Answer: D. The answer is transfer of the property. Specific performance means sue to perform. The seller, if suing, would be suing the buyer to buy the property. The buyer is suing the seller to sell the property.

Reference: Agency Relationships and Contracts > Purchase Contracts (contracts between seller and buyer)

225. Under which of the following listing agreements can owners of listed property sell the property on their own without having to pay the listing broker a commission?:

A. Exclusive-right-to-sell listing and exclusive-agency listing

B. Exclusive-agency listing only

C. Open listing and exclusive-agency listing

D. Open listing only

Answer: C. The answer is open listing and exclusive-agency listing. In an exclusive-agency listing, one brokerage is authorized to act as the exclusive agent of the principal. However, the seller retains the right to sell the property without obligation to the brokerage. In an open listing, the seller retains the right to employ any number of brokers to sell the property. In an open listing, the seller is obligated to pay the listing broker a commission only if the listing broker is the procuring cause of the sale. In an exclusive-right-to-sell listing, if the property is sold while the listing is in effect, the seller must pay the broker a commission regardless of who sells the property.

Reference: Agency Relationships and Contracts > Service/Listing Buyer Contracts (contracts between licensee and seller or buyer)

226. A listing taken by a real estate salesperson is technically an employment contract between the seller and the:

A. local multiple listing service.

B. brokerage firm.

C. salesperson and principal broker together.

D. salesperson.

Answer: B. The answer is brokerage firm. Only a principal or employing broker for the brokerage firm may enter into brokerage agreements. The broker's salespeople have authority only to assist in negotiating the agreements. The salesperson is merely the sub-agent of the broker, but only the broker is the agent of the client and a party to the representation agreement. The salesperson is not a party to it.

Reference: Agency Relationships and Contracts > Service/Listing Buyer Contracts (contracts between licensee and seller or buyer)

227. MOST states require that listing contracts contain:

A. a broker protection clause.

B. a multiple listing service (MLS) clause.

C. a definite contract termination date.

D. an automatic extension clause.

Answer: C. The answer is definite contract termination date. If brokers fail to specify a specific listing contract termination date in a listing, they may be subject to suspension or revocation of their real estate license in many states. In some states, automatic extension clauses that extend a listing past its expiration date are illegal. A listing may contain a broker protection clause which provides that within a specified period of time a property owner will pay the listing broker a commission if the owner transfers the property to someone the broker originally introduced to the seller. Many listing contracts do contain a multiple listing clause permitting the broker to share the listing with other brokers through the MLS, but states do not usually require such a clause.

Reference: Agency Relationships and Contracts >

Service/Listing Buyer Contracts (contracts between licensee and seller or buyer)

228. All of the following are valid reasons for terminating a listing contract EXCEPT:

A. agreement of the parties.

B. sale of the property.

C. destruction of the premises.

D. death of the salesperson.

Answer: D. The answer is death of the salesperson. A listing contract is a personal service contract between a brokerage and a seller, not between a salesperson and a seller. If the salesperson who secures the listing dies, the listing contract still exists between the brokerage and the seller. A listing contract may be terminated upon the sale or destruction of a property, or by agreement of the parties to the contract, or if the seller or brokerage/broker die.

Reference: Agency Relationships and Contracts >

Service/Listing Buyer Contracts (contracts between licensee and seller or buyer)

229. A buyer who is a client of the broker wants to purchase a house that the broker has listed for sale. Which of the following statements is TRUE?:

A. The seller and buyer must be informed of the situation and agree, usually in writing, to the broker's representing both of them.

B. The broker must treat the buyer as a consumer/customer and proceed to write an offer on the property and submit it.

C. The buyer should not have been shown a house listed by the broker.

D. The broker must refer the buyer to another broker to negotiate the sale.

Answer: A. The answer is the seller and buyer must be informed of the situation and agree, usually in writing, to the broker's representing both of them. Both buyer and seller must give informed consent, generally written, for dual representation. The broker is not required to treat the buyer as a client or to refer the buyer to another broker. In many areas it may be common for buyer-clients to purchase a home listed by their broker, however, both the seller and buyer must agree to the dual agency in writing.

Reference: Agency Relationships and Contracts > Agency Relationships

230. A brokerage firm has an Exclusive-Right-to-Sell listing and represents the owner in the sale of the owner's property. Which of the following events will terminate that agency relationship?:

A. The broker engages other brokers to help sell the property.

B. The owner abandons the property.

C. The owner declares personal bankruptcy.

D. The broker discovers that she will not make an adequate commission due to the low market value of the property.

Answer: C. The answer is the owner declares personal bankruptcy. The bankruptcy of a principal in an agency relationship terminates the agency contract, as title to the property transfers to a court-appointed receiver. The agency relationship remains in effect with any of the other events.

Reference: Agency Relationships and Contracts > Agency Relationships

231. The type of listing contract that provides for payment of a commission to the broker even though the owner makes the sale without the broker's aid is called an:

A. option listing.

B. exclusive-right-to-sell listing.

C. open listing.

D. exclusive-agency listing.

Answer: B. The answer is an exclusive-right-to-sell listing. In an exclusive-right-to-sell listing, if the property is sold while the listing is in effect, the seller must pay the broker a commission regardless of who sells the property. An open listing clause states that any number of brokers may work simultaneously to sell the property, with the commission going to the broker who secures a buyer able to purchase the property. An exclusive-agency listing provides the brokerage firm or a co-op broker will receive a commission if the property sells, but the owner reserves the right to sell the property without owing a commission if the owner sells the property on their own. An option listing permits the broker to retain an option to purchase the property for the broker's own account.

Reference: Agency Relationships and Contracts > Service/Listing Buyer Contracts (contracts between licensee and seller or buyer)

232. A buyer's agent reveals to a listing agent that the buyer is moving into the area for a new job and must be in a new home as soon as possible. The buyer's agent:

A. has violated her duty of confidentiality to the buyer.

B. may share this information with anyone as it is not relevant to the transaction.

C. is required to share this information with the seller or the seller's agent as a material fact relevant to the transaction.

D. terminates the agency relationship by revealing this information to the seller's agent.

Answer: A. The answer is has violated her duty of confidentiality to the buyer. Confidentiality about the principal's personal affairs is an important element of an agent's fiduciary duties. Providing the information to the listing agent may weaken the bargaining power of the buyer. The buyer's agent is not allowed to share confidential information with anyone without explicit permission from the buyer.

Reference: Agency Relationships and Contracts > Agency Relationships

233. The electrical wiring in a house is defective. The broker who listed the house is aware of this and intentionally deceives a potential buyer about it. The buyer purchases the home and later suffers a financial loss due to the faulty wiring. This is an example of:

A. mistake of law.

B. novation.

C. fraud.

D. mistake of fact.

Answer: C. The answer is fraud. Fraud is lying or covering up a known fact. Mistake of law or fact would be when a party does not have knowledge of a situation or material fact. Novations are new contracts.

Reference: Agency Relationships and Contracts > Purchase Contracts (contracts between seller and buyer)

234. If upon receipt of an offer to purchase his property the seller makes a counteroffer, the original offer is:

A. contingent on the counteroffer.

B. binding on the seller but not the buyer.

C. terminated.

D. binding on the buyer but not the seller.

Answer: C. The answer is terminated. When the original offer is rejected by the seller, it ceases to exist and is considered to be terminated. The buyer may accept or reject the seller's counteroffer, which is in effect a new offer.

Reference: Agency Relationships and Contracts > Purchase Contracts (contracts between seller and buyer)

235. A landowner subdivides her acreage and offers the lots for sale. A broker tells her that he can sell the lots. After the broker sells some of the lots, the landowner refuses to pay him a commission. The broker can:

A. do nothing.

B. file a lien against the landowner's remaining lots.

C. report the landowner to the real estate licensing authorities.

D. sue the landowner for breach of contract.

Answer: A. The answer is do nothing. An oral agreement does not constitute a valid agency contract entitling the broker to a commission. Unless the broker has been employed by the seller under a valid written agency contract, the broker is not entitled to a commission. The broker has no grounds for a lien or for a suit. Real estate licensing authorities do not regulate or arbitrate commission disputes between a broker and a prospective client.

Reference: Agency Relationships and Contracts > Service/Listing Buyer Contracts (contracts between licensee and seller or buyer)

236. All of these are essential elements of a contract EXCEPT:

A. earnest money.

B. consideration.

C. a lawful objective.

D. mutual agreement.

Answer: A. The answer is earnest money. The five essential elements of real estate contracts are lawful objective, consideration, mutual agreement, competent parties, and in writing.

Reference: Agency Relationships and Contracts > Purchase Contracts (contracts between seller and buyer)

237. On discovering a latent defect in a property, a salesperson should discuss the problem with the seller and then:

A. tell the seller that the defect must be repaired.

B. contact the city building inspector about the defect.

C. arrange for the repairs.

D. inform any prospective buyers of the defect.

Answer: D. The answer is inform any prospective buyers of the defect. A salesperson or broker is also expected to disclose information about material defects in the property to prospective buyers. The seller is not required to correct the defects, but the salesperson should inform the seller that not repairing the defects may result in lower offers from buyers. The salesperson should not arrange for repairs without explicit instructions from the seller and is not required to contact a city inspector about the defect. The salesperson should be sure that the defect is included in any property inspection report to the buyer if not corrected by the seller.

Reference: Agency Relationships and Contracts > Service/Listing Buyer Contracts (contracts between licensee and seller or buyer)

238. A property manager is hired to manage a property while the owner is overseas for two years. The property manager is a(n):

A. special agent.

B. universal agent.

C. general agent.

D. attorney-in-fact.

Answer: C. The answer is general agent. A general agent may represent a principal in a broad range of matters related to a particular business or activity. A property manager is usually considered a general agent. A special agent may represent a principal in one specific act or business transaction under detailed instructions, such as when an agent represents a seller under a listing agreement. A universal agent is a person empowered through a general power of attorney to do anything the principal could do personally. The power of attorney makes the agent an attorney-in-fact.

Reference: Agency Relationships and Contracts > Agency Relationships

239. An example of specific performance for breaching a real property purchase contract would be:

A. a court action to force compliance with the contract.

B. the forfeiture of the earnest money deposit.

C. damages for the taking of private land for public use.

D. recovery of money lost as a result of the breach.

Answer: A. The answer is a court action to force compliance with the contract. Specific performance means that if one breaks the promise, the other party has the legal right to sue in court to make the defaulting party perform.

Reference: Agency Relationships and Contracts > Purchase Contracts (contracts between seller and buyer)

240. minor signed a sales contract to purchase a home. Which of the following describes this contract?:

A. Valid and binding

B. Void

C. Voidable by the seller

D. Voidable by the minor

Answer: D. The answer is voidable by the minor. Minors who are parties to a contract always make the contract voidable. It is incumbent upon the seller to not allow a minor to enter into a contract. The seller will have to wait for the minor to cancel or move forward.

Reference: Agency Relationships and Contracts > General Legal Principles, Theory and Concepts about Contracts

241. A buyer has signed a contract with a broker to compensate the broker even if the buyer purchases the property from a relative. This is called a(n):

A. open buyer agency contract.

B. exclusive-agency buyer agency contract.

C. invalid contract.

D. exclusive buyer agency contract.

Answer: D. The answer is exclusive buyer agency contract. An exclusive buyer agency contract binds the buyer to compensate the agent whenever the buyer purchases a property of the type described in the contract, even if the buyer finds the property independently. An exclusive-agency buyer agency limits the broker's right to a commission; the broker is entitled to payment only if the broker locates the property the buyer purchases. An open buyer agency contract permits the buyer to enter into similar agreements with an unlimited number of brokers, with commission limited to the broker who locates/procures the property the buyer purchases.

Reference: Agency Relationships and Contracts > Service/Listing Buyer Contracts (contracts between licensee and seller or buyer)

242. An agency relationship in which a broker represents both the seller and the buyer in the same transaction would require all of following EXCEPT:

A. that both the seller and buyer must agree in writing that the broker may share confidential information with the other party.

B. that the principals agree in writing that the broker is representing both sides of the transaction.

C. that the broker will not disclose confidential information about one party to the other party.

D. that commissions are to be collected according to the provisions of agreements with both parties.

Answer: A. The answer is that both the seller and the buyer must agree in writing that the broker may share confidential information with the other party. Real estate licensing laws may permit dual agency only if the buyer and seller are informed and give written consent to the broker's representation of both in the same transaction. The broker may not provide confidential information from one party to the other party in the transaction. Commissions are determined by the listing contracts with both parties or by agreement by both parties upon acceptance of the sales contract.

Reference: Agency Relationships and Contracts > Agency Relationships

243. An executed contract means:

A. only one party to the contract must perform.

B. a party has the right to sue for specific performance.

C. all of the parties have fully performed their duties.

D. contingencies do not have to be met.

Answer: C. The answer is all of the parties have fully performed their duties. An executed contract means all of the parties have fully performed their duties and if a purchase contract title was passed via a deed. The remedies for default, specific performance, or liquidated damages are created in the contract and exist until the contract is executed.

Reference: Agency Relationships and Contracts > General Legal Principles, Theory and Concepts about Contracts

244. All of the following are essential elements of a contract EXCEPT:

A. mutual agreement.

B. words of conveyance.

C. consideration.

D. lawful objective.

Answer: B. The answer is words of conveyance. The essential elements of a valid contract are the following: competent parties, mutual agreement, lawful objective, consideration, and in writing. Words of conveyance are required in deeds.

Reference: Agency Relationships and Contracts > Purchase Contracts (contracts between seller and buyer)

245. Which of the following is NOT required to create a valid sales contract?:

A. Earnest money

B. Signatures

C. Offer and acceptance

D. Consideration

Answer: A. The answer is earnest money. Earnest money is not consideration and is not necessary to create a binding contract.

Reference: Agency Relationships and Contracts > Purchase Contracts (contracts between seller and buyer)

246. A real estate agent acting as a single agent owes either fiduciary or statutory agency duties to any of the following EXCEPT:

A. a seller.

B. a landlord.

C. a customer.

D. a buyer.

Answer: C. The answer is a customer. In single agency, the agent represents only one party in any single transaction. The agent owes fiduciary or statutory agency duties exclusively to one principal, who may be a seller, buyer, landlord, or tenant. The customer is the other party not represented by the agent in the transaction.

Reference: Agency Relationships and Contracts > Agency Relationships

247. A contract for the sale of real estate that does not state the consideration and is not signed by the parties is considered to be:

A. valid.

B. executory.

C. enforceable.

D. void.

Answer: D. The answer is void. A contract is void when no consideration is stated; consideration is an essential element of a contract. An executory contract is one that has been signed by both parties but all the requirements of the contract have not yet been performed. A contract that lacks all the essential elements is not valid but void and unenforceable.

Reference: Agency Relationships and Contracts > Purchase Contracts (contracts between seller and buyer)

248. An amendment to a contract is created:

A. only if using fill-in-the-blank agreements.

B. by adding provisions to an accepted contract.

C. only by attorneys before the closing.

D. before the original contract is written.

Answer: B. The answer is by adding provisions to an accepted contract. An addendum is a change to an original contract. An amendment is created to make changes or to add provisions after the original contract is created.

Reference: Agency Relationships and Contracts > General Legal Principles, Theory and Concepts about Contracts

249. The seller told the buyer that the property had no roof leaks. But when the buyer had the property inspected, a roofing contractor found leaks and said they had been leaking for months. The contract between the seller and the buyer is probably:

A. implied.

B. voidable.

C. valid.

D. void.

Answer: B. The answer is voidable. Duress, fraud, misrepresentation, and minors always make contracts voidable. The seller either misrepresented the property or committed fraud, which means the contract is voidable by the buyer. The buyer may choose to move forward and continue the sale or terminate the contact. If the buyer terminates the seller would have to return the earnest money.

Reference: Agency Relationships and Contracts > General Legal Principles, Theory and Concepts about Contracts

250. During the period of time after a real estate sales contract is signed, but before title actually passes, the status of the contract is:

A. voidable.

B. unilateral.

C. executory.

D. executed.

Answer: C. The answer is executory. An offer becomes an executory contract upon acceptance and executed upon completion of the duties. Duress, fraud, misrepresentation, and minors always make contracts voidable. Only one party is bound in a unilateral contract.

Reference: Agency Relationships and Contracts > General Legal Principles, Theory and Concepts about Contracts

251. A void contract is one that is:

A. does not have earnest money listed as consideration.

B. has all the essential elements of a contract.

C. unenforceable.

D. can be terminated by one party but not the other.

Answer: C. The answer is unenforceable. A void contract lacks some or all of the essential elements of a valid contract and so was never a contract in the eyes of the law. Earnest money is not a requirement of a valid contract so not having earnest money in a contract does not make the contract void. A valid contract can be rescinded by agreement of all parties but is not voidable by an action of only one of the parties.

Reference: Agency Relationships and Contracts > Purchase Contracts (contracts between seller and buyer)

252. A contract that exchanges a promise for performance is:

A. implied.

B. bilateral.

C. executory.

D. unilateral.

Answer: D. The answer is unilateral. In a unilateral contract like an option the seller promises to sell if the buyer decides to buy (perform). Bilateral contracts have both parties promising to each other. An implied contract is created by actions and an executory contract is yet to be performed.

Reference: Agency Relationships and Contracts > General Legal Principles, Theory and Concepts about Contracts

253. The sales contract says the buyer will purchase the property only if an attorney approves the sale by the following Saturday. The attorney's approval is a:

A. contingency.

B. lis pendens.

C. warranty.

D. consideration.

Answer: A. The answer is contingency. A contingency requires something to happen or the contract can be terminated and the earnest money returned. A lis pendens is notice of a pending law suit. A warranty promises that certain stated facts are true. Consideration is one of the essential elements of the contract to make it valid and is something of value offered in exchange for something from another.

Reference: Agency Relationships and Contracts > Purchase Contracts (contracts between seller and buyer)

254. Shortly before closing on her home, a seller learns that her listing broker is related to the buyer. The listing broker has not disclosed that relationship to the seller. If the seller later refuses to pay the listing broker his commission, will the broker likely prevail in a lawsuit to recover the commission?:

A. No, because the broker has violated his fiduciary duties to the seller.

B. Yes, because the disclosure of a relationship between the buyer and the listing broker is not relevant to the transaction.

C. No, because the seller may rescind a listing agreement at any time prior to closing.

D. Yes, because a seller must pay commission if the broker produces a ready, willing, and able buyer.

Answer: A. The answer is no, because the broker has violated his fiduciary duties to the seller. The broker has violated the duty of disclosure to his client, as the relationship may be relevant to the seller's decision to accept the buyer's offer. The broker may have also established an undisclosed dual agency in bringing a relative into the transaction. The broker's actions do not automatically provide the seller with a reason to terminate the listing contract.

Reference: Agency Relationships and Contracts > Agency Relationships

255. All listing agreements must contain a:

A. automatic extension clause.

B. broker protection clause.

C. multiple listing service (MLS) clause.

D. definite contract termination date.

Answer: D. The answer is definite contract termination date. Failing to specify a definite termination date in a listing can be grounds for suspension or revocation of a license. Broker protection clauses, MLS clauses, and automatic extensions of the contract are not required.

Reference: Agency Relationships and Contracts > Service/Listing Buyer Contracts (contracts between licensee and seller or buyer)

256. A broker associate and salesperson of the firm have been found guilty of violating the state real estate license law and have had their real estate licenses revoked. In this case the principal broker:

A. may be found guilty of improper supervision.

B. should not be concerned since broker associates do not need to be supervised.

C. would most likely have to pay a civil fine in addition to having his license revoked.

D. might have to make a claim against his E&O insurance.

Answer: A. The answer is may be found guilty of improper supervision. A principal broker is responsible to supervise all licensees in the firm. Errors and Omissions (E&O) insurance would not cover this type of issue. Civil fines are created in civil court not through a hearing at a real estate Commission.

Reference: Agency Relationships and Contracts > Service/Listing Buyer Contracts (contracts between licensee and seller or buyer)

257. A contract between two parties that legally binds one party to perform, but allows the other party to disaffirm it, is:

A. bilateral.

B. executed.

C. voidable.

D. void.

Answer: C. The answer is voidable. Voidable contracts have one side obligated but the other party able to rescind the contract if they wish. A contract with a minor is always voidable for example if an adult agrees to buy a property a minor owns the contract is voidable by the minor. Executed contracts are closed and completed. Void contracts lack an essential element and bilateral contracts exchange promises.

Reference: Agency Relationships and Contracts > General Legal Principles, Theory and Concepts about Contracts

258. When hiring an employee rather than an independent contractor, a broker is obligated to:

A. give paid vacations.

B. not split commissions.

C. withhold employment taxes.

D. guarantee a set schedule.

Answer: C. The answer is withhold employment taxes. A broker hiring an employee must withhold from the employee's wages employment taxes such as income and social security taxes. The broker is not required to give paid vacations, guarantee a set schedule, or split commissions, but may do so if agreed to by both the broker and the employee.

Reference: Agency Relationships and Contracts > Service/Listing Buyer Contracts (contracts between licensee and seller or buyer)

259. A seller accepts the buyer's offer to purchase his property. Before closing, the seller changes his mind, and the buyer sues for specific performance. What is the buyer seeking in this lawsuit?:

A. New contract

B. Deficiency judgment

C. Conveyance of the property

D. Money damages

Answer: C. The answer is conveyance of the property. A suit for specific performance is a lawsuit to require the breaching party perform as promised, in this case for the seller to sell the home. A suit for specific performance will not result in a new contract, deficiency judgment, or money damages for the buyer.

Reference: Agency Relationships and Contracts > Purchase Contracts (contracts between seller and buyer)

260. A broker would have the right to dictate which of the following to an independent contractor?:

A. Work schedule the person would have to follow

B. Sales meetings the person would need to attend

C. Number of hours the person would have to work

D. Compensation the person would receive

Answer: D. The answer is compensation the person would receive. Brokers may dictate the compensation their independent contractors will receive for work not yet done, but they may not dictate working schedules or sales meetings to be attended. The Internal Revenue Service would most likely classify persons employed with defined work schedules, including the numbers of hours worked, and required sales meetings as employees rather than independent contractors for income tax purposes.

Reference: Agency Relationships and Contracts > Service/Listing Buyer Contracts (contracts between licensee and seller or buyer)

261. A contract that conveys the right to quiet enjoyment and use of property but does NOT convey title is a:

A. lease.

B. bill of sale.

C. quitclaim deed.

D. dedication.

Answer: A. The answer is lease. Lease contacts give a tenant the owner's right of possession in exchange for rent. A bill of sale, deed, and dedication are not contracts.

Reference: Agency Relationships and Contracts > Purchase Contracts (contracts between seller and buyer)

262. The principal to whom an agent gives professional opinions and counsel is a:

A. subagent.

B. fiduciary.

C. client.

D. customer.

Answer: C. The answer is client. The client is the principal to whom the agent owes fiduciary duties. The customer is the third party or non-represented consumer for whom some level of service is provided and who is entitled to fairness and honesty. A subagent is the agent of a person already acting as an agent for the client.

263. Last month a broker took a listing on a property. She now learns that her client has been declared incompetent by the court. Her listing now is:

A. the basis for a commission if the broker produces a buyer.

B. terminated.

C. binding as the broker was acting in good faith.

D. still valid.

Answer: B. The answer is terminated. A listing contract may be terminated if either party dies or becomes incapacitated. Once terminated, the contract is not binding, and there is no basis for a commission to the broker.

Reference: Agency Relationships and Contracts > Service/Listing Buyer Contracts (contracts between licensee and seller or buyer)

264. Breach of contract is refusal or failure to comply with the terms of a contract. If the seller breaches the purchase contract, the buyer may do all of the following EXCEPT:

A. sue the seller for specific performance.

B. sue the seller for damages.

C. sue the broker for nonperformance.

D. rescind the contract and recover the earnest money.

Answer: C. The answer is sue the broker for nonperformance. The broker is not a party to a real estate purchase contract and could not be sued for nonperformance in the event of a seller breach. The buyer may take any of the other actions stated in the remaining answers.

Reference: Agency Relationships and Contracts > Purchase Contracts (contracts between seller and buyer)

265. A real estate broker's responsibility to keep the principal informed of all of the facts that could affect a transaction is the duty of:

A. obedience.

B. care.

C. accounting.

D. disclosure.

Answer: D. The answer is disclosure. It is the real estate professional's duty to keep the consumer informed of all facts or information that could affect a transaction. The broker also owes the principal care and accounting. The broker must act with reasonable care while acting on behalf of the consumer.

Reference: Agency Relationships and Contracts > Agency Relationships

266. Which of the following gives the BEST evidence of the buyer's intention to carry out the terms of the real estate purchase contract?:

A. The provision that "time is of the essence."

B. The earnest money deposit.

C. The agreement to seek mortgage financing.

D. he "subject to" clause.

Answer: B. The answer is the earnest money deposit. The earnest money deposit is customary in real estate transactions to provide evidence of a buyer's intention to carry out the terms of the contract in good faith. It is also the seller's only remedy in a liquidated damages contract. A buyer may pay cash and not require mortgage financing, so an earnest money deposit is the best evidence of the buyer's intention to purchase, even though earnest money is not consideration and not required to have a valid sales contract. The "subject to" clause and the "time is of the essence" clause do not relate to the buyer's intentions but are requirements of the contract.

Reference: Agency Relationships and Contracts > Purchase Contracts (contracts between seller and buyer)

267. All of the following are true about contingencies EXCEPT:

A. they must identify who will pay for any costs involved.

B. they must be met within the time given in the contract.

C. common contingencies include finance and inspection contingencies.

D. they must be worded loosely to allow reasonable satisfaction.

Answer: D. The answer is they must be worded loosely to allow reasonable satisfaction. Contingencies create a voidable contract; if the contingencies are rejected or not satisfied, the contract is void. A loosely worded contingency that is not specific and detailed may create an unenforceable contract.

Reference: Agency Relationships and Contracts > Purchase Contracts (contracts between seller and buyer)

268. A minor inherited a commercial real estate property and has entered into a sales contract with a buyer to

purchase the property. In this situation, the sales contract is considered to be:

A. legal and binding because it was an inheritance.

B. voidable by the minor.

C. voidable by the buyer.

D. unenforceable by the buyer.

Answer: B. The answer is voidable by the minor. A contract with a minor is always voidable, in this case by the minor.

Reference: Agency Relationships and Contracts > General Legal Principles, Theory and Concepts about Contracts

269. Which statement is TRUE of a listing contract?:

A. It obligates the brokerage firm to work diligently for both the seller and the buyer.

B. A seller must transfer the property if the brokerage firm produces a ready, willing, and able buyer.

C. The contract usually includes an automatic extension clause upon expiration of its term.

D. The contract is an employment contract for the professional services of a brokerage firm.

Answer: D. The answer is the contract is an employment contract for the professional services of a brokerage firm. The listing contract obligates the brokerage firm to work only for the seller. The seller may negotiate terms through the brokerage with a ready, willing, and able buyer, and refuse to sell to a buyer who is not willing to come to terms with the seller. A contract usually specifies a definite termination date and may not include an automatic extension of the term.

Reference: Agency Relationships and Contracts > Service/Listing Buyer Contracts (contracts between licensee and seller or buyer)

270. All of the following events terminate an agency relationship EXCEPT:

A. destruction of the property.

B. an appraisal with a value less than the selling price.

C. completion of the purpose of the agency.

D. bankruptcy of the principal.

Answer: B. The answer is an appraisal with a value less than the selling price. If an appraisal reveals a market value less than the stated selling price in a contract, the parties will have to renegotiate their contract if both parties are still interested in the sale. The appraisal does not affect any agency relationship. Completion of the agency's purpose, destruction of the property, and bankruptcy of the principal terminate an agency relationship.

Reference: Agency Relationships and Contracts > Agency Relationships

271. The listing contract on a residential property states that it expires on May 2. Which event would NOT terminate the listing?:

A. The owner dies on April 29.

B. The contract is not renewed prior to May 2.

C. The house is destroyed by fire on

D. On April 15, the owner tells the listing broker that the owner is dissatisfied with the broker's marketing efforts.

Answer: D. The answer is on April 15, the owner tells the listing broker that the owner is dissatisfied with the broker's marketing efforts. A mere complaint to the broker by the principal does not end the listing, whereas expiration of the listing with no renewal, death of the owner, or destruction of the property would end the listing.

Reference: Agency Relationships and Contracts > Service/Listing Buyer Contracts (contracts between licensee and seller or buyer)

272. Designated agency will most likely occur under what circumstance?:

A. The buyer is a client of the firm and the seller is the customer of the firm.

B. The buyer and the seller in the same transaction are both represented by the same brokerage firm.

C. Both the buyer and the seller are customers of the firm.

D. The seller and the buyer are represented by different brokerage firms.

Answer: B. The answer is the buyer and the seller in the same transaction are both represented by the same brokerage firm. Designated agency occurs when one brokerage firm practices dual agency in representing both the seller and the buyer in the same transaction. Both parties are clients of the firm. In many states, designated agency is a process that permits the firm's broker to appoint one agent to represent the seller, and another agent from the same firm to represent the buyer. Each of the agents is a designated agency for her respective client, the seller or the buyer and may not share confidential information about the party they represent.

Reference: Agency Relationships and Contracts > Agency Relationships

273. Who is ultimately responsible for a salesperson's mistakes in writing a sales contract?:

A. The salesperson's office manager.

B. The salesperson's principal broker.

C. The managing associate broker.

D. The salesperson and the managing associate broker.

Answer: B. The answer is the salesperson's principal broker. A real estate brokerage firm's principal broker has ultimate responsibility for all activities of the real estate licensees in the firm. Salespersons may be held accountable for any of their mistakes in a sales contract, but the principal broker holds ultimate responsibility for the salesperson's actions. A managing broker or office manager may share responsibility for the salesperson's actions.

Reference: Agency Relationships and Contracts > Service/Listing Buyer Contracts (contracts between licensee and seller or buyer)

274. Under the provisions of the Electronic Signatures in Global and National Commerce Act (ESIGN Act):

A. businesses must retain evidence of contractual agreements signed in electronic format.

B. every type of documentation is covered and can be approved electronically.

C. consumers may not withdraw their consent to the electronic contracting process.

D. consumers do not have to give prior consent to the electronic contracting process.

Answer: A. The answer is businesses must retain evidence of contractual agreements signed in electronic format. Evidence must be maintained to fulfill legislative requirements and to clarify any future questions about the legitimacy of a contract or the details of specific terms. This is true whether a document is in paper or electronic format.

Reference: Agency Relationships and Contracts > General Legal Principles, Theory and Concepts about Contracts

275. The final decision on a property's listing price should be made by the:

A. seller's attorney.

B. appraiser.

C. listing broker.

D. seller.

Answer: D. The answer is seller. The seller must determine the listing price of the seller's property. It is the responsibility of the broker to advise and assist the seller in making that decision. A broker or salesperson may use a competitive market analysis (CMA) to help the seller determine a reasonable listing price.

Reference: Agency Relationships and Contracts > Service/Listing Buyer Contracts (contracts between licensee and seller or buyer)

276. The status of a contract that meets all the essential elements and is enforceable is called a(n):

A. valid contract.

B. voidable contract.

C. unenforceable contract.

D. void contract.

Answer: A. The answer is valid contract. When a contract meets all of the essential elements and is enforceable, it is a valid contract. Duress, fraud, misrepresentation, and minors always make contracts voidable. Void or unenforceable real estate contracts lack an essential element and do not exist in the eyes of the court for enforcement.

Reference: Agency Relationships and Contracts > General Legal Principles, Theory and Concepts about Contracts

277. A buyer's agent duty of care to a buyer includes all of the following EXCEPT:

A. helping the buyer to evaluate a seller's counteroffer.

B. helping the buyer to locate a suitable property.

C. sharing with a listing agent that the buyer is willing to pay more for the property.

D. evaluating neighborhood and property conditions.

Answer: C. The answer is sharing with a listing agent that the buyer is willing to pay more for the property. Sharing with a seller how much a buyer is willing to pay for a property violates the buyer's agent's duty of care and confidentiality to the buyer-client. All of the other activities are examples of a buyer's agent exercising the duty of care for the buyer.

Reference: Agency Relationships and Contracts > Agency Relationships

278. In most real estate brokerage firms, a real estate salesperson may expect to work:

A. a minimum forty-

B. for two principal brokers at the same time.

C. on salary with an employee benefit plan.

D. on a commission based on the salesperson's productivity.

Answer: D. The answer is on a commission based on the salesperson's productivity. Most brokers hire salespersons as independent contractors with a commission payment plan based on the salesperson's participation in sales and/or rentals. A broker may not pay an independent contractor any company benefits, or mandate regular work hours or meetings for the independent contractor. A salesperson may work only for one principal broker at a time.

Reference: Agency Relationships and Contracts > Service/Listing Buyer Contracts (contracts between licensee and seller or buyer)

279. A listing agent is frustrated that a property has been on the market for over two months, and the agent wants to sell the home quickly. The listing agent shares with a non-represented buyer that the home has been on the market for

a long time, so the seller would welcome any offer on the home. The buyer makes an offer at a price lower than he had expected to offer. Has the agent violated any duties to the seller?:

A. Yes, the agent has violated his fiduciary duty because license law prohibits any discussion of how long a property has been on the market.

B. No, because the agent has served the seller's interest by producing a ready, willing, and able buyer.

C. No, because the agent is not required to disclose that information to any party in the transaction.

D. Yes, the agent has violated his fiduciary duty by disclosing a fact that could benefit the buyer.

Answer: D. The answer is yes, the agent has violated his fiduciary duty by disclosing a fact that could benefit the buyer. The agent has duties of care and loyalty to the seller, and although he must disclose any material fact to a buyer, disclosing this information directly benefits the buyer. The license law does not prohibit or require disclosing information about how long a property has been on the market. The license laws of most states do require agents to disclose any material facts to clients and customers.

280. The listing contract on a residential property states that it expires on June 30. Which event would NOT terminate the listing?:

A. The listing contract is not renewed prior to June 30.

B. The house is destroyed by fire on June 1.

C. The owner dies on April 29.

D. The salesperson who signed the listing dies on March 15.

Answer: D. The answer is the salesperson who signed the listing dies on March 15. The salesperson is not a party to the contract so his death would not terminate the contract. A listing contract is terminated if one of the parties to the agreement dies; if the property is destroyed by a force outside the seller's control; or if the listing contract's term expires.

Reference: Agency Relationships and Contracts >

Service/Listing Buyer Contracts (contracts between licensee and seller or buyer)

281. A broker helps a buyer and a seller with paperwork but does not have fiduciary obligations to either party. The broker's activity in this situation is that of a:

A. dual age

B. transaction broker.

C. single agent.

D. design

Answer: B. The answer is transaction broker. In some states, a broker may be an agent of neither party to a transaction, but help both the buyer and the seller with necessary paperwork and formalities in a transaction. The broker acts as a transaction broker or facilitator but not as an agent of either party.

Reference: Agency Relationships and Contracts > Agency Relationships

282. If, upon the receipt of an offer to purchase a property, the seller makes a counteroffer, the prospective buyer is:

A. relieved of the offer which is now void.

B. relieved of the original offer which has terminated.

C. bound to accept the counteroffer.

D. bound by the original offer which is still active.

Answer: B. The answer is relieved of the original offer which has terminated. Countering an offer terminates the original offer and creates a new offer. The original offer is terminated not void.

Reference: Agency Relationships and Contracts > Purchase Contracts (contracts between seller and buyer)

1. Federal income tax regulations allow homeowners to reduce their taxable income by amounts paid for:

A. real estate property taxes.

B. hazard insurance premiums.

C. repairs and maintenance.

D. both principal and interest.

Answer: A. The answer is real estate property taxes. Real estate property taxes, mortgage interest, points for loans, and some origination fees can be deducted on income tax returns. The law does not permit tax deductions for ordinary repairs, home maintenance, and hazard insurance premiums.

Reference: Finance > Lending Process

2. A seller agrees to sell a house to a buyer for $100,000. The buyer is unable to qualify for a mortgage loan for this

amount, so the seller and buyer enter into a contract for deed. The legal interest the buyer has in the property under a contract for deed is:

A. joint title.

B. legal title.

C. equitable title.

D. bare title.

Answer: C. The answer is equitable title. The buyer in a contract for deed holds equitable title to the property. Equitable title gives the borrower the rights of possession and use of the property, while the seller retains the legal title during the contract term. If the buyer defaults, the seller can evict the buyer and keep any money the buyer has already paid, which is considered rent.

Reference: Finance > Methods of Financing

3. A homeowner has owned her house for over 50 years. It has fallen into disrepair, but because she lives on a fixed

income, she does not have the money to make the needed repairs. She has a considerable amount of equity in the house. What type of loan would BEST provide her the funds to make the necessary repairs?:

A. Reverse-mortgage

B. Home equity loan

C. Open-end loan

D. Blanket loan

Answer: A. The answer is reverse-mortgage. A reverse mortgage allows people 62 years of age or older who have considerable equity in their homes to borrow money against that equity. No payments are due until the property is sold or the borrower defaults, moves, or dies. A home equity loan uses the equity in the home as a source of loans but requires monthly payments of principal and interest that may be burdensome to older persons on a fixed income. A blanket loan covers more than one parcel or lot and permits the borrower to obtain a release of a parcel or lot from the mortgage lien when the lot is sold. An open-end mortgage is an expandable loan in which borrowers are given a limit up to which they may borrow, with each advance secured by the same mortgage.

4. A broker was accused of violating antitrust laws. Of the following, he was MOST likely accused of:

A. not having an equal housing opportunity sign in her office window.

B. price-fixing.

C. blockbusting in a community.

D. undisclosed dual agencies.

Answer: B. The answer is price-fixing. Antitrust laws prohibit competing brokers from setting a standard commission rate, a practice known as price-fixing. Practicing undisclosed dual agency would violate agency law. Not posting the required fair housing sign in her office violates fair housing law. Blockbusting is violating fair housing laws not antitrust laws.

Reference: Finance > Government Oversight

5. A purchaser negotiates a mortgage loan in which she will make equal monthly payments over a period of 30 years, with the balance of the loan being zero at the end of that term. The purchaser has negotiated a(n):

A. partially-amortized loan.

B. straight mortgage.

C. balloon mortgage.

D. fully-amortized loan.

Answer: D. The answer is fully-amortized loan. A loan with equal, constant payments which result in a zero balance at the end of the term is a fully-amortized loan. A balloon mortgage is one type of partially-amortized loan. In a partially-amortized loan, the principal and interest payments do not pay off the entire loan; a balance remains and is due at the end of the term. A straight mortgage is a loan that requires periodic interest payments to the lender but nothing is applied to the principal balance. A construction loan is a type of straight loan in which the borrower receives money in draws and makes periodic payments of interest on those draws.

Reference: Finance > Basic Concepts and Terminology

6. A borrower obtained a $7,000 second mortgage loan for five years at a 6% interest annual interest rate. Monthly payments of principal and interest were $50. The final payment included the remaining outstanding principal balance. What type of loan is this?:

A. Accelerated loan

B. Partially amortized loan

C. Fully amortized loan

D. Straight loan

Answer: B. The answer is partially amortized loan. A partially amortized loan is a loan with a partial balloon payment. Principal is still owed at the end of the term, because periodic payments are not enough to fully amortize the loan and the final payment is larger than the others. A straight or interest only is a loan in which the borrower makes periodic payments of interest only, followed by a lump sum balloon payment of the full principal at the end of the term. In a fully amortized loan, the borrower pays both principal and interest in equal periodic payments over the life of the loan. An accelerated loan is a loan paid-off early in which the borrower pays the full balance owed at a time of default, sale of the property, or to redeem the property prior to foreclosure.

Reference: Finance > Basic Concepts and Terminology

7. To increase yield on a loan, the lender charges:

A. discount points rates.

B. origination fees and points prepayment fees.

C. loan origination fees.

D. setup fees interest.

Answer: A. The answer is discount points rates. The lender charges the borrower discount points to increase the yield, the true rate of return required by investors. Discount rates increase the lender's yield on loans. Loan origination fees cover the lender's costs in generating a loan. Interest is a charge for the use of the lender's money. A lender may recover unearned interest for payments made ahead of schedule by charging a prepayment penalty to a borrower who pays off a loan early.

Reference: Finance > Basic Concepts and Terminology

8. The total balance due on a mortgage loan is the:

A. principal.

B. interest.

C. equity.

D. rate of return.

Answer: A. The answer is principal. In finance terminology the principal is the balance owed on the original loan amount. The interest is the charge for the use of the money. The rate of return is the return on the investment in a property, one way to measure its profitability. An owner's equity is the amount of money remaining once current liens, including the mortgage, are subtracted from the current market value of the property.

9. The term of a loan is the:

A. years required to pay private mortgage insurance.

B. time required to underwrite the loan.

C. length of time the borrower has to repay the loan.

D. time period in which a borrower may cancel a loan contract.

Answer: C. The answer is length of time the borrower has to repay the loan. For residential loans, a borrower generally negotiates with the lender a term of between fifteen to thirty years. A longer term to repay the loan results in a lower monthly payment. A shorter term results in a higher monthly payment.

Reference: Finance > Basic Concepts and Terminology

10. A borrower has just made the final payment to her lender for her home's mortgage. A lien on her property will remain until the lender records a(n):

A. alienation of mortgage.

B. reconveyance of mortgage.

C. reversion of mortgage.

D. satisfaction of mortgage.

Answer: D. The answer is satisfaction of mortgage. A satisfaction of mortgage, also known as a release or discharge, is executed by the lender when a note has been fully paid. This document returns to the borrower all ownership interest in the real estate originally conveyed to the lender. This release must be recorded in the public record to show that the debt has been removed from the property.

Reference: Finance > Financing Instruments (Mortgages, Trust Deeds, Promissory Notes)

11. With a construction loan the borrower makes:

A. periodic payments of interest during the construction period.

B. principal payments only during the construction period.

C. monthly payments of interest and part of the principal.

D. constant payments of principal and interest during the construction period.

Answer: A. The answer is periodic payments of interest during the construction period. A construction loan is a type of non-amortized loan in which periodic interest payments are made to the lender but nothing is applied during the construction period to the principal balance. When the construction is complete, the borrower must secure long-term financing that will pay off the entire principal balance.

Reference: Finance > Methods of Financing

12. According to TRID rules, when must the Closing Disclosure be given to consumers?:

A. Within three business days after the loan application is submitted by the consumer

B. At least three business days before the closing

C. Three business days after the Loan Estimate Disclosure Form is given to the consumers

D. Three business days after the sales contract is signed

Answer: B. The answer is at least three business days before the closing. The creditor is responsible for ensuring the borrower (consumer) receives the form no later than three business days before consummation of the loan. Consumation is typically the day of closing.

Reference: Finance > Government Oversight

13. When a homeowner with an existing mortgage gets a home equity loan to consolidate existing credit card loans, the:

A. original mortgage loan remains in place.

B. lender will usually require the homeowner to refinance the existing mortgage.

C. home equity loan amount is added to the existing mortgage balance.

D. home equity loan takes a senior position to the original mortgage.

Answer: A. The answer is original mortgage loan remains in place. Home equity loans are a source of funds using the equity built up in a home and are an alternative to refinancing an existing mortgage. The original mortgage loan remains in place, and the home equity loan takes a junior position to the original mortgage lien. The home equity loan is a separate loan contract, with its own balance and repayment schedule.

Reference: Finance > Methods of Financing

14. Which law requires any advertisement that references mortgage financing terms to contain certain disclosures?:

A. Fair Housing Act

B. Equal Credit Opportunity Act

C. Real Estate Settlement Procedures Act

D. Truth in Lending Act

Answer: D. The answer is Truth in Lending Act. Truth in Lending Act requires that trigger terms about mortgage financing in any kind of advertising must also include additional disclosures in the advertisement. The Fair Housing Act prohibits discrimination against protected classes in residential real estate advertising and practice. RESPA (Real Estate Settlement Procedures Act) deals with closings and settlement and does not apply to advertisement. The Equal Credit Opportunity Act prohibits lenders and others who grant or arrange credit to consumers from discriminating against protected credit applicants.

Reference: Finance > Government Oversight

15. An individual who obtains a real estate loan and signs a note and a mortgage is known as the:

A. optionee.

B. mortgagor.

C. optionor.

D. mortgagee.

Answer: B. The answer is mortgagor. The borrower who receives a loan and in return gives a note and mortgage to the lender is the mortgagor. The lender is called the mortgagee. An optionor is an owner who gives an optionee, a prospective purchaser or lessee, the right to buy or lease the owner's property at a fixed price within a certain period of time.

Reference: Finance > Lending Process

16. According to TRID disclosure rules, when must the Loan Estimate form be provided to consumers?:

A. No later than three calender days prior to the closing

B. No later than three business days after the loan application is received by the lender

C. No later than three calender days after the loan application is received by the lender

D. No later than three business days prior to the closing

Answer: C. The answer is no later than three business days after the loan application is received by the lender. A business day includes Saturdays the lender is open for business.

Reference: Finance > Government OversightThe answer is no later than three business days after the loan application is received by the lender. A business day includes Saturdays the lender is open for business.

Reference: Finance > Government OversightThe answer is no later than three business days after the loan application is received by the lender. A business day includes Saturdays the lender is open for business.

Reference: Finance > Government Oversight

17. What is the major difference between conventional and government loans?:

A. A government loan is sold on the secondary market, while a conventional loan is not.

B. A conventional loan is sold on the secondary market, while a loan is not.

C. A conventional loan is guaranteed or insured by the government, while a government loan is not.

D. A government loan is insured or guaranteed by the government, while a conventional loan is not.

Answer: D. The answer is a government loan is insured or guaranteed by the government, while a conventional loan is not. Government loans, such as FHA or VA loans, are insured or guaranteed by the government. Conventional loans are not insured or guaranteed by the government. Both government and conventional loans may be sold on the secondary market.

Reference: Finance > Methods of Financing

18. When real estate is sold under an installment land contract and the buyer takes possession of the property, the legal title is:

A. transferred to a land trustee.

B. transferred to the buyer.

C. kept by the seller until the purchase price is paid according to the contract.

D. subject to a purchase-money mortgage.

Answer: C. The answer is kept by the seller until the purchase price is paid according to the contract. In a land contract, the seller retains legal title to the property during the contract term, and the buyer is granted equitable title and possession. At the end of the loan term, the seller delivers a clear title to the buyer.

Reference: Finance > Methods of FinancingThe answer is kept by the seller until the purchase price is paid according to the contract. In a land contract, the seller retains legal title to the property during the contract term, and the buyer is granted equitable title and possession. At the end of the loan term, the seller delivers a clear title to the buyer.

Reference: Finance > Methods of Financing

19. The clause in a mortgage instrument that would prevent the assumption of the mortgage by a new purchaser is a(n):

A. due-on-sale clause.

B. acceleration clause.

C. defeasance clause.

D. power of sale clause.

Answer: A. The answer is due-on-sale clause. A due-on-sale clause, or alienation clause, provides that when property is sold, the lender may either declare the entire debt due immediately or permit the buyer to assume the loan at an interest rate acceptable to the lender. The due-on-sale clause allows the lender to prevent a future purchaser of the property from being able to assume the loan, particularly if the original interest rate is low. A defeasance clause requires a lender to execute a satisfaction of mortgage once the loan has been fully repaid. The acceleration clause is used if the borrower is in default.

Reference: Finance > Financing Instruments (Mortgages, Trust Deeds, Promissory Notes)

20. A couple refinances their home with a new lender under a new loan agreement. They currently have a separate line of credit under their original lender. The original lender granting the line of credit agrees to take a second lien position on the property, granting first position to the new lender. The lenders have made this arrangement through a(n):

A. acceleration clause.

B. subordination agreement.

C. defeasance clause.

D. due-on-sale clause.

Answer: B. The answer is subordination agreement. The lenders sign a subordination agreement which places the line of credit in a junior position to the new loan created through the refinancing of the property. A defeasance clause requires a lender to execute a satisfaction (release or discharge) of a loan when the borrower fully pays off the loan. A due-on-sale clause provides that when the property is sold the lender may declare the entire debt due or permit the buyer to assume the loan. The acceleration clause in a mortgage permits the lender to declare the entire debt due and payable immediately if the borrower defaults on payments.

Reference: Finance > Financing Instruments (Mortgages, Trust Deeds, Promissory Notes)

21. When a person buys a house using a mortgage loan, the difference between the amount owed on the property and its market value represents the homeowner's:

A. capital gain.

B. equity.

C. replacement cost.

D. tax basis.

Answer: B. The answer is equity. Equity is created by a down payment and is the portion of the property held free of any mortgage. An owner's equity increases as a loan is paid down. The tax basis of a property is the amount of money the owner invests in the property. Replacement cost is one way to look at the construction cost of a building for appraisal purposes. It is the cost required to construct an improvement similar to the subject property using current materials and standards. Capital gain is the taxable gain from the sale of a property, the difference between the sales price and the tax basis of the property.

Reference: Finance > Basic Concepts and Terminology

22. Two salespersons both work for the same real estate firm. One afternoon they agree to divide their town into a northern region and a southern region. One will handle listings in the northern region, and the other will handle listings in the southern region. Their agreement:

A. is an illegal boycott of other salespeople in their office.

B. violates the Sherman Antitrust Act and makes the salespersons liable for triple damages.

C. constitutes illegal price-fixing.

D. does not violate antitrust laws.

Answer: D. The answer is does not violate antitrust laws. Antitrust laws prohibit price-fixing and other antitrust activities between competing firms. Because both salespersons work for the same firm, their agreement is not an agreement between competing companies to divide markets. The salespersons are merely fixing responsibilities within one company. Their agreement is quite proper and not subject to antitrust law.

Reference: Finance > Government Oversight

23. A couple purchased a home for cash over 25 years ago. Today they receive monthly checks from a lender that supplement their retirement income. The couple most likely have obtained a(n):

A. interest-only loan.

B. adjustable-rate mortgage.

C. reverse mortgage.

D. home equity loan.

Answer: C. The answer is reverse mortgage. A reverse mortgage allows people 62 or older to borrow money against the equity they have built in their home. The borrower is charged a fixed rate of interest and no payments are due until the property is sold or the borrower defaults, moves, or die. Adjustable-rate mortgages and interest-only loans require payments on the loans and do not provide any income to the borrower during the life of the loan. In a home equity loan, a borrower uses the equity built up in the home as a source of cash; the original mortgage remains in place, with the home equity loan being junior to the original lien.

Reference: Finance > Methods of Financing

24. A homeowner has equity in their property and would like to consolidate some of his debt. Which of the following loans would be the best for the homeowner?:

A. A new term loan

B. A home equity loan

C. A reverse mortgage

D. An ARM loan

Answer: B. The answer is a home equity loan. This loan is designed to allow the homeowner to tap into equity to pay off bills. A reverse mortgage may only be used by those over 62 and would not consolidate debt. A term and an ARM loan would not be used in this situation.

Reference: Finance > Methods of Financing

25. The provision in a mortgage or deed of trust that permits the lender upon the default of the borrower to proceed to a foreclosure sale without a court action is the:

A. acceleration clause.

B. power-of-sale clause.

C. alienation clause.

D. hypothecation.

Answer: B. The answer is power-of-sale clause. A power-of-sale clause in a mortgage permits the lender to foreclose and sell a mortgaged property that is in default without any court action. An acceleration clause permits the lender to demand payment of a loan balance immediately when a buyer defaults on mortgage payments. An alienation clause permits the lender to require payment of a loan balance when a buyer sells the property to another purchaser. Hypothecation is the pledging of specific real property as security for a debt while maintaining possession of the property.

Reference: Finance > Financing Instruments (Mortgages, Trust Deeds, Promissory Notes)

26. Funds for Federal Housing Administration (FHA) loans are usually provided by:

A. the FHA.

B. the Federal Reserve

C. the seller.

D. qualified lenders.

Answer: C. The answer is qualified lenders. An FHA loan is insured by the FHA, and funds must be made available by FHA-approved lenders. Funds are not provided by the Federal

Reserve, the FHA, or the seller.

Reference: Finance > Methods of Financing

27. What is the definition of "business day" for purposes of the three-business-day time frame to issue a Loan Estimate under the TRID rules?:

A. Monday through Saturday

B. Any day the lender's offices are open to the public for conducting business

C. Any calender day except national holidays

D. Monday through Friday

Answer: B. The answer is any day the lender's offices are open to the public for conducting business. The Loan Estimate must be delivered to the consumer within three business days of the lender's receipt of the loan application.

Reference: Finance > Government Oversight

28. A borrower defaulted on a loan and the lender foreclosed. The lender obtained the property, which sold for less than what the borrower owed. In this case the lender may:

A. file for a default judgment and attach all the borrower's real and personal property .

B. start a new foreclose suit to collect the balance due from the borrower.

C. do nothing since the property has gone through foreclosure.

D. seek a deficiency judgment, which can be used to collect the balance owed.

Answer: D. The answer is seek a deficiency judgment, which can be used to collect the balance owed. After the buyer defaulted and the loan has been foreclosed, lenders may seek deficiency judgments.

Reference: Finance > Financing Instruments (Mortgages, Trust Deeds, Promissory Notes)

29. Fannie Mae is an agency that:

A. buys mostly FHA loans.

B. operates mostly in the primary mortgage market.

C. guarantees payment of Freddie Mac mortgages.

D. operates mostly in the secondary mortgage market.

Answer: D. The answer is operates mostly in the secondary mortgage market. Fannie Mae provides a secondary market for mortgage loans. Fannie Mae does buy FHA loans but deals primarily in conventional loans. Fannie Mae does not provide loans in the primary mortgage market or guarantee payment of loans.

Reference: Finance > Lending Process

30. A lender will take certain factors into consideration when deciding whether to grant a borrower a mortgage

loan. A decision based on which factor is a violation of the Equal Credit Opportunity Act (ECOA)?:

A. Ability of the borrower to make the payments

B. Amount of the borrower's income

C. Creditworthiness of the borrower

D. Age of the borrower

Answer: D. The answer is age of the borrower. ECOA prohibits lenders from discriminating against credit applicants on the basis of several factors, including age, race, sex, and marital status. A lender may consider a borrower's income, creditworthiness, and ability to make payments in determining whether or not to make a loan.

Reference: Finance > Government Oversight

31. A contract for deed provides for the:

A. sale of unimproved land only.

B. sale of real property under an option agreement.

C. immediate transfer of legal title to the buyer at closing.

D. conveyance of legal title at a future date.

Answer: D. The answer is conveyance of legal title at a future date. In a contract for deed, the seller retains legal title to the property. When the buyer pays off the loan and all requirements under the land contract have been met, the buyer receives legal title to the property. A land contract may be used in the sale of improved and unimproved land. The buyer receives possession upon closing of the contract but will not get legal title until the final payment is made.

Reference: Finance > Methods of Financing

32. The borrower with a construction loan receives the loaned amount in:

A. two payments at the beginning and at the end of the construction period.

B. stages, called draws, during the construction period.

C. one sum at the beginning of the construction period.

D. one sum at the end of the construction period.

Answer: B. The answer is stages, called draws, during the construction period. With a construction loan, the borrower receives money in stages, called draws, and makes periodic payments of interest. At the end of the construction period, the borrower must secure long-term financing to pay off the entire balance of the loan.

Reference: Finance > Methods of Financing

33. The loan-to-value ratio (LTV) may be defined as the ratio of a mortgage loan principal to the:

A. interest rate on the loan.

B. property's value.

C. listed price of the property.

D. assessed value of the property.

Answer: B. The answer is property's value. Mortgage loans are generally classified based on their LTV, which is the ratio of the mortgage loan principal to the value of the property. The value the lender will use is the sales price or the appraised value, whichever is less.

Reference: Finance > Basic Concepts and Terminology

34. Many states permit a mortgagors to redeem their property after default but before a foreclosure sale. This right is called a(n):

A. owner's right of redemption.

B. mortgagee's right of redemption.

C. equitable right of redemption.

D. statutory right of redemption.

Answer: C. The answer is equitable right of redemption. If a borrower in default pays the lender the amount in default, plus costs, before the foreclosure sale, the debt will be reinstated in some states. This right is known as an equitable right of redemption. Certain states also have a period of time after a foreclosure sale in which the borrower in default may redeem the property if the borrower pays the court; the right to redeem the property within the period is called a statutory right of redemption.

Reference: Finance > Financing Instruments (Mortgages, Trust Deeds, Promissory Notes)

35. The clause in a mortgage or deed of trust which gives a lender the right to demand the entire loan balance to be due upon the buyer's default is the:

A. defeasance clause.

B. alienation clause.

C. due-on-sale clause.

D. acceleration clause.

Answer: D. The answer is acceleration clause. The acceleration (speedup) clause allows the lender to declare the entire loan balance due on a borrower's default. The alienation/due-on-sale clause allows the lender to accelerate the balance due if borrowers alienate/sell their mortgaged property. The defeasance clause requires the lender to release its lien claim against the property when the entire debt has been paid.

Reference: Finance > Financing Instruments (Mortgages, Trust Deeds, Promissory Notes)

36. A lender offers to take over the title of a property that is in foreclosure without going through the foreclosure process. This is called a(n):

A. subordination agreement.

B. deed in lieu of foreclosure.

C. reconveyance deed.

D. assumption.

Answer: B. The answer is deed in lieu of foreclosure. A deed in lieu of foreclosure is an alternative to foreclosure and is carried out by mutual agreement between the lender and the borrower rather than by a lawsuit. A reconveyance deed is used by a trustee under a deed of trust to return title to the trustor. In an assumption, a buyer purchases a property by assuming the seller's debt and becoming personally obligated for the payment of the entire debt. A subordination agreement moves a first mortgage lien to a secondary position by mutual agreement of the two lenders.

Reference: Finance > Financing Instruments (Mortgages, Trust Deeds, Promissory Notes)

37. A financing instrument that establishes a third party to hold title on behalf of the lender is a:

A. mortgage.

B. trustee.

C. deed of trust.

D. promissory note.

Answer: C. The answer is deed of trust. A deed of trust is a three-party financing instrument that conveys the deed to the property to a trustee who holds legal title on behalf of the lender, who holds the promissory note as the beneficiary of the trust. The trustee is the third party in this arrangement and is usually chosen by the lender. A mortgage is a two-party financial instrument in which the borrower, the mortgagor, signs a promissory note to repay the lender and provides the mortgage as a security for the debt.

Reference: Finance > Financing Instruments (Mortgages, Trust Deeds, Promissory Notes)

38. When compared with a 30-year payment period, taking out a loan with a 20-year payment period would result in:

A. higher monthly payments.

B. slower equity buildup.

C. lower monthly payments.

D. greater impound requirements.

Answer: A. The answer is higher monthly payments. A 20-year loan is paid off faster than a 30-year loan, with the payments spread out over a shorter period of time. This arrangement results in payments that are higher than those in a 30-year loan. The borrower's equity would build up quicker in the 20-year loan, as the borrower is paying more toward the principal each month than with a 30-year payment.

Reference: Finance > Basic Concepts and Terminology

39. A buyer wants a loan that has no adjustments or balloons and that will pay all the monthly taxes and insurance along with principal and interest. The buyer also wants to have the loan fully paid off when the last payment is made. The lender will most likely recommend which loan?:

A. Partially amortized budget loan

B. Fully amortized budget loan

C. Term budget loan

D. ARM budget loan

Answer: B. The answer is fully amortized budget loan. Budget loans include payments for taxes and insurance and can be used

with any loan payment type. The buyer also wanted the loan
fully paid off with the last payment and only a fully amortized
loan can do that without a balloon.

Reference: Finance > Methods of Financing

**40. The defeasance clause in a mortgage requires the
mortgagee to execute a(n):**

A. satisfaction of mortgage.

B. assignment of mortgage.

C. partial release agreement.

D. subordination agreement.

Answer: A. The answer is satisfaction of mortgage. A
defeasance clause requires the lender to execute a satisfaction,
also known as a release or discharge, when the note has been
fully paid. Satisfaction of the mortgage returns to the borrower
all interest in the real estate originally conveyed to the lender. A
mortgagee may assign a note to a third party, such as investor or
another mortgage company (the assignee). When the debt is paid

in full, the assignee is required to execute the satisfaction of the mortgage.

Reference: Finance > Financing Instruments (Mortgages, Trust Deeds, Promissory Notes)

41. In evaluating a prospective borrower's qualifications for a residential loan, a lending institution may consider all of the following EXCEPT:

A. the buyer is retired so does not have a regular paycheck.

B. credit score and debit ratio.

C. the appraised value of the property.

D. the total amount of revolving debt the borrower has.

Answer: A. The answer is the buyer is retired so does not have a regular paycheck. The Equal Credit Opportunity Act prohibits discrimination in granting credit on the basis of age, in particular because the borrower is retired, marital status, national origin, or dependence on public assistance. A credit score, appraised value, and total debt are used as part of a loan application evaluation process.

Reference: Finance > Government Oversight

42. With a VA-guaranteed mortgage:

A. the borrower must apply for a certificate of eligibility.

B. the borrower may have a prepayment penalty clause in the loan.

C. discount points must be paid by the seller.

D. the funding fee amounts are negotiable.

Answer: A. The answer is the borrower must apply for a certificate of eligibility. A borrower must apply for a certificate of eligibility which sets forth the maximum guarantee to which the veteran is entitled. Discount points can be paid by either the buyer or the seller. Prepayment penalties are prohibited. Funding fees are determined by the VA (Veterans Affairs).

Reference: Finance > Methods of Financing

43. Which of the following act as security for the loan?:

A. Deed of trust

B. Conveyance deed

C. Promissory note

D. Subordination agreement

Answer: A. The answer is deed of trust. A deed of trust or a mortgage are the two security instruments used in loans. The promissory note is a promise to pay the debt. A conveyance deed conveys title to real property and a subordination agreement is used to hold positions when new documents are recorded.

Reference: Finance > Financing Instruments (Mortgages, Trust Deeds, Promissory Notes)

44. A person who assumes an existing mortgage loan is:

A. generally released from liability, but not always.

B. not personally liable for the repayment of the debt.

C. not in danger of losing the property by default.

D. personally responsible for paying the principal balance.

Answer: D. The answer is personally responsible for paying the principal balance. A buyer who purchases property and assumes the seller's debt becomes personally obligated for the payment of the entire debt. If the buyer defaults on the loan the buyer is in danger of losing the property.

Reference: Finance > Financing Instruments (Mortgages, Trust Deeds, Promissory Notes)

45. A couple purchased a residence for $195,000. They made a down payment of $25,000 and agreed to assume the seller's existing mortgage, which had a current balance of $123,000. The buyers financed the remaining $47,000 of the purchase price by executing a mortgage and note to the seller. The

type of loan, in which the seller becomes the mortgagee, is called a:

A. balloon note.

B. reverse mortgage.

C. package mortgage.

D. purchase money mortgage.

Answer: D. The answer is purchase money mortgage. A purchase money mortgage is created when a seller agrees to finance all or part of the purchase price. In this case the seller agrees to finance $47,000 of the purchase price and takes back a mortgage and note from the buyer. The term purchase money mortgage can mean either owner financing or any mortgage used as acquisition debt in the purchase of a property. Here the owner-seller took back a mortgage for $47,000. An owner take back is a purchase money mortgage. In a package mortgage, a borrower secures a loan with both real and personal property. A balloon note includes a final payment called a balloon payment that is larger than the periodic payments made on the note. A reverse mortgage is created when the bank makes payments to an older home owner who wants to stay in the home but take advantage of equity.

Reference: Finance > Methods of Financing

46. What does PMI (private mortgage insurance) purchased by a buyer provide?:

A. Funds for the buyer to pay interest over the life of the loan

B. Funds for the buyer to pay closing costs

C. Funds to pay discount points required by the lender

D. Funds for the lender in the event that the buyer defaults on the loan

Answer: D. The answer is funds for the lender in the event that a buyer defaults on the loan. The borrower purchases insurance from a private mortgage insurance company as additional security to insure the lender against default.

Reference: Finance > Basic Concepts and Terminology

47. Conventional loans are viewed as the most secure loans because:

A. their loan-to-value ratios are often lower than other types of loans.

B. they are not purchased by investors in the secondary mortgage market.

C. they are government insured loans.

D. private mortgage insurance protects the lender for the full amount of the loan.

Answer: A. The answer is their loan-to-value ratios are often lower than other types of loans. The borrower with a conventional loan usually makes a down payment of at least 20%, so that the loan-to-value ratio is 80%. The security for the loan is provided by the mortgage, and the payment of the debt rests on the borrower's ability to pay. Conventional loans are not insured or guaranteed by the government, unlike FHA or VA loans. Private mortgage insurance (PMI) protects the lender only for the excess of the loan amount over 80% of the property's appraised value. Conventional loans are often purchased from the original lenders through the secondary mortgage market.

48. That portion of the value of an owner's property that exceeds the amount of the mortgage debt is called the:

A. principal.

B. interest.

C. equity.

D. escrow.

Answer: C. The answer is equity. An owner's equity represents the ownership interest (the paid-off share) in the property that increases as the mortgage debt (the principal) is reduced. The value of the property minus the mortgage debt equals equity. The principal is the amount of money owed by a borrower on a property loan. The interest is the amount paid by a borrower to a lender in return for the use of money. Escrow is the process by which a third party holds money provided by one party in a transaction (usually a buyer) until the transaction is closed.

49. The borrower discovers that the loan is not assumable. What clause did the borrower find?:

A. Due on sale

B. Defeasance

C. Subordination

D. Acceleration

Answer: A. The answer is due on sale. The alienation/due-on-sale clause requires when the property is sold the loan must be paid off and is not assumable. Acceleration is used when the borrower is in default and allows the lender to call the note due and payable.

Reference: Finance > Financing Instruments (Mortgages, Trust Deeds, Promissory Notes)

50. A home is purchased using a fixed-rate, fully amortized mortgage loan. With this loan,:

A. the principal amount in each payment is greater than the interest amount.

B. a balloon payment will be made at the end of the loan.

C. each mortgage payment reduces the principal by the same amount.

D. each mortgage payment amount is the same.

Answer: D. The answer is each mortgage payment amount is the same. In a fully amortized loan, there will be no balloon payment because the periodic payments fully repay the loan by the end of the term period. Each mortgage payment reduces the principal by a slightly different (increasing) amount, but each mortgage payment (principal and interest) is the same.

Reference: Finance > Basic Concepts and Terminology

51. RESPA (Real Estate Settlement Procedures Act) applies to the activities of:

A. lenders only.

B. title companies only.

C. real estate brokers only.

D. lenders, title companies, and real estate brokers.

Answer: D. The answer is lenders, title companies, and real estate brokers. RESPA requirements apply to lenders primarily. RESPA also requires real estate brokers and title companies that package services for consumers to inform consumers of the relationship between the companies and to inform consumers that they are free to choose other companies for services.

Reference: Finance > Lending Process

52. The component of an adjustable-rate mortgage (ARM) that limits the percentage that the interest rate may increase over a specific time period, usually a year, is the:

A. payment cap.

B. life-of-the loan rate cap.

C. rate cap.

D. margin.

Answer: C. The answer is rate cap. The rate cap limits the amount an ARM's interest rate may change over a specific period of time, usually a year. The life-of-the loan rate cap limits the amount the rate may increase over the entire life of the loan. The payment cap sets a maximum amount the borrower will have to pay for a mortgage payment. The margin is the premium added to the index rate to adjust an ARM's interest rate.

Reference: Finance > Methods of Financing

53. Buyers seeking a mortgage on a single-family residence would be LEAST likely to obtain the mortgage from a:

A. mutual savings bank.

B. credit union.

C. commercial bank.

D. life insurance company.

Answer: D. The answer is life insurance company. Life insurance companies make mortgage loans on large projects but rarely, if ever, on individual home purchases. Mutual savings banks, credit unions, and commercial banks are all sources of mortgages for individual residences.

Reference: Finance > Methods of Financing

54. A homeowner has been making periodic payments of principal and interest on a loan, but the final payment will be larger than the others. This is a(n):

A. home-equity loan.

B. balloon payment loan.

C. fully amortized loan.

D. FHA loan.

Answer: B. The answer is balloon payment loan. When the periodic payments of principal and interest or interest only are not enough to fully pay the loan by the time the final payment is due, the final payment is known as a balloon. A fully amortized loan requires equal periodic payments of principal and interest. An FHA loan is a fixed-interest loan with equal periodic loans of principal and interest and is insured by the FHA. A home-equity loan typically does not have a balloon payment.

Reference: Finance > Methods of Financing

55. If a property sold at a mortgage foreclosure does NOT bring an amount sufficient to satisfy the outstanding mortgage debt, the mortgagor may be responsible for:

A. a default judgment.

B. a deficiency judgment.

C. punitive damages.

D. liquidated damages.

Answer: B. The answer is a deficiency judgment. A deficiency judgment entitles the mortgagee to a personal judgment against the borrower for the unpaid balance when a foreclosure sale does not produce enough cash to pay the loan balance in full after deducting expenses and accrued unpaid interest. It may also be obtained against any endorsers or guarantors of the note and against any owners of the mortgaged property who assumed the debt by written agreement. The mortgagee is not entitled to any damages. A default judgment is a judgment in favor of a plaintiff when a defendant does not appear in court.

Reference: Finance > Financing Instruments (Mortgages, Trust Deeds, Promissory Notes)

56. The federal Equal Credit Opportunity Act (ECOA) allows lenders to discriminate against potential borrowers on the basis of:

A. age.

B. dependence on public assistance.

C. amount of income.

D. race.

Answer: C. The answer is amount of income. Lenders may reject applicants who have insufficient income for the loans they are requesting or for their lack of ability to repay the loans. Lenders may not discriminate against potential borrowers on the basis of race, color, religion, national origin, sex, marital status, age, or dependence on public assistance.

Reference: Finance > Government Oversight

57. A purchaser is qualified to obtain an FHA loan for his new home. Which of the following would he apply to?:

A. An FHA lender

B. Fannie Mae

C. Freddie Mac

D. The FHA

Answer: A. The answer is an FHA lender. The FHA does not negotiate loans. The FHA insures loans, which means the loan is backed by the government. Loans are made through an FHA-approved lending institution. Fannie Mae does not lend money directly to homebuyers but purchases mortgages in the secondary market. Freddie Mac is a federally chartered corporation that purchases mortgages in the secondary market.

Reference: Finance > Methods of Financing

58. An eligible veteran made an offer of $225,000 to purchase a home contingent upon obtaining a no-down-payment VA-guaranteed loan. Three weeks after the offer was accepted, the VA issued a certificate of reasonable value (CRV) for $222,000 for the property. In this case, the veteran may:

A. purchase the property by making a $3,000 cash payment.

B. withdraw from the sale with a three-point penalty.

C. withdraw from the sale on payment of a commission to the seller's broker.

D. seek secondary funding for the $3,000.

Answer: A. The answer is purchase the property by making a $3,000 cash payment. When the purchase price of a property is greater than the VA-issued certificate of reasonable value, the veteran may pay the difference in cash to purchase the property because secondary financing is somewhat restricted under VA regulations. Since the veteran's contract in this case was contingent on a no-down-payment VA-guaranteed loan, the veteran could also choose not to purchase the home and to seek another property to buy with no penalty.

Reference: Finance > Methods of Financing

59. A fixed-rate home loan that is fully amortized according to the original payment schedule:

A. permits the borrower to pay the same amount each payment period.

B. has an interest rate that fluctuates based on an economic index.

C. cannot be sold in the secondary market.

D. requires a monthly payment amount that fluctuates each month.

Answer: A. The answer is permits the borrower to pay the same amount each payment period. A fully amortized loan is a level-payment loan, with the same amount being paid by the borrower each payment period (usually monthly). The loan can be sold in the secondary market. An adjustable-rate mortgage has an interest rate that in fluctuates based on an economic index.

Reference: Finance > Basic Concepts and Terminology

60. The charge for the use of the lender's money in a loan is the:

A. equity.

B. rate of return.

C. principal.

D. interest.

Answer: D. The answer is interest. Interest is the sum paid or accrued in return for the use of a lender's money. Interest on a promissory note is usually due in arrears at the end of each payment period. The rate of return is the return on the investment in a property. An owner's equity is the amount of money remaining once current liens, including the mortgage, are subtracted from the current value of the property. The principal is the balance owed on the original loan amount.

Reference: Finance > Basic Concepts and Terminology

61. Which of the following BEST expresses the concept of equity?:

A. Current market value minus capital gain

B. Replacement cost minus depreciation

C. Current market value minus property debt

D. Current market value minus cost of land

Answer: C. The answer is current market value minus property debt. Equity is the amount of money remaining after owners sell their property at market value and then pay off any mortgage debt. Equity is that portion of a property's value that exceeds the debt remaining on the property's loan. Current market value minus capital gain equals the actual total a property owner would acquire after selling a property and paying any capital gain taxes owed as a result of the sale. Current market value minus the cost of land provides the value of the improvements (home, garage, etc.) of a property. Replacement cost plus the cost of land minus depreciation equals the depreciated value of a structure.

Reference: Finance > Basic Concepts and Terminology

62. Antitrust laws prohibit all of the following EXCEPT:

A. real estate companies agreeing not to cooperate with a broker because of that broker's fees.

B. competing brokers allocating market shares based on the value of homes.

C. a broker setting a company commission schedule.

D. competing property management companies agreeing to standardized management fees.

Answer: C. The answer is a broker setting a company commission schedule. All the other actions are violations of antitrust laws. Real estate brokers must independently determine commission rates or fees for their firms only. Commission decisions must be based on a broker's business judgment and revenue requirements and without input from other competing brokers.

Reference: Finance > Government Oversight

63. A mortgage broker generally:

A. provides credit qualification and evaluation reports.

B. handles the escrow procedures.

C. brings the borrower and the lender together.

D. rants real estate loans using investor funds.

Answer: C. The answer is brings the borrower and the lender together. A mortgage broker is an intermediary who brings borrowers and lenders together. A mortgage broker locates potential borrowers, processes preliminary loan applications, and submits the applications to lenders for final approval. Mortgage brokers do not provide loans, handle escrow funds, or check borrowers' creditworthiness for loans.

Reference: Finance > Lending Process

64. A land contract, contract for deed, or installment contract has been reached between the seller and buyer. It MOST likely means that the:

A. mortgagee finances the property and retains title until the final payment is made by the mortgagor.

B. mortgagor finances the property and retains title until the final payment is made by the mortgagee.

C. seller finances the property and retains title until the final payment is made by the buyer.

D. buyer finances the property and retains title until the final payment is made by the seller.

Answer: C. The answer is seller finances the property and retains title until the final payment is made by the buyer. In a land contract, the seller will finance the property and retain title until final payment from the buyer is made. Mortgagor/borrower and mortgagee/lender are used when a mortgage is being used not a land contract.

Reference: Finance > Methods of Financing

65. A real estate loan payable in periodic installments that are sufficient to pay the principal in full during the term of the loan is a(n):

A. straight loan.

B. fully amortized loan.

C. interest-only loan.

D. partially amortized loan.

Answer: B. The answer is fully amortized loan. The payment in an amortized loan partially pays off both principal and interest. The mortgagor pays a constant amount, usually monthly. At the end of the term, the full amount of the principal and interest due is reduced to zero. In straight loan and interest only loans, the borrower makes periodic payments of interest only, followed by a lump sum balloon payment of full principal balance at the end of the loan term. In a partially amortized loan, the periodic payments are not enough to pay the principal balance, so a final payment (a balloon payment) is larger than the other payments to satisfy the debt.

Reference: Finance > Basic Concepts and Terminology

66. When a loan requires payments that do not fully pay off the loan balance by the final payment, which term BEST describes the final payment?:

A. Variable

B. Acceleration

C. Balloon

D. Adjustment

Answer: C. The answer is balloon. When the term of the loan is over and the payments made have not paid off the debt, the last payment is a balloon payment. The loan is called a balloon loan. Acceleration occurs when a lender calls for full payment of a loan before its term has ended. The adjustment in an adjustable rate mortgage establishes how often the rate may be changed. A variable payment is one that may change over time depending on the mortgage agreement.

Reference: Finance > Methods of Financing

67. An FHA-insured mortgage loan is obtained from:

A. any FHA-approved insuring institution.

B. the Department of Housing and Urban Development.

C. any FHA-approved lending institution.

D. the Federal Housing Administration.

Answer: C. The answer is any FHA-approved lending institution. The FHA (Federal Housing Administration) operates under HUD (Department of Housing and Urban Development).

The FHA neither builds homes nor lends money itself. The FHA insures loans. Loans must be obtained from FHA-approved lending institutions.

Reference: Finance > Methods of Financing

68. What best describes a fraud scheme known as a rescue scam?:

A. An investor creates a fictional buyer and false loan documentation to obtain a loan.

B. A false identity is used on a loan application without the knowledge of the rightful property owner.

C. Homeowners behind on their mortgage are told that their home can be saved by paying upfront fees and transferring the deed to the defrauder.

D. A property is knowingly appraised with a higher-than-market value by an appraiser acting in collusion with a borrower or lender.

Answer: C. The answer is homeowners behind on their mortgage are told that their home can be saved by paying upfront fees and transferring the deed to the defrauder. The rescuer runs off with the upfront fees, gets a second loan on the property, and takes that money or sells the home and takes the proceeds.

Reference: Finance > Government Oversight

69. Three years ago a couple moved from the house they had owned for 20 years but did not sell it. They decided to travel and bought a mobile home as their residence. They now decide to sell the house. How much of their capital gain on the house will be taxable?:

A. 15%, depending on their tax bracket.

B. None of it, if the capital gain is less than $500,000.

C. 28%, depending on their tax bracket.

D. All of it, if the capital gain is over $500,000.

Answer: B. The answer is none of it, if the capital gain is less than $500,000. Federal law requires that the couple must have lived in the house for two out of the last five years to receive the $500,000 exemption from capital gains tax. The couple lived in the house for two years before they purchased the mobile home three years ago. The couple qualifies for the capital gain exception of $500,000.

Reference: Finance > Lending Process

70. The principal distinction between the primary mortgage market and the secondary mortgage market is in the:

A. insuring versus the guaranteeing of mortgage loans.

B. use of mortgages versus the use of deeds of trust.

C. use of discount points versus the use of origination fees.

D. origination versus the purchase of mortgage loans.

Answer: D. The answer is origination versus the purchase of mortgage loans. Loans are originated in the primary mortgage market and bought and sold in the secondary mortgage market after they have been funded. The use of mortgages or deeds of trust is determined by state law. Insuring, guaranteeing, and use of discount points and loan origination fees all occur in the primary lending market.

Reference: Finance > Lending Process

71. The Truth in Lending Act requires the lender or credit institution supply borrowers with information applying to:

A. the HUD-1 and final settlement costs.

B. the true cost of credit or annual percentage rate.

C. an estimate of all the closing costs on the residential property.

D. any environmental issues impacting the property.

Answer: B. The answer is the true cost of credit or annual percentage rate. Truth in Lending requires the disclosure of the APR (annual percentage rate) or the true cost of credit on the loan. RESPA requires a new loan estimate of closing costs and the new loan closing disclosure prior to settlement.

Reference: Finance > Government Oversight

72. In a land contract, the buyer:

A. has possession during the term of the contract.

B. does not pay interest and principal.

C. obtains legal title at closing.

D. is not responsible for the real estate taxes on the property.

Answer: A. The answer is has possession during the term of the contract. In a land (installment) contract, the buyer has possession of the property during the term of the contract. The buyer holds equitable title, while the seller holds legal title to the property. The buyer pays interest and principal on the loan, and in most cases, real estate taxes on the property during the term of the contract.

Reference: Finance > Methods of Financing

73. A salesperson has been trying for weeks to list a spectacular house for sale. The homeowners tell the salesperson that a competing company will charge a commission rate that is 2% lower than the commission rate charged by the salesperson's brokerage firm. In order to get the listing, the salesperson should tell the owner that:

A. his company provides excellent services to market its sellers' properties.

B. most brokers in the area charge a standard rate of commission.

C. the competing firm cannot provide good services because it charges less commission.

D. salespersons in the area will not show the competing firm's listings because of its lower commission rates.

Answer: A. The answer is his company provides excellent services to market its sellers' properties. The other possible statements imply that there is a standard commission rate among competing brokers. Antitrust laws prohibit price-fixing, the practice of setting prices for services rather than letting competition in the open market establish those prices. The salesperson should only focus on what his company can offer. Antitrust laws also forbid brokers from "boycotting" other brokers because of their fees.

Reference: Finance > Government Oversight

74. A loan fee charged by a lender to increase the lender's yield on a loan is:

A. the interest.

B. the yield.

C. the principal.

D. a discount point.

Answer: D. The answer is a discount point. Discount points are used to increase the lender's yield on its investment. The yield is the profit the lender makes on a loan, the spread between the cost of acquiring the funds lent to the borrower, and the interest rate charged to the borrower. Interest is the sum paid or accrued in return for the use of a lender's money. The principal is the balanced owed on the original loan amount.

75. The primary activity of Fannie Mae is to:

A. guarantee mortgages with the full faith and credit of the federal government.

B. act in tandem with Ginnie Mae to provide special assistance in times of tight money.

C. buy and pool blocks of conventional mortgages and sell bonds that use them as security.

D. buy and sell only VA and FHA mortgages.

Answer: C. The answer is buy and pool blocks of conventional mortgages and sell bonds that use them as security. Fannie Mae buys and gathers existing conventional mortgages into bundles (pools) and raises money to do this by selling bonds backed by these pools of mortgages. Ginnie Mae is a division of HUD that administers programs using VA and FHA loans as collateral.

Reference: Finance > Lending Process

76. The clause in a trust deed or mortgage that permits the lender to declare the entire unpaid balance immediately due and payable upon default is the:

A. alienation clause.

B. judgment clause.

C. forfeiture clause.

D. acceleration clause.

Answer: D. The answer is acceleration clause. An acceleration clause gives the lender the right to declare the entire debt due and payable immediately if the borrower has defaulted. The alienation/due-on-sale clause allows the lender to accelerate the balance due if borrowers alienate/sell their mortgaged property. A forfeiture clause in a contract for deed requires the borrower to forfeit all amounts paid if the borrower defaults. A judgment clause permits a lender to file a lien against a borrower without having to initiate court proceedings.

Reference: Finance > Financing Instruments (Mortgages, Trust Deeds, Promissory Notes)

77. Real estate firms are often affiliated with title insurance companies or mortgage brokers. RESPA permits these business arrangements as long as:

A. companies disclose their relationships with one another to the consumer.

B. consumers are unaware of these arrangements.

C. consumers are required to use the services of the affiliated companies.

D. companies pay referral fees between them.

Answer: A. The answer is companies disclose their relationship with one another to the consumer. RESPA permits such arrangements as long as a consumer is clearly informed of the relationship among the affiliated companies and provided information that the consumer may use other service providers for the same services. The companies may not require a consumer to use the services of any affiliated company. The companies may not pay one another referral fees.

Reference: Finance > Government Oversight

78. A promissory note:

A. is an agreement to perform or not to perform certain acts.

B. may not be executed in connection with a real estate loan.

C. is a guarantee by a government agency.

D. makes the borrower personally liable for the debt.

Answer: D. The answer is makes the borrower personally liable for the debt. A promissory note is the borrower's personal promise to repay a debt according to agreed-on terms. A promissory note is a contract, an agreement to perform a certain act. A borrower of real estate securing a mortgage loan will sign a promissory note agreeing to repay the loan.

Reference: Finance > Financing Instruments (Mortgages, Trust Deeds, Promissory Notes)

79. Brokerage commissions charged to sellers in listing contracts for the sale of real property are MOST typically set by the:

A. principal broker then negotiated with the seller.

B. negotiation between local brokerage firms.

C. brokerage firm and board of REALTORS®.

D. state Commission and the principal broker negotiations.

Answer: A. The answer is principal broker then negotiated with the seller. The principal broker has the right to set the minimum commission for the firm and then the broker associates and salespeople can negotiate the level of commission they need to complete the job as created by the listing contract. The Commission, local firms, and the board of REALTORS® may not be a party to the firm's commission decision or negotiations.

Reference: Finance > Government Oversight

80. Institutions in the secondary mortgage market:

A. provide loans to lenders in the primary mortgage market to raise capital for new loans.

B. make direct loans to purchasers for second mortgages.

C. purchase a number of mortgage loans already funded and assemble them into packages to form marketable securities for investors.

D. set the interest rates required for loans made in the primary mortgage market.

Answer: C. The answer is purchase a number of mortgage loans already funded and assemble them into packages to form marketable securities for investors. In the secondary mortgage market, loans are bought and sold only after they have been funded by lenders in the primary mortgage market. The secondary market activity enables lenders to sell mortgage loans to raise capital for new loans.

Reference: Finance > Lending Process

81. The type of loan that will MOST likely have the lowest loan-to-value ratio is a(n):

A. PMI loan.

B. VA loan.

C. conventional loan.

D. FHA loan.

Answer: C. The answer is conventional loan. Conventional loans are viewed as the most secure loans because their loan-to-value ratios are often the lowest. Buyers in conventional loans make larger down payments than borrowers in FHA, PMI, or VA loans. Usually with the larger down payment in a conventional loan, no additional insurance or guarantee on the loan is necessary to protect the lender's interest.

Reference: Finance > Methods of Financing

82. The type of mortgage loan that uses both real and personal property as security is a:

A. purchase-money mortgage.

B. package loan.

C. term loan.

D. blanket loan.

Answer: B. The answer is package loan. A package loan includes not only the real estate but also all personal property and appliances installed on the premises. A blanket loan covers more than one parcel or lot and permits the borrower to obtain a release of a parcel or lot from the mortgage lien when the lot is sold. A purchase-money mortgage refers to the instrument given by a borrower to a seller who takes back a note for part or the entire mortgage. A term/straight or interest only loan secures only real property.

Reference: Finance > Methods of Financing

83. A purchaser buys a home using a mortgage loan from a local lender. The lender promptly recorded the mortgage.Three years later, the homeowner needs additional cash, so he places a second mortgage with a different lender. Based on these facts, which statement is TRUE?:

A. The new lender cannot hold a security interest in the property already held as collateral by the original lender.

B. The loan from the original lender has priority over the loan made three years later with the new lender.

C. The loan from the original lender is a subordination loan.

D. Because it is older, the loan from the original lender is subject to the loan from the new lender, which assumes priority in time.

Answer: B. The answer is the loan from the original lender has priority over the loan made three years later with the new lender. The dates of the recording of the liens establishes their priority. The loan from the new lender is made and recorded more recently and is subject to (second in line behind) the loan from the original lender. If a second mortgage has a higher amount than a first mortgage, the second lender may require a subordination agreement in which the first lender lowers its lien position to that of the second lender; both lenders must sign the agreement.

Reference: Finance > Financing Instruments (Mortgages, Trust Deeds, Promissory Notes)

84. In an FHA insured loan transaction, the:

A. mortgage insurance premium must be paid by the seller.

B. interest rate is set by the FHA.

C. discount points may be paid by the seller or the buyer.

D. mortgage insurance premium may be paid by the seller or the buyer.

Answer: C. The answer is discount points may be paid by the seller or the buyer. Either the seller or the buyer may pay discount points in an FHA loan transaction. Interest rates are not set by the FHA, but are negotiated between the lender and the buyer. An FHA loan includes a one-time upfront mortgage insurance premium (MIP), which can be financed, paid by the buyer, with an additional 1/2% MIP added to the monthly payments.

Reference: Finance > Methods of Financing

85. A couple applying for a residential mortgage loan has a combined monthly gross income of $8,000. Their total housing expense with a new loan would be $1,770, including PITI. Their total debt expense, including housing expenses, would be $2,800. Under these conditions, would the couple qualify for a conforming loan under Fannie Mae guidelines?:

A. Yes, because their debt to income ratios are within criteria set by Fannie Mae.

B. Yes, because their total housing expense is less than 60% of their total debt expense.

C. No, because their total housing expense is more than 50% of their total debt expense.

D. No, because their debt to income ratio exceeds the limits set by Fannie Mae.

Answer: A. The answer is yes, because their debt to income ratios are within criteria set by Fannie Mae. A conforming loan is one that qualifies under debt to income ratios set by Fannie Mae. The borrower's total housing expense must be no more than 28% of gross monthly income, and the borrower's total debt expense including housing must be no more than 36% of gross monthly income. To find the total housing expense ratio, divide the total housing expense ($1,770) by the monthly gross income ($8,000): 1,700 ÷ 8,000 = 22%. To find the total debt expense, divide that expense ($2,800) by the monthly gross income ($8,000): 2,800 ÷ 8,000 = 35%. In this situation, if their credit score and history are considered good by the lender, the couple would qualify for a conforming conventional loan.

Reference: Finance > Lending Process

86. The right of borrowers who have defaulted on a loan to redeem their property after foreclosure for a certain period of time established by law is called a(n):

A. equitable right of redemption.

B. owner's right of redemption.

C. mortgagee's right of redemption.

D. statutory right of redemption.

Answer: D. The answer is statutory right of redemption. Certain states have a period of time after a foreclosure sale in which the borrower in default may redeem the property if the borrower pays the court; the right to redeem the property within the period is called a statutory right of redemption. If a borrower in default pays the lender the amount in default, plus costs, before the foreclosure sale, the debt will be reinstated in some states. This right is known as an equitable right of redemption.

Reference: Finance > Financing Instruments (Mortgages, Trust Deeds, Promissory Notes)

87. Which of the following is a TRUE statement about interest on a fully amortized loan?:

A. The interest is paid each period without any payment on the principal.

B. The interest requires that the final interest payment will be determined after the last loan payment is made.

C. The interest is paid in arrears.

D. The interest increases throughout the term of the loan.

Answer: C. The answer is the interest is paid in arrears. A fully amortized loan requires a constant payment for both the principal and interest with each payment for the life of the loan. Interest or principal do not increase in a fully amortized loan because the terms are set in the original loan documents and don't change.

Reference: Finance > Basic Concepts and Terminology

88. All the following clauses in a loan agreement enable the lender to demand the entire remaining debt be paid immediately EXCEPT:

A. an acceleration clause.

B. a due-on-sale clause.

C. a defeasance clause.

D. an alienation clause.

Answer: C. The answer is a defeasance clause. A defeasance clause requires a lender to execute a satisfaction when the note has been fully paid. An alienation clause, also known as a due-on-sale clause, provides that when the property is sold the lender may declare the entire debt due immediately. An acceleration clause permits the lender to demand payment of a loan balance immediately if the buyer defaults on the loan payments.

Reference: Finance > Financing Instruments (Mortgages, Trust Deeds, Promissory Notes)

89. A purchaser cannot qualify for conventional financing and negotiates a contract for deed with a seller. The buyer in this arrangement:

A. has a full legal interest in the property.

B. has possession and pays the property expenses and taxes.

C. receives a deed to the property at closing.

D. must lease the property from the seller for the duration of the contract term.

Answer: B. The answer is has possession and pays the property expenses and taxes. In a contract for deed arrangement, the buyer takes full possession of the property and gets equitable title to the property. The buyer agrees to pay real property taxes, insurance premiums, and for the upkeep of the property. The seller is not obligated to execute and deliver the deed for the property to the buyer until all the terms of the contract have been satisfied.

Reference: Finance > Methods of Financing

90. All of the following clauses in a loan agreement enable the lender to demand that the entire remaining debt be paid immediately EXCEPT:

A. an alienation clause.

B. a due-on-sale clause.

C. a defeasance clause.

D. an acceleration clause.

Answer: C. The answer is a defeasance clause. A defeasance clause requires the lender to execute a satisfaction of the loan when the loan has been fully paid. A due-on-sale clause provides that when the property is sold, the lender may declare the entire debt due or permit the buyer to assume the loan. An alienation clause states that the lender may collect full payment on a loan if the property is conveyed to another party without the lender's consent. An acceleration clause permits the lender to declare the entire debt payable immediately if the borrower defaults on payments on the loan.

Reference: Finance > Financing Instruments (Mortgages, Trust Deeds, Promissory Notes)

91. A mortgage loan in which the borrower only pays interest for a stated period of time and pays off the principal balance at the end of that term is a(n):

A. package loan.

B. interest-only loan.

C. balloon loan.

D. amortized loan.

Answer: B. The answer is interest-only loan. Interest-only mortgages require payment of interest only for a certain period of time with the principal balance and interest recalculated over the remaining years of the loan. A balloon payment loan is a partially amortized loan in which the periodic payments are not enough to fully amortize the loan by the time the final payment is due so that the final payment (called a balloon payment) is larger than the others. In a package loan the borrower secures the loan with both personal and real property. In an amortized loan the monthly payment partially pays off both principal and interest so that both are paid off slowly, over time, in equal payments.

Reference: Finance > Methods of Financing

92. Homeowners may deduct all of the following expenses when preparing their income tax return EXCEPT:

A. homeowners' association dues.

B. some origination fees.

C. mortgage interest.

D. real estate taxes.

Answer: A. The answer is homeowners' association dues. Homeowners may not deduct homeowners' association dues from annual tax returns. Points for loans, some origination fees, mortgage interest and real estate property taxes, can be deducted on income tax returns (remember POIT).

Reference: Finance > Lending Process

93. A lender that charges a rate of interest in excess of that permitted by state law may be guilty of:

A. misrepresentation.

B. truth-in-lending violations.

C. fraud.

D. usury.

Answer: D. The answer is usury. Usury is the act of charging a rate of interest in excess of limits established by law. Fraud is a form of deceit or misrepresentation by which a lender or some other party attempts to gain some unfair advantage over a borrower or another person. Truth-in-lending violations involve improper disclosures or the lack of disclosures regarding the cost of credit from a lender. Truth-in-lending laws do not establish any set minimum or maximum interest rate in lending transactions.

Reference: Finance > Basic Concepts and Terminology

...continued in Volume Two

Made in the USA
Columbia, SC
25 September 2019